T0385776

HOW SHERLOCK PULLED THE TRICK

How Sherlock Pulled the Trick

Spiritualism and the Pseudoscientific Method

BRIAN MCCUSKEY

The Pennsylvania State University Press
University Park, Pennsylvania

Library of Congress Cataloging-in-Publication Data

Names: McCuskey, Brian, 1967– author.
Title: How Sherlock pulled the trick : spiritualism and the pseudoscientific
    method / Brian McCuskey.
Description: University Park, Pennsylvania : The Pennsylvania State
    University Press, [2021] | Includes bibliographical references and index.
Summary: "Reconsiders Sherlock Holmes in light of Arthur Conan Doyle's
    spiritualism. Brings together literary study and author biography
    to return the iconic Holmes to his mystical origins"—Provided by
    publisher.
Identifiers: LCCN 2021010047 | ISBN 9780271089874 (cloth)
Subjects: LCSH: Holmes, Sherlock. | Doyle, Arthur Conan, 1859–1930—
    Characters. | Doyle, Arthur Conan, 1859–1930—Religion. | Detective
    and mystery stories, English—History and criticism. | Spiritualism
    in literature. | Literature and spiritualism. | Private investigators in
    literature.
Classification: LCC PR4624 .M19 2021 | DDC 823/.8—dc23
LC record available at https://lccn.loc.gov/2021010047

The Pennsylvania State University Press is a member of the Association of
University Presses.

It is the policy of The Pennsylvania State University Press to use acid-free
paper. Publications on uncoated stock satisfy the minimum requirements
of American National Standard for Information Sciences—Permanence of
Paper for Printed Library Material, ANSI Z39.48–1992.

For my parents

CONTENTS

ACKNOWLEDGMENTS

Portions of chapter 5 were previously published as "Sherlock Holmes and Intelligent Design," *Quarterly Review of Biology* 87, no. 3 (2012): 225–35 (© 2012 by The University of Chicago), and "221B–9/11: Sherlock Holmes and Conspiracy Theory," in *Transatlantic Literature and Culture After 9/11*, edited by Kristine Miller (London: Palgrave Macmillan, 2014), 50–67, reproduced with permission.

My deepest thanks to:
  colleagues and students in the Department of English and the College of Humanities and Social Sciences at Utah State University;
  editors and readers at Penn State University Press, especially Kathryn Yahner;
  librarians and staff at Utah State University, the University of Minnesota, the Harry Ransom Center, the Portsmouth Central Library, and the British Library;
  teachers at the University of Michigan, the University of North Carolina at Chapel Hill, Harvard School, and St. Augustine by-the-Sea School;
  friends in Austin, Texas; London, England; Montevideo, Uruguay; Nelson, New Zealand; Salt Lake City, Utah; Santa Monica, California; Stockholm, Sweden; Woodstock, Vermont; and Cache Valley, Utah;
  family in Casco Bay, Maine, and Big Sky, Montana, especially Dylan, Caitlin, and Kris.

Introduction

The Book of Life

"Why does the mystique of Sherlock persist?" the journalist Christopher Hitchens asked in 1999, reviewing the latest biography of Holmes's creator, Arthur Conan Doyle. "It is sheer power of mind that does the trick," he answered admiringly, "and that turns the tables not just on evil but—by letting in the light—on superstition and nameless dread as well."[1] In the same year, Hitchens engaged Holmes to turn the tables on President Bill Clinton, whose administration had bombed a Sudanese pharmaceutical plant. The White House claimed that Osama bin Laden was manufacturing nerve gas there, but officials refused to name confidential sources or provide classified evidence. Hitchens compared those officials who would not speak on the record to Doyle's famous watchdog that did not bark in the nighttime: "In the Sherlock Holmes tale 'Silver Blaze,' the failure of such a beast to give tongue—you should pardon the expression—was the giveaway that exposed his master as the intruder." Clinton must be behind the cover-up, Hitchens reasoned, which left only the question of motive. Listing and crossing off possible reasons to destroy the plant, he again took a page from Doyle: "Take away every exploded hypothesis, says Sherlock Holmes—this time in 'The Adventure of the Beryl Coronet'—and the one you are left with, however unlikely, will be true." In this case, Hitchens concluded, the truth was that Clinton authorized the bombing to appear more presidential during the Monica Lewinsky scandal.[2]

After the terrorist attacks on September 11, 2001, Hitchens argued that President George W. Bush had better reason to authorize bombing. In his view, the Iraq War was a necessary defense of core liberal principles, especially the separation of church and state. Over the next decade, Hitchens attacked not just Islamic fundamentalism but all organized religion as dreadful superstition. An outspoken atheist, he debated the existence of God with creationists and debunked their arguments for intelligent design in nature. In a 2009 essay on faith-based versus evidence-based thinking, Hitchens pointed to Doyle, who spent the last decade of his life on a worldwide mission for spiritualism, writing less about Sherlock Holmes and more about everything from ectoplasm to fairies. "The case of Sir Arthur Conan Doyle's unshakeable belief in fairies is not precisely an instance of religious tomfoolery," said Hitchens, "but does show that certain kinds of belief are evidence-proof."[3] Despite Doyle's mission, Hitchens could still believe in the rationalist Holmes, but only if he distanced the character from the author in his mind. Finishing Doyle's biography, Hitchens was "grateful that, when he took himself over the precipice and into the maelstrom of babble and superstition, Conan Doyle left his main man behind on the ledge, there to bear witness to the beauties of deduction."[4]

Emancipated from religion, Holmes now has the power to enlighten his readers, at least according to many how-to handbooks. In *Success Secrets of Sherlock Holmes* (2011), David Acord reads the Holmes canon as "a kind of Victorian-era self-help manual" that will "teach us the philosophy and mind-set we need to succeed beyond our wildest dreams."[5] Daniel Smith's *How to Think Like Sherlock* (2012) recounts "Holmes's fantastic feats of intellect" and promises "all sorts of information, advice and tips on how you can more closely resemble him."[6] Maria Konnikova makes the same promise in *Mastermind: How to Think Like Sherlock Holmes* (2013), which "takes Holmes's methodology to explore and explain the steps necessary for building up habits of thought that will allow you to engage mindfully with yourself and your world." *Mastermind* has heftier credentials than its competitors: much of it was originally published as a guest blog for *Scientific American*, in which Konnikova presented Holmes as "an ideal model for how we can think better than we do."[7] Her book thus belongs in both the self-help and the popular science sections of the bookstore, alongside other guides that employ the detective to illustrate principles and methods. Explaining quantum physics in *The Strange Case of Mrs. Hudson's Cat*

(1997), Colin Bruce quotes the same stories as Hitchens, because they "describe just those rules that good scientific investigation should follow."[8] James O'Brien uses those stories to teach forensics in *The Scientific Sherlock Holmes* (2013), agreeing with Hitchens that "the character's ongoing appeal and success" is due to "his knowledge of science and frequent use of the scientific method."[9]

To rest their cases on Holmes's methods, however, both O'Brien and Konnikova must distance the rational character from his author's beliefs, just as Hitchens did. O'Brien argues that Doyle "began to leave science out" of the stories once his "shift to spiritualism" started; it is therefore "no coincidence that the stories that are short on science are generally viewed as inferior."[10] Konnikova concedes that "Doyle failed the test of Holmesian thinking" when he accepted photographic evidence of fairies, but she excuses him because he meets the different standard of "what passes for rationality *given the context of the times*," during the spiritualist revival after World War I.[11] To accept that excuse, we might appeal to the authority of Albert Einstein, who endorsed the "pure thinking" of "the great detective" in *The Evolution of Physics* (1938), a survey for general readers.[12] For additional evidence, we might refer to the cover illustrations of *Beeton's Christmas Annual*, the magazine in which Holmes first appeared at the end of 1887. On the front, a scientific gentleman rises from his laboratory table to light a lamp overhead. The back advertises Beecham's Pills, "universally admitted to be a marvelous antidote" to a variety of intestinal disorders. Sandwiched between these illustrations of pure research and modern medicine is *A Study in Scarlet*, the origin narrative of "a supremely ingenious detective," as its publisher announced in the *Times*, "whose performances, while based on the most rational principles, outshine any hitherto depicted."[13] The *Beeton's* cover may fit that billing, but the title of the magazine produces dramatic irony. Sherlock Holmes, the scientific method incarnate, was originally packaged and presented as a Christmas story, a supernatural genre better known for ghosts and fairies than detectives.

Rather than distancing the character from his author, leaving spiritualism out of the stories, this book considers Holmes in light of Doyle's beliefs. Each chapter investigates the detective at a different stage of his shining career, from his first appearance in 1887 to his current wide release on the internet. The chapters all proceed inductively, keeping an eye on Holmes while gathering documentary evidence from other sources, from Victorian periodicals to television shows, from séance notes to website posts, following a trail that weaves in and out of the stories themselves. As the evidence accumulates, the trail loops back on itself to revisit previous scenes, seeking corroboration and noting correspondences. Continual cross-reference illuminates the spiritual aura of Sherlock Holmes, revealing the sources of his mystique.

Chapter 1 surveys the religious questions being debated in the London press when Holmes appeared at the end of 1887, focusing on arguments between natural scientists and Christian apologists about who knows best, and how they know it. Which will enlighten us: reason or revelation? What should we trust: evidence or authority? Why are we here: chance or design? Where are we headed: extinction or apocalypse? To the Victorians, those choices seemed stark. Even if many scientists faithfully attended church and many clergymen closely studied nature, the cultural debate itself was highly polarized. As various writers staked out their positions, both marking and mediating their differences, the figure of an ingenious detective began to emerge, between the lines and within the margins. While Holmes does not come fully into focus until the next chapter, which takes up *Beeton's Christmas Annual* again, these contemporaneous periodicals set the terms that would define him.

Those terms preoccupied the young Doyle, who fell away from his family's Catholicism during his medical studies at the University of Edinburgh. While he rejected organized religion, he retained strong spiritual yearnings. Chapter 2 follows his personal religious development up through the creation of Holmes in *A Study in Scarlet*, a biographical approach that shifts our point of view of both the character and the novel. While the detective is no spiritualist, he encouraged and enabled his author to become one; writing *Scarlet* was the tipping point in Doyle's search for an evidence-based faith. To be successful, that search required a strange detour halfway through the novel to Utah, where Holmes cannot follow—and where many readers would prefer not to go at all. Upon returning, however, we find the detective wonderfully transfigured: Holmes was Doyle's good faith solution to the irreconcilable differences between scientists and apologists.

Once Doyle found spiritualism, Holmes seemed disposable. Doyle pushed him over the precipice of Reichenbach Falls in 1893, only to pull him back eight years later in *The Hound of the Baskervilles* (1901–2). Holmes was still too valuable, both financially and psychologically, for his author to let him go. Chapter 3 follows the born-again detective along the path to his author's public conversion in 1916, when Doyle became known as the Saint Paul of spiritualism. Like Hitchens, the arch-skeptic Martin Gardner insists on a healthy distance between author and character: "There is scarcely a page in any of Doyle's books on the occult that does not reveal him to be the antithesis of Holmes."[14] However, as Doyle built his case for a new revelation, bearing witness to the beauties of the afterlife, there is scarcely a page that does not recycle the language and logic of his detective fiction. The author took over the role of his character, whom he could then finally retire; without Holmes to hold him back, Doyle plunged deep into what he called the "illimitable ocean" of spiritualist thought.[15]

After Doyle's death in 1930, both of his known universes—the fictional address of 221B Baker Street and the spiritual afterlife called "Summerland"—continued to expand outward. Chapter 4 examines how the two universes functioned in parallel. Doyle's widow spent the rest of her life defending her husband's spiritualist legacy from overzealous followers; her sons spent the rest of their lives defending their father's literary estate from overzealous fans. Doyle's followers started conjuring up the author at their own séances; Holmes's fans started writing about the character in their own stories. In both cases, the family prohibited the unauthorized use of such likenesses, reserving its right to decide how best to conserve those universes and preserve the spirit of Doyle. The family's problem was that he had designed both universes to function smoothly and remotely without himself as the cosmological constant. In his absence, followers and fans were free to keep the faith however they liked, beyond the reach of both reason and the law. The chapter concludes with its own detour to Utah, this time to explore a third Sherlockian universe: the mystical field of literary criticism, which grounds itself on the dirty work of detection. Readers of this book wondering why it does not begin with a literature review of Holmes scholarship will find both the review and the reason buried there.

Chapter 5 traces Holmes once he departs the text, hits mass media, and goes viral. The television series *Sherlock* and *Elementary* bring Holmes up to the present day, when the ultramodern cities of London and New York simultaneously start to revolve around the Victorian detective, to strange effect. After more than a century, Doyle's good faith solution to the cultural conflicts of his day has evolved into a new problem: the language and logic of his detective fiction now informs parallel universes and alternate realities in our public sphere, especially intelligent design creationism and 9/11 conspiracy theory. On the internet, babble and superstition have no antidote, not even Sherlock Holmes, whose rational principles only make things worse.

Yet that is all Holmes has ever done, because he is only what passes for rationality, in any context. His performances make a show of science, as Régis Messac argued in 1929, but his methods are closer to "une science dégradée ou une pseudo-science" (a degraded science or a pseudoscience).[16] Everybody knows that Holmes's logic is not deductive, deriving a priori truth from rational first principles, as Aristotle taught. Nor is it inductive, generalizing a posteriori knowledge from past empirical observation and experience, as Francis Bacon demonstrated. If anything, his logic is abductive, making inferences to the best explanation that covers the known facts, although in Holmes's case "best" usually means "first that comes to mind." He is always right, even when the facts are only loosely covered. But that is not a worry; that is the beauty. Because everybody also knows that he is fictional, we humor those leaps and lapses. On the one hand, Holmes's methodology "amounts only to an incoherent, even contradictory, store of alluring maxims," as Peter McDonald observes; on the other, there is no point "subjecting the stories to such close critical scrutiny," because they are "an exercise in mythopoeic image-making," not a guide to best practices.[17] However, if we don't scrutinize the stories, then they will lure us into forgetting that the maxims are bunk. "It is only deduction if the reader can be made to believe that it is," says Ronald Pearsall, "by suspending his critical faculties."[18] Once that happens, image becomes everything. Wearing a deerstalker seems like enough to make you a mastermind, when in fact you have stopped making sense. Holmesian thinking is not a test of logic: it is a waiver, an excuse for not testing your reasons, on the grounds that you are always right when it counts and only wrong when it doesn't. The mystique of Sherlock persists because it is pure mystification—a powerful trick of the mind.

When reading fiction, there is no harm in suspending one's critical faculties, but reality is another story. Beginning with Beecham's cure-all on the back cover, Holmes keeps bearing witness to faith-based pseudoscience, helping to confuse logical and magical thinking and licensing quackery that goes from harmless to poisonous. Citing Holmes is a risky move, because it tends to encourage flawed reasoning, whether conscious or not, especially when a desired end is in view. Hitchens was so bent on indicting the president for conspiracy that he was willing to overstretch the analogy between Clinton's White House and a criminal's doghouse; by that logic, which takes discretion for confession, everyone is always guilty of something. Konnikova is so intent on elevating Holmes as a mastermind that she is willing to lower the bar for his credulous author; by that logic, which gives excuse to error, no one is ever wrong about anything. Both writers make themselves believe their own deductions.

Despite all those recent how-to handbooks, *Beeton's Christmas Annual* works more like a cartoon flipbook, merrily converting good faith into bad science. Read cover to cover, the page-turning mystery in the middle gradually transforms the science lab on the front into the sales pitch on the back, *lux et veritas* into a laxative, so that useful knowledge turns to mere excrement. Sherlock Holmes is not the scientific antithesis of his spiritualist author; he is the pseudoscientific thesis of spiritualism itself. The quality or truth of spiritualist belief is not the concern here; the problem is the quality of spiritualist logic. Its false claim to scientific authority becomes truly dangerous when applied elsewhere, in bad faith.

Dr. Watson senses that something is off from the start, soon after moving into Baker Street. Picking up a magazine to read over breakfast, Watson sees that his new flatmate has pencil-marked the heading of one particular article, which explains "how much an observant man might learn by an accurate and systematic examination of all that came in his way." From "a momentary expression" the logician can "fathom a man's inmost thoughts," while from "a drop of water" he can "infer the possibility of an Atlantic or a Niagara without having seen or heard of one or the other." The anonymous author calls his method "the Science of Deduction and Analysis." Its results show that "all life is a great chain, the nature of which is known whenever we are shown a single link." Watson has his doubts. "The reasoning was close and intense," he allows, "but the deductions appeared to me to be far fetched and exaggerated." Anticipating the objection, the author explains that those who are "uninitiated" in his method will "consider him as a necromancer," because his conclusions are "as infallible as so many propositions of Euclid." While the article proceeds to tell deduction from divination, Watson notes that its "somewhat ambitious title" has already blurred the distinction: "The Book of Life" invokes Revelation rather than *Elements of Geometry* as a model of total knowledge. On the grounds of its having no grounds, Watson concludes that this so-called science is "rubbish," neither empirical nor logical. He exclaims, "What ineffable twaddle!"[19]

Amused, Holmes outs himself as the anonymous author, and then goes on to spend the next four decades proving to Watson that "the theories which I have expressed there, and which appear to you to be so chimerical, are really extremely practical" (23–24). Before following them into those future stories, let us linger over breakfast to ask what other recent magazines and newspapers might be within reach of the table. Holmes spends so much time clipping articles from the London press that we will begin by doing the same, immersing ourselves in 1887 periodical literature that documents the state of play between religion and science during the advent of the detective. The logic of those arguments will inform the detective's theories; the language of those writers will resonate in his stories. For the moment, let us set aside the strangeness of Holmes writing an anonymous article about himself in the third person, marking its title, and then leaving it out for his new friend to find and read. "What is it?" he asks innocently, as if he were not observant enough to know what Watson is reading. To begin answering his question, the next chapter serves as a long contextual footnote to "The Book of Life," with its biblical allusion to the list of faithful Christians who will be saved on Judgment Day. Everyone else, prophesies Revelation, will be thrown into the lake of fire, and so the first step is to ask who, at the end of 1887, was trying to make the cut.

CHAPTER 1

Reason and Revelation, 1887

THE DEFENSE OF THE CHURCH

Christmas 1887 was a Sunday, and on that Christmas Eve, as it did every Saturday, the *Times* of London listed the next day's church services. None of them would have drawn Sherlock Holmes, who stays home to receive clients on Christmas morning in "The Blue Carbuncle." Although the detective seems to have little to do with the religion of his time, that historical context summoned him. By the end of this background chapter, which gradually calls him into being, Holmes will be ready to materialize fully in the next.

The *Times* divided the list of services into two parts, on two separate pages, which reflect the history and the hierarchy of religious institutions in Victorian Britain. As befits the established Church of England, its Anglican "Preachers for To-morrow" appear first, while non-Anglican "Sermons, Lectures, &c." follow later.[1] The Anglican column emphasizes the authority of the Church, a modern institution of state resting on a medieval foundation of stone. At the top are St. Paul's Cathedral, mother church of the Diocese of London, and Westminster Abbey, under the jurisdiction of the queen. Next in line are her three Chapels Royal in St. James's Palace, Whitehall, and the Savoy. The citywide tour of establishment services concludes in legal London, at the Inns of Court and their chapels, where the Church's own system of ecclesiastical courts also has jurisdiction, enforcing canon law.

After a schism of four pages, the list of non-Anglican services begins with a latitudinarian sermon at the Foundling Hospital's chapel, where the morning preacher espoused religious views broad enough to make him an outlier, if not yet an outsider. In that sermon, Alfred Momerie, a professor of logic at King's College, criticized institutional Christianity: "From being a religion of conduct it has been made into a religion of ceremony and of creed."[2] The controversial Momerie would soon have to resign from both the chapel and the college; the bishop of London banished the logician to preaching in a public hall on Baker Street, of all places. From this hetero-dox edge of Anglicanism, the list then descends into the aftermath of the Reformation. First, a cluster of Roman Catholic high masses surrounds two Presbyterian sermons, as if the pope were still trying to contain the outbreak of Calvinism. But Catholic dogma is no match for Protestant dissent, which races down the remaining list of a dozen nonconformist services across London, with diverse spiritual tenets, from Congregation-alist gathering to Methodist outreach, from Apostolic revelation to Theistic reflection, all of which make faith a matter of individual conscience.

At the very bottom of the list, the Reformation starts to lose its religion. The penultimate service is Unitarian, at Bedford Chapel in Bloomsbury, where Stopford Brooke preached the humanity of Christ after quitting his post as chaplain to Queen Victoria. The final option is not a sermon but a "discourse," offered by the South Place Religious Society, a group of Unitar-ians turned humanists who had just voted to rename themselves an Ethical Society. Invited to lecture was George Griffith, agnostic author of articles published in the *Secular Review* and poems collected in *The Dying Faith* (1884).

As proof of life, Anglican reverends could point to the recently con-secrated Truro Cathedral in Cornwall, which the *Times* called "a stone of stumbling to the critical agnostic, who wonders how it can be that the Church still commands the adherence of men of intelligence."[3] The cathe-dral, the first newly built since the Reformation, was the culmination of fifty years of church building and restoration work all across England, as the Church labored to boost attendance. A London curate observed that while "the deadness of the last century" had allowed both apathy and dissent to flourish, leaving "terrible arrears of work to make up," Truro Cathedral was a heartening sign that "the Church had awakened" and "was now full of energy."[4]

At the end of 1887, the Church needed all the energy it could muster to defend its position at the top of the *Times* list of services, since there were multiple threats to its authority from the groups below. The first threat was foreign: Rome. Queen Victoria and Pope Leo XIII both celebrated their Jubilee that year. The previous summer, the pope had sent a special envoy to London to congratulate the queen; in December, she did the same for him, sending the Duke of Norfolk, a prominent English Catholic, to Rome. Rumors swirled that the duke would offer to establish diplomatic relations between Britain and the Vatican, in exchange for the pope's public condemnation of the Plan of Campaign, an anti-British resistance movement in Ireland, where Catholic priests were helping distressed tenant farmers to organize against their landlords. The prospective deal alarmed all denominations "who entertain apprehensions of danger to the Protestant religion from such friendly relations with the Pope."[5] Dissenters loathed the pope, whom the Methodist *London Quarterly Review* called a "galvanized anachronism," while the militant Church Association decried the "gross materialistic perversions" of Anglo-Catholic vestments and ornaments.[6] At the Association's conference in November, its chairman announced that "the action of the Romanizing clergy in violating the laws of the national Church had become a national danger," warning that "a great struggle for the maintenance of Protestantism could not be far off."[7]

The second threat was closer: Ireland. In an October speech in Nottingham, William Gladstone, party leader of the Liberal minority, made a newly aggressive pitch for Irish home rule. The previous year, Gladstone had split his majority and lost his ministry over the issue, when Liberals opposed to home rule—among them, Arthur Conan Doyle—broke away to form the Liberal Unionist Party.[8] Twenty years earlier, during his first ministry, Gladstone had passed the Act of Parliament that disestablished the Church of Ireland. Now he floated the possibility of also disestablishing the Church in Scotland and Wales, "when the Irish difficulty is so far disposed of as to permit it," hoping to win back some of the Scottish and Welsh dissenters he had lost to the Liberal Unionists. Gladstone was careful not to overcommit himself, even as he made his pitch to reformers. Stating that disestablishment was "unquestionably ripe for consideration in Scotland and Wales," he also suggested, "I daresay many or some of you think it is also ripe in England," bringing cheers from his audience.[9] Conservatives were horrified by what they called "an appeal to the baser feelings of sectarian animosity," rebuking Gladstone for offering a false promise at best and a cheap bribe at worst.[10] Lord Salisbury, the Conservative Party prime minister, pledged the reverse: "To the Established Churches of this island we are attached by every sentiment, by conviction, and by affection, and no motive of political expediency shall ever divert us from the duty of defending them."[11]

The problem for Conservatives was that sectarian animosity in Wales had already passed the tipping point toward disestablishment. As in Ireland, tenant farmers in Wales were struggling to pay rent after a decade of agricultural depression. Unlike Ireland, however, the Church of England was still established in Wales, though the majority denomination was Methodism; many Welsh farmers were thus also having to pay tithes to a Church not their own. Once they started refusing, the British government began seizing and selling their stock to make up the arrears, which had led to violent clashes in the summer of 1887. (Ireland had its own Tithe War in the 1830s, when Catholic farmers made the same protest.) Now, with winter coming, there were *Times* reports of tithe collectors being pelted with rotten eggs and manure, while those farmers who did pay then found their cattle mutilated. Liberals seized the moment to argue for both Welsh disestablishment and Irish home rule on the same grounds. "In Wales, as in Ireland," said George Trevelyan in a speech to fellow Liberals, "there is not even the pretence of arranging the institutions of the country in accordance with the wishes of the great mass of the people."[12] Conservatives warned of a slippery slope. "Welsh disestablishment would inevitably be the prelude to disestablishment in England," prophesied Henry Reed, a leader of the Church Defence Institute.[13] His allies against Gladstone included the Earl of Selborne, a Liberal Unionist whose *A Defence of the Church of England Against Disestablishment* (1886) was already in its third edition. At an Institute meeting in December, Selborne stressed "the historical character of the Church," which "had existed in this land from the time when the name of Christ was first named here," but such appeals to tradition did not convince reformers.[14] "The Church must be in a bad way indeed," laughed the Liberal chairman who introduced Trevelyan, "if they had to go back to the eighth century to defend it."[15]

The *Times* at the end of 1887 was thus full of heated debate about established religion, prompting one reviewer of Selborne's book to comment drily, "The Church of England has recently grown 'interesting.'"[16] None of these articles, however, would have much interested Sherlock Holmes. His knowledge of politics, Watson notes, is "feeble," though he knows enough about dissent to disguise himself later as a nonconformist clergyman, with the right costume and "general look of peering and benevolent curiosity" (21, 170). Chapter 5 will return to the question of why the current events discussed in this chapter matter so little to Holmes. Nonetheless, the political battles over religious difference raised a philosophical question about religious belief, one that involves Holmes more directly, though his knowledge of philosophy is also "next to nothing" (21). The broader issue is not which Christian denomination will be judged true believers, their names listed in the Book of Life at the end of days, but how on earth they all know that the Book of Revelation is true in the first place.

WHAT THE CANONS SAW

Despite the mounting threats to Anglican authority, the mood was optimistic at the annual Church Congress, where clergy and laity gathered in October 1887 to review the past, discuss the present, and debate the future of their faith. In doing so, the Church pointedly contrasted itself with the Vatican, whose doctrine of papal infallibility was condemned, in the bishop of Durham's opening sermon, as "a denial of history and a stultification of reason." Speakers asked questions about how best to unify the Church during these interesting times of growing "spiritual conflict" and "political antagonism."[17] Could Anglican worship be broad enough to include both Anglo-Catholic communion and evangelical conversion? Could nonconformist clergy be won back to the Anglican fold, checking the spread of dissent? Could religious teaching at home be made more systematic, and missionary work abroad more effective? Could the working classes be convinced to choose Christianity over socialism, the gateway to atheism? As a rule, the speakers answered such questions affirmatively, insisting that the Church was stronger and more successful than ever.

On the final day of the Congress, one speaker demurred. "It is pleasant, amid the plaudits of a great audience, to proclaim the triumphs of the Faith," said the Reverend Isaac Taylor, canon of York, "but it is disheartening to have to tell the story of a lamentable failure." At a panel on the Church mission in Africa, Taylor delivered the bad news: "It must be confessed that over a large portion of the world, Islam, as a missionary religion, is more

successful than Christianity."[18] Taylor's thesis outraged the audience, causing what the next day's *Times* reported as a "sensation."[19] Crediting Islam
would also have outraged Watson, who introduces himself as a wounded
veteran of the Second Anglo-Afghan War against "the murderous Ghazis"
(15). Even though Taylor concluded that Islam was successful because it
better suited "lower races," whereas Christianity aimed higher, the rest of
the panel rejected both his testimonial and his statistical evidence. One
Anglican reverend retorted that he had personally seen the mission in Central Africa advancing with "rapid strides," having himself "worked for seven
years in its field," while another called Taylor's figures "fallacious" and his
description "fanciful."[20] At the end of October, Taylor defended himself
in the *Times*, having been "repeatedly challenged to give my authority for
statements which have aroused surprise and indignation," and even feeling
himself to have been "violently attacked." He cited further statistics from
Indian missions and additional testimonies from African travelers.[21] Eager
to promote this "very active controversy" in its pages, the *Times* printed
replies to Taylor throughout November, most of them criticizing "the perversion of figures and misrepresentation of facts into which he has been
hastily led."[22]

The correspondence staged a philosophical debate about the rules
of logic and the laws of evidence. Its main points prefigured Holmes's
maxims, as if both sides were jointly drafting the detective's forthcoming article on the Science of Deduction and Analysis. For example, the
Reverend Malcolm MacColl objected that Taylor's "facts, even if we were
to grant them without reserve, are very far from sufficient to support his
conclusion."[23] He was drawing the same distinction as Holmes between
"a good working basis" of information and the "mere surmise and conjecture" of speculation (34). Taylor countered that "a single mistake in
statistics does not invalidate a whole army of facts which no one has ventured to dispute."[24] He was showing the same confidence in his data set
as Holmes, who knows that "when a fact appears to be opposed to a long
train of deductions, it invariably proves to be capable of bearing some
other interpretation," requiring only the correction of one point rather
than the rejection of all the rest (49).

The argument soon turned personal. Having presented his evidence,
Taylor attacked his opponent, recalling another controversy involving Mac-
Coll, a zealous anti-Ottoman campaigner. When steaming down the Sava

River in 1876, on the lookout for evidence of Turkish barbarity, MacColl
claimed to have seen the corpse of a Christian impaled on the shore. He
and his fellow traveler, the Reverend Henry Liddon, reported their sighting
to the British consul in Sarajevo, who concluded "after much reflection"
that it was probably not a body but a large bundle of drying haricot beans,
hanging from a tall garden stake.[25] Undeterred, MacColl continued making
the extreme allegations for which *Vanity Fair* later rebuked him "and other
imaginative atrocity-mongers."[26] Taylor could thus remind *Times* readers
that his opponent was an unreliable eyewitness: "Canon MacColl is, we
know, able to discern impaled Christians where his fellow travelers are
only able to discover scarecrows and beanstacks."[27] The canon sees only
and exactly what he expects to see because he breaks Holmes's first rule
of investigation: "It is a capital mistake to theorize before you have all the
evidence. It biases the judgment" (27).

His objectivity called into question, MacColl defended himself by
attacking the bias of the British consul, whose theory was "one of the most
grotesque travesties of the ordinary laws of evidence that the annals of controversy supply." No bundle of beans had been observed firsthand; instead,
the idea had simply "evolved," MacColl protested, "out of the depth of the
consular mind, sagely ruminating far away at Sarajevo!"[28] In other words,
the consul does not rank among the "few people," as Holmes says of himself,
"who, if you told them a result, would be able to evolve from their own consciousness what the steps were which led up to that result" (84). Seconding
MacColl in the *Times*, his friend Liddon denied that anyone could have
such power of mind, arguing that the two canons "were better judges of
what we did and did not see than were critics who settled the matter, however peremptorily, but on *a priori* grounds, in London drawing-rooms."[29]
The staunch empiricist Watson initially makes the same objection to
Holmes's article, which he calls "the theory of some armchair lounger,"
refusing to believe "that without leaving your room you can unravel some
knot which other men can make nothing of, although they have seen every
detail for themselves." Holmes explains that he occasionally does "have
to bustle about and see things with my own eyes," but that he can usually
just draw on "a lot of special knowledge which I apply to the problem, and
which facilitates matters wonderfully" (23–24). Watson must soon revise
his opinion of "The Book of Life," but MacColl continued to object in the
same terms, calling the consul's theory "rubbish."[30]

Over the next two weeks, a dozen other writers shared their views on "What the Canons Saw," as the *Times* styled the debate, offering both travel accounts of the region and armchair analyses of those accounts. The correspondence devolved into a go-around of contradictions between different eyewitnesses, competing hypotheses, and opposed premises. As the argument grew legalistic, with both sides citing multiple sources, the question of the Church mission in Africa dropped away altogether. However, more fundamental questions emerged. When settling the truth, what matters most: Statistical probability or individual testimony? Empirical evidence or ecclesiastical authority? Human reason or divine revelation? The answers were important enough for the Church to devote a session of its Congress to "Christian Evidences" for the truth of the risen Christ. Speakers insisted that there were simply too many eyewitness accounts then, as well as conversion testimonies now, for the Resurrection to be anything but an unquestioned fact.[31] At the end of the month, Liddon deployed that argument against his opponents in the *Times*, likening them to nonbelievers who still doubted Christ's resurrection, even though it had been "seen by a great many persons." He argued that skeptics were the ones guilty of bias, for "when the human will is strongly disposed to ignore the practical consequences of a fact it has a subtle and almost unlimited power of blinding the intellect even to the most elementary laws of evidence."[32]

His opponents immediately took that point and turned it back against the canons. The folklorist John Stuart-Glennie sharply observed, "The inferences that may be drawn from it with respect to the question of the Resurrection may differ from Canon Liddon's."[33] At the beginning of December, another skeptic called the question on impalement. Unless the canons "wish their evidence to be regarded in the same light as that upon which rest such miracles," they must "produce independent corroborative evidence." Barring that, their account will be relegated "from the regions of fact to the regions of faith."[34] After one last round of letters, in which the canons insisted that they had "the best of reasons for having no doubt at all about a fact" and for "believing the evidence of our own eyes," even the *Times* editors had seen enough, declaring "This correspondence must now close."[35]

The question of what exactly the canons had seen in 1876 remained open, however, because there was no one yet present in 1887 who had enough special knowledge to facilitate matters—reviewing all the evidence, hearing all the testimony, noting all the biases, and weighing all the inferences—and thus to distinguish fact from faith. That ultimate logician was definitely on the way: Liddon's appeal to "elementary" laws of evidence seemed almost to summon him. Four days later, the *Times* announced the publication of *A Study in Scarlet*, which "is certain to be read, not once, but twice by every reader; and the person who can take it up and lay it down again unfinished must be one of those people who are neither impressionable nor curious."[36] Had they known Sherlock Holmes was coming, the canons would have believed his rational principles to be hostile to their revealed knowledge and religious authority. And they would also have sworn that his impressionable and curious readers, fascinated by the Science of Deduction and Analysis, belong among the sinners whose names will be struck from the Book of Life.

A DANGEROUS POSSESSION

One day the world would learn "that there is nothing—and can be nothing—antagonistic between true Science and revealed Truth," predicted the president of the Church Congress, hoping even that "Religion may find in Science its handmaid and its friend." In 1887, that day had not yet come. The chairman of the Christian Evidences panel, worrying that "science is becoming popularised," seemed to have Holmes in mind. He exhorted his audience to remember that because "popular science is of necessity superficial, and cannot be deep and far-reaching," it "may be a dangerous possession."[37] Science was popular enough to feature in advertisements for last-minute Christmas presents. The publisher of *Beeton's Christmas Annual* also promoted *Science Made Easy*, its English translation of Gaston Tissandier's *Les récréations scientifiques* (1880), with a blurb promising that "science is not only made easy, but rendered absolutely delightful."[38] Science was so easy and delightful that Henry and Edward Dale, brothers who manufactured electrical and optical equipment, also advertised "Scientific Toys" as "The Best Presents for Children."[39]

Other signs of science's far-reaching popularity at the time were newspaper reports of the many lectures, both academic and popular, being given all over London. In November, the astronomer Norman Lockyer, one of the founders of the journal *Nature*, delivered his "Preliminary Notes on the Spectra of Meteorites" to the Royal Society. The *Times* praised the lecture as "the mature result of an arduous and sustained series of investigations, supported by a vast mass of cumulative and converging evidence which amounts in many respects to actual demonstration." Lockyer's chain of reasoning, whose "starting-point is the meteorite" and whose "goal is the orderly evolution and cycle of the universe," was just as ambitious as Holmes's links from a drop of water to an unknown Atlantic or Niagara.[40] At the previous week's meeting of the Middlesex Natural History Society, the popular science writer William Mattieu Williams read a paper on "the chemistry of the London clay, in which he gave a lucid explanation of the component parts of the clay, illustrating his remarks by some interesting experiments."[41] Holmes's own muddy experiments in *Scarlet* are just as interesting: by analyzing the "splashes upon his trousers," he can tell "by their colour and consistence in what part of London he had received them" (22).

During the 1880s Williams wrote "Science Notes," a column for the popular *Gentleman's Magazine*, presenting his thoughts on everything from chlorophyll to water purification to whale extract to human body weight—and that was just the November 1887 issue. Most Victorian middle-class journals and magazines contained science writing, pitched at various educational levels, from features like "A Fossil Continent" in the *Cornhill Magazine*, which marveled at "the levelling and topsy-turvy view of evolutionary biology," to summaries of recent experiments, including "a new method of determining the density of the earth" documented in the *Contemporary Review*. The periodicals also kept readers up to speed with all the latest books, such as the astronomer Richard Proctor's *Other Suns Than Ours* (1887), which the *Westminster Review* praised as "a conspicuous example of a scientific man adopting the popular literary method with success."[42] Proctor's book was a collection of his writings for the illustrated magazine *Knowledge*, which he founded with the aim of educating the public about scientific knowledge. Its subtitle: *Plainly Worded—Exactly Described.*

Plain speaking about science, however, meant contradicting fundamental Christian beliefs. Proctor had to reassure readers that *Knowledge* was not directly attacking their faith: "If anyone objects to a scientific statement about facts because he cannot reconcile it with his own ideas about matters theological, I may be at the pains to point out that the facts alone concern us here."[43] At best, too much popular science might make readers feel unpleasantly topsy-turvy. "There is in many people's minds a painful uneasiness about the relation of the Bible to modern science and philoso-phy," acknowledged William Elmslie, a Presbyterian minister writing about Genesis and geology.[44] At worst, popular science would cause a fall from grace into "the abyss of indifference," Celestine Edwards told the Christian Evidences panel in October. "Philosophical speculations adverse to Chris-tianity—and, indeed, all religions—have, and are being, let loose from the educated few to the multitude," warned the Dominican evangelist, "where they receive a cordial welcome without being questioned."[45] Proving the preacher's point, a chatty article that month in *All the Year Round* debunked the miracle of faith healing as a purely psychosomatic effect. "How is it possible for people in this sceptical, practical nineteenth century of ours," it asked, "to have this blind, irrational faith in the miraculous, which would have brought joy to the heart of a medieval Bishop?"[46] Sherlock Holmes would second the question. Even though he and Watson seem to be "deal-ing with forces outside the ordinary laws of Nature" in *The Hound of the Baskervilles*, the detective firmly sets aside "the supernatural explanation," explaining that "we are bound to exhaust all other hypotheses before falling back upon this one" (684).

Mixed in with the discourses of critical agnostics at the bottom of the *Times* list of services were what Edwards called "the absurdities of athe-ism."[47] On Sunday, November 6, the Theistic Church promised "Reason Without Atheism," but just below were two science lectures: the naturalist Ramsay Traquair on "Paleontology and the Doctrine of Descent," and the chemist Percy Frankland on "Micro-organisms: Their Place in Nature."[48] Those lectures were the trapdoors through which one fell on the way from universal theism above to secular humanism below. On that Sunday, the radical minister James Picton lectured on "The Christ of Mythology" at the South Place Ethical Society, while the historian Edward Beesly lectured on the French Revolution at the Positivist Society. Positivism, as formu-lated by the philosopher Auguste Comte earlier in the century, rejected theological explanations of a natural world fully knowable through human reason, itself part of that world. Sharing Holmes's "passion for definite and exact knowledge," Comtean positivists also gave people the same unpleas-ant first impression as the detective, seeming "a little too scientific" in their worldview, which "approaches to cold-bloodedness" (17). As Emilio Cas-telar complained, positivists "play endless funeral marches at the fancied burial of all abstractions and of all gods. Listen to them and you would take metaphysical religion for dead."[49] Positivists could argue, as did James Morison in *The Service of Man: An Essay Towards a Religion of the Future* (1887), that a rational and ethical humanism is a stronger basis for moral self-sacrifice than Christianity, but the conservative *National Review* was doubtful, finding "little in this book tending to the edification and comfort of a sceptic, who looks back with regret to a religion which he can no longer hold."[50] Wilfrid Ward, a Catholic essayist, bluntly refused to discuss Morison's conclusions, "from which all Christians would shrink with horror."[51]

At the end of November, the *Pall Mall Gazette* looked back with some horror at the secular and scientific lectures delivered that first Sunday, observing that the threat of nonbelief was not only moral but also political. "The London Sunday is fast becoming revolutionized," it warned, thanks to "the vast machinery at work throughout the metropolis for the propagation of Liberal, Radical, Socialistic, and anti-Christian principles."[52] The phrase neatly summarized the chain of associations through which conservative politicians linked liberalism to atheism, with some justification. Even the social reformer William Rossiter, founder of the South London Working Men's College, worried in July that "artisan atheism" was spreading through secular clubs that "denounce the Church as the enemy of truth."[53] And Gladstone himself, on the morning of his controversial October speech, addressed the Nottingham Congregational Institute to discuss the "one great controversy, greater than all others, which has been developed in unusual and menacing dimensions," between "belief on the one side and no belief on the other." A devout Christian, Gladstone emphasized that he was on the side that accepted "the great and fundamental and essential verities of the Christian religion," arguing that disestablishing the Church would not entail disavowing faith.[54] Gladstone's apologist rhetoric in Nottingham did not sway his opponents. An anonymous "Unionist" wrote the *Times* to tell Gladstone "to keep the Almighty out of his perorations," since he worshiped instead "the hideous Moloch of party."[55] Conservatives had been playing the same divisive anti-Christian card against Gladstone since 1880, when they accused him of being "on the side of atheism, disloyalty and immorality" for supporting the atheist Charles Bradlaugh's request, as a newly elected Liberal MP, to affirm rather than swear his oath of office on the Bible.[56] Trevelyan now accused Conservatives opposed to Irish independence of once again faking moral outrage for political reasons. "Will anybody tell me," he demanded, "that they conscientiously believed that they would have their consciences painfully affected by seeing a man of unsound religious views sitting in the House of Commons? (Laughter.)"[57]

Despite the Liberal laughter, atheism was no joke in late 1887. It was both a direct spiritual threat to the Church and a divisive political issue for Parliament. In 1886, Bradlaugh had finally been allowed to affirm, after being imprisoned and fined for refusing to swear the oath. Now he was struggling to get his Oaths Act through Parliament, to change the law itself, at a moment when public support was low. In warning that "anti-Christian meetings are numerous," the *Gazette* may have been indulging in conspiracy theory, but the threat of a London Sunday revolution in November 1887 was not a fantasy. It was real enough that the *Gazette* had been obliged to go back and choose the month's first Sunday as "an ordinary and fairly representative day" of lecture meetings because "the last two or three Sundays have been somewhat disorganized owing to the action of the police."[58] This was a somewhat understated reference to Bloody Sunday on November 13, when thousands of protestors marched into Trafalgar Square, demanding the release of William O'Brien, a radical Irish MP who had been imprisoned for helping to organize a rent strike in County Cork. Tensions were already high in Trafalgar Square, where unemployed workers had been demonstrating throughout the summer and fall; the London police were also still on edge from the Fenian (Irish republican) bombing campaign that lasted from 1881 to 1885. In early November, the home secretary had approved the Metropolitan Police proposal to ban all meetings in the square. Secularists who championed free speech joined the radicals, socialists, and republicans in marching. Bradlaugh's colleague Annie Besant, a leader of the National Secular Society, rallied a crowd in Clerkenwell Green before the march, declaring the ban "not worth the paper upon which it was printed."[59] When the various processions all converged in Trafalgar Square, they met a massed police force, and a melee ensued. The Conservative politician Henry Richards immediately blamed Gladstone for his inflammatory Nottingham speech, describing the march as an anti-Christian crusade. "The Radical clergy and Nonconformist ministers who support Mr. Gladstone in his attack upon the London police," said Richards, "could hardly be gratified with the wholesale Sabbath desecration and lack of Sunday rest caused by their friends to-day."[60]

The religious dimension of Bloody Sunday explains why that month's question of "What the Canons Saw" escalated so quickly into a high-stakes argument about the evidence for miracles in general and resurrection in particular. During that argument, Liddon and MacColl threw a sharp counterpunch. The church canons described themselves as scientific observers of empirical facts, setting their shared objective knowledge against the singular subjective revelation of the British consul, whom they represented as an oracular "sage." That debate tactic—co-opting the opponent's method and reversing the burden of proof—was also executed on a grander scale during the panel discussion of Christian Evidences at the Church Congress. The bishop of Manchester set the many eyewitness testimonies to the risen Christ, who appeared "to more than five hundred brethren at once," against the mass delusion theory of the modern skeptic, who unreasonably believed that "above five hundred men could be brought together who had dreamt the same dream at the same time, and at the same place."[61] To rationalize their belief in miracles, the canons followed the same logic, but they also pointed to the history of "the advancement of Christendom in the arts and sciences" as evidence that science and religion have always been friends— and never better friends than today, despite misunderstandings in the past. Although "blunders on the part of Christian tribunals" once led to the persecution of Galileo, "no Christian of sense would now admit that any proved truth of physical science can be inimical to the creed of Christendom."[62]

In the same spirit, Liddon had already shown himself more than willing to accommodate geological truths within his religious creed. Preaching at St. Paul's Cathedral one year earlier, he argued that the coming "universal and final ruin" of Revelation is "only the extension of present facts," such as earthquakes and volcanoes. Turning science against itself, Liddon followed a different chain of evidence, from a drop of magma to the apocalypse: "As our globe was a ball of fire, at any moment the pent-up forces which surge and boil beneath our feet might be poured out."[63] In other words, the lake of fire is as real as the Atlantic Ocean or Niagara Falls; scientists have proved that truth. Whether or not they can save themselves from damnation remains to be seen.

DISPENSING WITH GOD

According to Watson, Holmes's knowledge of geology is "practical, but limited" to analyzing soil samples; geological theories of deep time and gradual change do not interest him (21). Those theories made Reverend Elmslie uneasy, but they were no longer as painful to contemplate in 1887 as a generation earlier, when John Ruskin complained about hearing the "dreadful Hammers" of geologists when reading Bible verses.[64] Liddon could now make a seismological case for Revelation, while the *Cornhill Magazine* could make light of timelines that include "a few million summers or so," quipping that "in geology we refuse to be bound by dates."[65] Yet Elmslie still wrestled with the "antagonism between the natural and the revealed accounts of creation." He tried to reconcile the two timelines by first questioning how much geologists had actually proved: "Of certainties in scientific theory there are few." He then emphasized how much room for error science always leaves, since "all that can be attained is probability, especially in speculative matters, such as estimates of time, explanations of formation, and theories of causation." While not hostile to science, Elmslie called attention to its past errors, which offset the Church's past mistakes; both scientists and theologians were then equally guilty of "the folly of pretended infallibility." Having leveled the regions of fact and faith, Elmslie could then describe creation as "a composite process," which "begins in the spiritual world and terminates in the material." The accounts complement rather than clash with each other: "The Bible shows us God creating; geology shows us the world being created."[66] In turn, Elmslie's account of the world's beginning complements Liddon's sermon on its end. The whole story comes full circle, from spiritual origin to material creation, and then from geologic upheaval to divine destruction.

Biology was more difficult than geology to reconcile with the Bible, although it, too, was less painful to contemplate than it had once been. At the end of 1887, Charles Darwin's son Francis published a biography of his father, and early reviews suggested that Darwinian theory was no longer any more controversial than Copernican. "The principle of evolution, so early broached and so long discredited," said the geologist Archibald Geikie in the *Contemporary Review*, "has now at last been proclaimed and accepted as the guiding idea in the investigation of Nature."[67] Recalling the 1859 publication of *On the Origin of Species*, the *Times* reviewer commented, "It is difficult for the present generation to project themselves backward 30 years and realize the shock to old-fashioned beliefs which must have been caused by the launching of Darwin's book."[68] The *Westminster Review* described "the storm of indignant fury and vituperation with which the book was received

by the majority of the clergy, a great number of naturalists, and a large proportion of the reading public," but explained that there was no longer any
doubt. "The links in the chain of his argument," it concluded, sounding like
Holmes, were "now almost self-evident propositions." Even *The Descent of
Man* (1871), which presented "the inevitable extension of his theory to the
human species," had by 1887 lost much of its power to shock.[69] Of *Descent*,
the *Times* said only that its publication "revived the storm to some little
extent, and drew forth malignant representation from certain quarters; but
opposition to the new doctrine, apart from genuine criticism, was seen to
be hopeless."[70] The *Illustrated London News* added that Darwinian evolution
"is no longer supposed to be hostile to spiritual religion, or to the sublimest
conceptions of Divine creation and of human destiny."[71]

While the general process of evolution was supposed to be compatible with religion, the specific mechanism of natural selection was not,
because it replaced providence with accident as the first cause and prime
mover. "There is no keener opposition in philosophy than between those
who look for design in nature, and those who shout 'Away with it, away
with it!'" declared the Duke of Argyll at the end of 1887.[72] Argyll was the
creationist author of *The Unity of Nature* (1884), in which he argued that
scientific reason leads to religious conviction. He described reason as "the
gift of seeing the necessity or the natural consequences of things." Because
"the links of consequence are the links of an endless chain" of causes and
effects, both material and moral, "there is no limit to this kind of following." It thus follows that the great chain leads to supernatural agency, since
the natural world is too interlinked not to be intelligently designed: "No
man can believe that its existing arrangements of Matter and of Force are
self-caused, self-originated, and self-sustained."[73] Argyll was pursuing the
same line of reasoning as William Paley, whose *Natural Theology* (1802)
formalized still the most popular argument from design. Just as a working
watch is evidence of its maker, so, too, does the natural world imply a creator, "for every indication of contrivance, every manifestation of design,
which existed in the watch, exists in the works of nature."[74] The debunking
of that argument has a history as long as the making of it. In 1887, while
he was fighting for the Oaths Act, Bradlaugh tried once again to settle the
question; with Besant, he issued a pamphlet asking "Is There a God?" Not
on any good evidence, he answered: "There is no sort of analogy between
a finite artificer arranging a finite mechanism and an alleged divine creator

originating all existence," because "from an alleged product you are only at liberty to infer a producer after having seen a similar product actually produced."[75] That logical objection to natural theology—which goes back to David Hume's *Dialogues Concerning Natural Religion* (1779)—did not stop Argyll from updating the argument. He contended that Darwinian evolution actually reaffirms "the instrumentality employed by the Divine Author of all living things," who is thereby producing the natural world before our very eyes. Furthermore, the phrase "natural selection" is an analogy so loose that it leaves a loophole, suggesting design even though it denies the designer. Darwin had regretted the phrase, but Argyll still held him to it, restoring divine cause to evolutionary theory, since that theory "says nothing whatever of the beginning of the whole series." Argyll thus repeated in a different scientific discipline the same apologetic maneuver as Elmslie, who reintroduced God to Genesis just before the beginning of geologic time. Argyll was not attacking Darwin, whom he claimed to admire, but rather his followers, the agnostic scientists and atheist philosophers who gleefully "thought that Darwin had dispensed with God."[76]

Argyll's argument from design in December came at the end of a year-long debate in the pages of *The Nineteenth Century* with the most famous of those followers: the agnostic biologist Thomas Huxley. Huxley was known as "Darwin's bulldog" after his 1860 Oxford debate with the Anglican bishop Samuel Wilberforce, who panned *Origin of Species* in the *Quarterly Review*. A generation later, that event had become almost mythical; the lack of contemporaneous notes meant that its winner was still debatable. The publication of Darwin's biography briefly renewed hostilities at the end of 1887, even though the bishop had died more than a decade earlier. Huxley had contributed a chapter discussing the early reception of *Origin of Species*, including Wilberforce's review, which he dismissed as "the insolence of a shallow pretender."[77] In a letter to the *Times*, the bishop's son Reginald protested that Huxley had willfully misrepresented his father, suggesting that the biologist still resented his "castigation" at Oxford. Huxley answered immediately, agreeing that "an effectual castigation was received by somebody," but that "respect for filial piety" prevented him from saying whom.[78] Huxley's sharp tongue and ironic tone was familiar to readers of his many articles for *The Nineteenth Century*, where he had been debating the devout Gladstone off and on since 1885. Their disagreements about biblical miracles, from the six days of creation in Genesis to the demonic swine in the Gospels, always remained gentlemanly. In contrast, over the course of the year, Huxley's exchange with Argyll turned nasty.

The origin of their dispute was Liddon's sermon on geology and the apocalypse, which pitted Darwin's view of "the graduated sequence and course of events" against Revelation's prophecy of their sudden and final end. Calling the theory of evolution merely "fashionable," Liddon concluded that "there are more important laws than those which surround our puny life, moral and not merely physical forces," and that "these royal and ultimate laws shall wreck the natural order of things which seems so stable."[79] In February, Huxley critiqued Liddon's misunderstanding about the laws of nature: to describe them as physical forces is "a mark of pseudo-science." Laws of nature cause nothing to happen; they prevent nothing from happening. Instead, they are "a mere record of experience upon which we base our interpretations of that which does happen and our anticipation of that which will happen." Apologists attack scientists for closing their minds in advance, refusing to believe that miracles can happen, but the record simply does not show that they have ever happened. Scientists must therefore "decline, on the ground of the utter insufficiency of the evidence, to put faith in the reality of that other world."[80] As Holmes suggests in *Hound*, scientific naturalism is methodological, not philosophical. It does not rule out supernatural explanations; it simply sets them aside, awaiting one that can be demonstrated rather than debunked. Until then, natural explanations will suffice.

Furthermore, Huxley continued, not even the events described in Revelation would necessarily wreck the natural order of things. For example, global cooling would produce a series of geologic disasters, "a scene of horror which even the lurid fancy of the writer of the Apocalypse would fail to portray," wiping out humanity. "And yet," he observed, "not a link in the chain of natural causes and effects would be broken." Huxley then imagined what it would be like to be able to follow that chain not only forward and backward forever in time but also outward infinitely in space, far past Niagara or the Atlantic. To that supreme logician, who makes Sherlock Holmes look like a child, the whole of creation is just a scientific toy: "If a being endowed with perfect intellectual and aesthetic faculties, but devoid of the capacity for suffering pain, either physical or moral, were to devote his utmost powers to the investigation of nature, the universe would seem to him to be a sort of kaleidoscope, in which, at every successive moment of time, a new arrangement of parts of exquisite beauty and symmetry would present itself; and each of them would show itself to be the logical consequence of the preceding arrangement, under the conditions which we call the laws of nature." And so, if scientists "put little faith in the wild vaticinations of universal ruin" envisioned in Revelation, then that is not because they "contradict scientific principles," but because they are visions of the future rather than a record of the past. As such, "the evidence of their scientific value does not fulfil the conditions on which weight is attached to evidence." Bringing his argument back around to evolution, Huxley concluded that "biologists who have not been asleep for the last quarter of a century" must therefore reject the notion of "a quasi-spiritual something" that shapes the developing form of individual organisms, though they will be called materialists at best and atheists at worst.[81]

In March, Argyll rebuked Huxley for taking "no cognisance of anything outside the beggarly elements of the Positive Philosophy," which admits only material objects, even though science itself traffics in ideas and abstractions, including the abstract idea of science itself. Rejecting that philosophy, Argyll again updated his argument from design, swapping out observation for inspiration. He proposed that the human mind has an innate faculty of "instantly and instinctively" recognizing the "specialty of purpose" that informs organic structures and natural relations. Argyll appealed to a "higher kind of rational order" than allowed by positivist principles, "which seem expressly devised to cover up and conceal from our own sight some of the most salient of the phenomena we are pretending to describe." Argyll was making the same point as Holmes does when Watson misses the big picture: "You see, but you do not observe" (162). But Argyll did not want his readers merely to observe nature, which is the sort of thing scientists like Huxley do; he wanted them to appreciate it, relying on faculties other than vision and reason, while still staying down to earth. "When we kneel down and put our ear to nature to listen to her divine music," he directed, "we must try to catch not only every note, but every tone and semitone and overtone, and all the transitions between them, if we desire to enjoy and to understand her harmonies to the full."[82] According to Argyll, Holmes needs revision: you see, but you do not feel.

Argyll was not the only writer in 1887 to base the argument from design on strong feeling rather than sound reasoning. Edmund Clay was a psychologist, not a natural scientist, and so he looked inward rather than outward for evidence of a higher power. In October's *Westminster Review*, Clay argued that the "common-sense" of human beings is a "special faculty." When science questions the existence of the soul, the mind rebels, since we feel that we actually do have souls, and have a hard time imagining that we do not. That innate feeling sets a limit on acquired knowledge: "To be a science, a system of explanations must be satisfactory to common-sense."[83] It does not take a two-time winner of the French national chess championship to point out the logical problem here, though one did so the following month. "It is the part of common-sense to adapt itself to science," replied Edward Chamier from Paris, "not the part of science to adapt itself to common-sense." Clay's "common-sense" is simply confirmation bias. Because we see so many intricate relations and useful adaptations in nature, "the inference is almost irresistible for common-sense that our world must be the work of a supreme Intelligence." But that inference is actually the premise, which begs the question. "To argue that our world must be the product of design because it is generally conformed to the requirements which have been abstracted from itself," Chamier explained, "is equivalent to arguing that the course of rivers has been ordered providentially with reference to the cities which stand upon their banks."[84] The analogy neatly illustrates the circular logic that informs all arguments from design. As one review of Argyll's *Unity of Nature* observed, "The plan and treatment of the book is essentially dogmatic and *a priori*, i.e., theological rather than inductive or scientific."[85]

To deflect that criticism, Argyll redirected it toward Huxley, accusing the scientific approach of being essentially theological. Darwin's followers were guilty of not only a priori dogmatism, refusing in advance to believe in divine miracles, but also post hoc animism, invoking the law of natural selection as if it were a divine principle. With their "bad physics and worse metaphysics," scientists had succumbed to "the fumes of worship and of incense raised before the fetish of a Phrase."[86] In other words, "natural selection" was just ineffable twaddle, as Watson would say, no more meaningful a phrase than Holmes's "Science of Deduction and Analysis," the capitalization suggesting that it, too, has been fetishized. Unlike Holmes, Huxley accepted the criticism, conceding that "as is the case with all new doctrines, so with that of Evolution," which meant that "the enthusiasm of advocates has sometimes tended to degenerate into fanaticism, and mere speculation has, at times, threatened to shoot beyond its legitimate bounds."[87] Huxley therefore cautioned his readers: "The scientific imagination always restrains itself within the limits of probability." That line was a tribute to his lifelong friend and fellow materialist John Tyndall, who had recently retired from the Royal Institution. In his "Discourse on the Scientific Use of the Imagination" (1870), Tyndall argued that scientists are free to speculate when making hypotheses, so long as they are also "able to surround imagination by the firm frontiers of reason."[88] Lack of restraint, however, encourages both intellectual promiscuity and religious enthusiasm, as Huxley suggested with a wicked final metaphor: "The spirit of pseudo-science has impregnated even the imagination of the Duke of Argyll."[89]

Having accused scientists of reasoning in bad faith, Argyll attacked again in September, making an ad hominem argument against Huxley himself. He first praised Darwin for bringing "no preconceived theories" aboard the Beagle. Because the young naturalist's mind was "receptive, not constructive," he avoided confirmation bias when exploring the Galapagos Islands. Huxley, on the other hand, had once made "a ridiculous error" because of his "theoretical preconceptions" about evolution. In 1868, studying an ocean floor mud sample that had grown slimy after years of being preserved in alcohol, he thought he had discovered a new form of life, perhaps even its origin, which he called Bathybius. Seven years later, Huxley retracted his theory when another researcher found that Bathybius was just gypsum, precipitated out of the seawater by the alcohol. Argyll gloated that Huxley's mistake "teaches us that neither the beauty—nor the imposing character—nor the apparent sufficiency of an explanation may be any proof whatever of its truth."[90] In the same issue, Wilfrid Ward also criticized Huxley's imposing character. Darwin's bulldog denied miracles because he insisted on "the undeniableness of the facts he adduces, their bearing being presupposed in his sense, and no other interpretation being suggested as possible."[91]

Huxley retorted in November that undeniable evidence, not infallible authority, was what counted for science, which was why Argyll's analogy between Darwinism and fanaticism could not hold. "Pending the production of further evidence," said Huxley, "I hold that the existence of people who believe in the infallibility of men of science is . . . purely mythical."[92] Pending publication for the end of the month, A Study in Scarlet would soon prove Huxley's point. On the other hand, the novel does score a point for

Argyll: the mythical detective is also fanatical. When introducing Holmes to Watson, Stamford calls him "an enthusiast in some branches of science," especially forensic research, which involves him "beating the subjects in the dissecting-rooms with a stick" (16–17).

To get the last word of 1887, Argyll extended his scientific/fanatic analogy even further, calling the theory of natural selection "a shibboleth," which is to say, "a sort of intellectual idol before which all the world has been called to bow, as the one all-sufficient and all-embracing explanation of the origin of species." He redirected all the scientific objections to religious authority back toward science itself, which was conducting its own version of the Spanish Inquisition: "It has become the fashion to deprecate even the suspicion of heresy on this cardinal tenet of the new philosophy."[93] The argument comes full circle. Just as Liddon had done a year earlier, Argyll wrote off Darwinism as merely trendy, a fad for quoting *Origin* instead of believing Revelation, whose lake of fire is full of fashion victims with the same bad taste and worse judgment.

OVERELABORATE DEDUCTIONS

In November, as the dispute with Argyll heated up, Huxley reflected on some other recent sermons on science and religion that "indicate the possibility of bringing about an honourable *modus vivendi* between the two."[94] That possibility seemed remote, however, given another mounting threat to Christianity: biblical criticism. Also called higher criticism, this historical approach to the Bible undermined its status as the authoritative word of God, transcribed by Moses. Instead, the "documentary hypothesis" of the German scholar Julius Wellhausen proposed that the Pentateuch is a collation of separately authored documents, all of which date from later than the time of Moses. In October, the *London Quarterly Review* took a good-humored shot at a German theological series—"It represents the critical school, and needs therefore to be weighed as well as read"—but the challenge to religious faith was serious.[95] In the *Contemporary Review*, archeologist Reginald Stuart Poole lamented the "destructiveness" of Wellhausen's argument, which "supposes the main body of the Hebrew legislation to have been constructed after the return from Babylon, with the direct object of clothing with the authority of Moses what he did not

write." Objecting to the notion that the Torah was "a pious fraud," Poole
critiqued the "suspicious result" of what he took to be the circular logic
and confirmation bias of Wellhausen and his colleagues, who used their
"wholesale process of elimination" against any textual evidence that con-
tradicted their historical claims. They were guilty of not-so-pious fraud:
"The interpolation and corruption of the text cannot be proved on *a priori*
grounds," Poole objected, "but the framers of the hypothesis are so firmly
persuaded of its truth that they do not scruple to clear away any passage
which tells against it."[96]

Against the critics who played interpretive games with texts, spinning
around in hermeneutic circles, Poole set the empirical methods of archeol-
ogists as they constructed timelines, basing interpretation on a foundation
of excavated stone. "They have depended upon facts," he emphasized, "and
they have maintained a due balance between external and internal evidence;
not working wholly within the document, nor yet neglecting the evidence
of its vocabulary and style." Demonstrating how best to date the Pentateuch,
he compiled the evidence of both documents and monuments, finding "its
whole weight is against the new critics."[97] Poole was not the only archeologist
pushing back against biblical criticism. The *London Quarterly Review* noted
approvingly that a recent book published by the Palestine Exploration Fund
"seizes upon every fact tending to throw light upon the Bible," showing both
"the most careful adherence to scientific method" and "an entire absence of
desire to use the evidence of the land *against* the book." The review spun
apologetic deference to the Bible as scientific neutrality, but this was the
same circular logic running in reverse, confirming the opposite bias. "The
facts are steadily accumulating," it insisted, "and their constant tendency is
to confirm the strict accuracy of the Biblical record."[98]

Biblical scholars like William Robertson Smith challenged that army of
facts. Ten years earlier, Smith been tried for heresy in the Free Church of
Scotland after writing an *Encyclopedia Britannica* entry that called Moses's
authorship into question. Now questioning Poole's argument, Smith found
nothing "that appears to have real weight either for or against the views of
the critics," concluding that the archeologist had "hampered and weakened
his argument by attempting to prove too much." Inadvertently, Poole had
even shown that "the Book of Genesis is not pure history throughout, but
contains a certain amount of matter closely allied to folk-lore."[99] Reducing
religion to folklore was precisely what biblical criticism threatened to do,

abetted by the rise of comparative religion. The *Times* was then running ads for Andrew Lang's *Myth, Ritual, and Religion* (1887), a two-volume anthropological and psychological analysis of religious practice, which stopped just short of questioning religious belief itself. Protesting this trend was Charles Spurgeon, a Baptist preacher who wrote a series of articles in 1887 objecting to the gradual decline—what he called "the Down-Grade"—of true faith among Protestants, accelerating thanks to both Darwin and Wellhausen. "The Holy Spirit is degraded into an influence," Spurgeon lamented, "the punishment of sin is turned into fiction, and the resurrection into a myth."[100]

Spurgeon opposed revelation to reason, but there were many Christian apologists seeking a modus vivendi, though the reviews were generally as mixed as the approaches. On the one hand, apologists could accept the historical data, while still offering their own testimony. "Criticism and religion are compatible," the Reverend James Wilson declared in his *Essays and Addresses: An Attempt to Treat Some Religious Questions in a Scientific Spirit* (1887), assuring readers that they could "become a Christian without having first believed in the divinely guaranteed accuracy of the Bible."[101] Wilson may have tried to avoid "reducing the Bible to the level of any other book," but one reviewer warned he was "treading on very dangerous ground."[102] On the other hand, apologists could reject the data, offering their own evidence instead. In his *Apologetics; or, The Scientific Vindication of Christianity* (1887), the German theologian Johannes Ebrard began by promising to "proceed from observed facts and with painful care, step by step, forwards," and ended after amassing three volumes worth of "evidence for the historical truth of the original biblical tradition."[103] While praising Ebrard for attacking "the current anti-Christian theory in minute detail and with much force," the *Contemporary Review* concluded that his treatise was "too rigid a demonstration to be wholly acceptable to the English mind, with its healthy instinct against over-elaborate deductions in theology."[104]

Somewhere between those two approaches was George Mivart, a Catholic biologist who had been Huxley's student. He accepted evolution but rejected natural selection, offering his own theories of "individuation" and design. In 1885, Mivart began a series of *Nineteenth Century* articles that explored "the essential harmony which exists between the truths of science and the dictates of religion." Knowing that he seemed to "deal in paradox," Mivart argued that Galileo himself had been a revelation from God, a sign that the Church should leave scientific questions to the scientists. The

Church therefore had no authority to restrict "the freedom thus so happily gained" for science in general, especially evolutionary biology, whose
evidence it must not simply reject.[105] In 1887, Mivart extended the same
freedom to biblical criticism, even though it suggested that much of biblical history was "mythical, legendary, or quite false." Because that history
underwrote the Church's authority, Mivart knew he was risking apostasy,
but he insisted that "as regards Biblical criticism, we are living in what may,
by analogy, be called a pre-Copernican period." Fortunately for Mivart,
because there were many inspirational passages in the Bible about which
historians and scientists had nothing to say, he could close his argument by
opening a loophole for faith. "If, then, Catholics at present are free to hold
as inspired, in some undefined sense of that word, only certain portions,
or passages, of the books set before them as canonical," he reasoned, "then
no difficulty to faith can arise from any historical research whatsoever, and
no detriment to science can spring from any such religious belief."[106]

   It does not take a veteran judge of Her Majesty's High Court to point
out the logical problem here, though one did so in October, when James
Stephen accused Mivart of "playing fast and loose with reason." According
to Stephen, the loophole opens into a rabbit hole, plunging down past doubt
into relativism. "Once allow full play," he explained, "to physical science, to
literary criticism, and to history, and it is impossible to be absolutely certain
either of the existence of God, the infallibility of the Church, or the truth
of any one of its dogmas." At that point, just as Spurgeon warned, religion
becomes a fiction in which anything goes. "Why may not we write our
novel as we like?" asked Stephen.[107] Mivart wrote back to defend himself:
his position "may seem the acme of unreason" to Stephen, but there was
nothing contradictory about it. Science does not lead to "the annihilation of
Christianity," because science cannot prove any negative claims about religion, such as the claim that "there is no knowable, personal First Cause."[108]
It is therefore perfectly rational, countered Mivart, to continue believing
that there is one.

   Stephen responded a month later, astonished by "a state of mind which
seems to me even stranger than the one which originally surprised me."
One by one, he debunked Mivart's theological claims, with their "practically impossible conditions of disproof," to demonstrate that the "whole
system is an elaborately disguised and inconsistent begging of the question." Mivart accepted the authority of the Church on all questions, other

than the ones with actual answers; he therefore adopted a peculiar view of Church history, in which ecclesiastical officials "were always right when they could not be tested, and generally wrong when they could." For that reason, Mivart's mind could only run in logical circles, repeating to itself, "I believe the Church to be infallible because the infallible Church says it is infallible."[109] According to Stephen, the only thing that still gave Mivart any reason to believe was this endless loop of appealing to an authority that appealed to itself.

Mivart did worry about losing his faith. "A Catholic who is so unhappy as to have become anyhow convinced that the essentials of his religion are untrue," he acknowledged, "cannot of course consistently make any further profession of Catholicity."[110] Despite his doubts, the biologist continued to profess his faith, searching for that modus vivendi, but the pressure was severe. The more he wrote, the more tightly his logic ran in circles. "We are not the creators of the things we know," he later insisted, "nor do we carry within us the reasons why they exist." To avoid falling into "absolute scepticism," we must trust in scientific truth, having faith in God as its origin, even when it contradicts dogma. The unacceptable alternative is "to suspect that a lying devil may be the cause of all things, deluding us in our fundamental intellectual perceptions."[111] Mivart thus reasoned that science itself saved him from heresy, but he also wondered about the eternal consequences for being wrong. In an 1892 essay, "Happiness in Hell," he asked if it were really true that "countless multitudes of mankind will burn for ever in hell fire." No need to worry, he answered: the horrors depicted in Revelation are only "startling symbols," connoting rather than denoting the difference between losing and gaining heaven.[112] That difference must be unimaginably and inexpressibly infinite, and so to take those horrors literally is, paradoxically, to forget what is due to God. Mivart thus offers an elegant solution for those who worry about whether their names are in the Book of Life. The best way to prove you are a true believer, saving yourself from the lake of fire, is to stop believing that it really exists.

RETROSPECTIVE PROPHECY

As fellow biologists, Mivart and Huxley had once been friends, united in their enthusiasm for Darwinian evolution, but natural selection eventually

REASON AND REVELATION, 1887 35

drove a wedge between the Catholic and the agnostic. In 1871, the same year Darwin published *Descent*, Mivart published *On the Genesis of Species*, a title that says it all. Mivart revised Darwin's *On the Origin of Species* to include a divine cause within evolutionary theory, which would then "completely harmonize with the teachings of science, philosophy, and religion."[113] He also wrote an anonymous review of *Descent* in which he accused Darwin of the same bad faith for which Argyll later attacked his followers: "The Author, starting at first with an avowed hypothesis, constantly asserts it as an undoubted fact, and claims for it, somewhat in the spirit of a theologian, that it should be received as an article of faith."[114] Huxley retaliated by panning Mivart's book, not a serious study but a children's toy, whose author was permitted only to "amuse himself with such scientific implements as authority tells him are safe and will not cut his fingers." In contrast, Huxley praised the courage of scientists who "follow reason and fact in singleness and honesty of purpose, wherever they may lead, in the sure faith that a hell of honest men will, to him, be more endurable than a paradise full of angelic shams."[115] For Huxley, it was better to reason straight from Holmes's drop of water to the lake of fire than to pretend that science could circle around it.

In between arguing with Mivart in the 1870s and Argyll in the 1880s, Huxley wrote a classic essay, "On the Method of Zadig." Zadig is Voltaire's fictional Babylonian philosopher, so wise that he can describe the queen's dog and the king's horse without ever having seen them, simply by reading their tracks in the forest. Huxley grouped together all the above historical sciences that threaten religion—archeology, geology, astronomy, paleontology, and evolutionary biology—and argued that they share the same method: knowing the distant past by closely observing the present. Huxley called it "retrospective prophecy," wishing there were such a word as "backteller."[116] His chief example of a backteller was the French paleontologist Georges Cuvier, famous for reconstructing extinct animals from a few fossilized bones, just as Holmes reconstructs crime scenes from a few dropped clues. "This power," as Holmes says in *Scarlet*, "is what I mean when I talk of reasoning backward" (84). Arthur Conan Doyle counted Huxley among the "chief philosophers" who informed his university education, when he became so unhappy with Catholicism that he could not continue in the faith.[117] There are strong clues that Holmes has Zadig in mind when writing "The Book of Life," especially when he notes that his approach, though strictly empirical, may look like necromancy. In Huxley's account, the philosopher spooks Babylonian authorities not only because his faculty of reason uncannily resembles the gift of revelation, but also because his scientific method undermines "all the sacred foundations" of their religion, casting doubt on revelation itself.[118] The Science of Deduction and Analysis, however, fully confirms the religion being practiced in the immediate neighborhood of Baker Street. To understand why, this book will next work its way backward, from the character to his author, who was following reason, seeking harmony, and finding paradox.

CHAPTER 2

Reasoning Backward, 1881–1887

In his 1924 autobiography, *Memories and Adventures*, Arthur Conan Doyle reflected on the cultural debates surveyed in the last chapter. Siding with natural scientists against Christian apologists, he described a generation gap that "opened between our fathers and ourselves so suddenly and completely that when a Gladstone wrote to uphold the Gadarene swine, or the six days of Creation, the youngest student rightly tittered over his arguments, and it did not need a Huxley to demolish them."[1] By 1924, however, Doyle was the world's most famous spiritualist, publicly debating both apologists and scientists, whom he riled for two different reasons. Recounting his recent lecture tour of the United States, where he spoke at both Carnegie Hall in New York City and the Mormon Tabernacle in Salt Lake City, Doyle insisted on the truth of spiritualism: "It is an absolute fact that when we do communicate with these emancipated souls they all tell us of a fate very different from any which we learn from the Churches."[2] Christian churches objected to the different fate, while the scientific community rejected the absolute fact. To locate the sources of his conviction, this chapter retraces Doyle's path to spiritualism in the 1880s, when he began practicing medicine, writing fiction, and attending séances in Portsmouth. The same path leads to Holmes's entrance in *A Study in Scarlet,* where it then backtracks to an earlier American adventure in Utah.

Born into an Irish family in Edinburgh in 1859, the same year as the publication of Darwin's *On the Origin of Species,* Doyle was raised Roman Catholic. At the age of nine, he was sent to a Jesuit boarding school in northwest England, where he began to reject "the uncompromising bigotry of the Jesuit theology," as he later said, which promised "sure damnation for everyone outside the Church." After a final year abroad at a Jesuit school in Austria, Doyle began studying medicine at the University of Edinburgh, where he met Dr. Joseph Bell, the brilliant diagnostician whom Doyle later credited as his model for Sherlock Holmes. Full of "all the new knowledge," Doyle renounced his old faith: "I found that the foundations not only of Roman Catholicism but of the whole Christian faith, as presented to me in nineteenth-century theology, were so weak that my mind could not build upon them." The apologists were so uncompromising, letting "manifest absurdities" stand in the Bible "without even a footnote to soften them," that their arguments were easily demolished by the young medical student. Upon receiving his degree in 1881, Doyle had settled almost to the bottom of the *Times* list of services, "a respectful materialist" floating somewhere between Unitarianism and agnosticism.[3]

But no lower, because not all was lost. Doyle's worldview "never for an instant degenerated into atheism, for I had a very keen perception of the wonderful poise of the universe and the tremendous power of conception and sustenance which it implied." His scientific education under Bell, however, meant that he insisted on "definite demonstration" and "positive proofs" as "the only conditions upon which I could resume any sort of allegiance to the unseen." In this state of "arrested development," Doyle attended an 1881 lecture entitled "Does Death End All?" by Joseph Cook, an American Protestant clergyman.[4] Attacking Huxley, Cook argued that agnosticism and atheism are "violently unscientific." Logic itself ordains that there must be a first cause and thus a divine will that preexists the natural world; if divine will gives life to matter, then human life must transcend matter, as the soul.[5] Writing to his mother after the lecture, Doyle found Cook's argument from design "clever" but "not convincing."[6]

In 1882, Doyle set up a general medical practice in suburban Portsmouth, although he declined to take advantage of his family's Catholic connections there. He continued to distinguish between convincing and

unconvincing proofs of the unseen. On the one hand, he praised bacte-
riologists for developing vaccines to fight "infinitesimal creatures," even
those that have "not been detected by the highest microscopic powers."[7]
On the other, when William Warner announced in the *British Journal of
Photography* that his camera had captured "Od," a radiant psychic energy,
Doyle wrote to debunk the claim. "Mr. Warner cites as facts things which
are incorrect, and that in a crisp and epigrammatic way which is delightful," Doyle scoffed. "From these so-called facts he draws inferences which,
even if they were facts indeed, would be illogical, and upon these illogical
inferences draws deductions which, once more, no amount of concession
would render tenable."[8] Warner defended himself by lumping Doyle with
all the other "men of science who know little or nothing of the laws of
nature, and when something is stated that is beyond their powers of com-
prehension they turn it into ridicule, and thus expose themselves as to their
want of knowledge in occult science."[9] Impatient with illogical occultism,
Doyle was even more so with illiberal Christianity. When a Portsmouth
clergyman objected on moral grounds that the local Young Men's Christian
Association had hired a young female singer to perform at a fundraiser,
Doyle publicly rejected this "so-called Christianity," declaring he would
rather "choose between Mohametanism and Atheism."[10]

During this period, when Doyle was not only practicing medicine but
also publishing short stories, he started a novel, *The Narrative of John Smith.*
The protagonist, a middle-aged gentleman suffering from gout, spends a
week confined to his sofa, reflecting on the same questions of science and
religion that absorbed his much younger author. The novel has no plot:
Smith talks to a few visitors but mostly to himself, showing off a highly educated and conflicted mind as he discourses on everything from molecular
biology to Trinitarian theology. Like his author, Smith accepts evolutionary
theory, but even though Darwin is on his bookshelf, he endorses Herbert
Spencer's spiritualized version of evolution, in which humanity ascends
toward higher and higher forms of being. Also like his author, he rejects
organized religion, which has become far too "narrow." Such broad views
would eventually force Alfred Momerie out of both his chapel and his college, but Smith foresees an alternate future in which a professor of logic
is the best possible preacher. As a thought experiment in creedless natural theology, Smith tells the story of a "lonely reasoner" who observes
the world so closely, finding there such perfect balance, that he is "able to

evolve from his own resources a religion" based on empiricism.[11] The novel thus introduces a series of fictional surrogates that served to distance the Edinburgh-educated doctor from unscientific questions. Doyle created a character who asks them instead, and that character imagines another who will one day answer.

Doyle finished *John Smith* in 1883, but when he mailed the only copy to a publisher, it went missing, and he told his mother he would have to begin all over again.[12] The rewritten novel, never published and not quite finished, turned up at an auction of his papers in 2004. Strangely, the manuscript contains heavy editing in its first but not its second half: Doyle not only doubled back to rewrite the whole novel but also doubled back, before reaching the end, to re-rewrite the beginning. It is also strange, given this redoubled effort, that Doyle denied the existence of this manuscript in early 1893, when he was famous enough for *The Idler* to invite him to reflect on his work before Sherlock Holmes. Telling the story of the missing novel, which had "a personal-social-political complexion," Doyle expressed "horror" at the thought of *John Smith* turning up, and relief that it was "safely lost."[13] Doyle recalled Smith only to bury him, just as he would try, at the end of that year, to bury Holmes.

In 2011, the British Library published the unearthed manuscript, now an uncanny artifact: a story compulsively repeated and then repressed, which finally returns after more than a century, twisted back on itself, doubling for its lost twin. The original narrative, at once fictional and autobiographical, was already divided against itself. Smith allowed Doyle not only to imagine following scientific methods toward a religion of the future, as the lonely reasoner does, but also to contradict scientific principles in the present. At the outset, Smith puts more faith in indestructible atoms than immortal souls, but he proceeds to chip away at materialism, until his beliefs can float upward from Darwinian to divine. Smith develops the same argument from design—reasoning that existence itself presupposes a first cause— that Doyle rejected when Cook proposed it. When Smith ridicules "the unimaginative complacent type of scientist," he repeats the same critique that Warner levied against Doyle. At that point, Smith flips the script, just as the Duke of Argyll did, calling naturalism a "scientific shibboleth," and comparing scientists to "zealots." He also adopts Canon Liddon's apologetic argument, the one that Huxley called a mark of pseudoscience, accusing biologists and geologists of laying down natural laws. By the end of *John Smith*, it is the agnostic, denying the obvious design in nature, who is "your pseudo-scientist."[14] The manuscript cuts off a few pages later, as if Doyle needed to go no further. The real end of this interior dialogue was to turn the tables on his own scientific education, convincing himself of the opposite view and pledging allegiance to the unseen. It was more important to rewrite the beginning twice, getting the questions right, than to rewrite the ending at all, leaving the answers open.

MANY MONTHS OF INQUIRY

His spiritual development no longer arrested, Doyle was free to investigate the paranormal experiences in person that he had previously explored only in print. By 1884, he had published enough stories crossing over from everyday realism to supernatural romance that he told his mother he was considering a collected edition entitled *Twilight Tales*.[15] Those stories exhibit what one critic calls "gothic materialism," showcasing "uncanny objects" that float along that boundary.[16] The project never materialized, but seven of the stories would eventually be reprinted in October 1887, just before Sherlock Holmes appeared, in an edited collection called *Dreamland and Ghostland*. Those lands are the home of "vast untouched sciences," which John Smith promises are reachable by clairvoyants and Buddhists.[17] In late 1883, soon after losing *John Smith*, Doyle began studying both those sciences—psychical research and theosophical wisdom—at the prompting of Alfred Drayson, the president of the Portsmouth Literary and Scientific Society, which Doyle joined in November. Drayson was a longtime spiritualist, as well as an amateur astronomer, who outdid Darwin in 1859, publishing two books. *The Earth We Inhabit* argued that our rapidly expanding planet was once small enough that the tropics began at the poles; *Great Britain Has Been and Will Be Again Within the Tropics* proposed that the earth goes through an oblique second rotation every thirty thousand years. The *Eclectic Review* called his work "a parade of pseudo-science," marveling that "no man naturally, or without long and painful cultivation, could become so inconsequent and absurd."[18]

Drayson's reputation did not improve as time went on. In 1873, he presented his newest astronomical calculations, predicting a regular cycle of future ice ages. Calling it "the theory of a paradoxer," the journal *Nature* admired only his earnestness: "He attempts to prove this, and, we believe, has succeeded in persuading himself that he has proved it."[19] Like George Mivart, Drayson dealt in paradox because he sought harmony. At the end of *Great Britain*, he anticipated one day publishing "a much larger volume, in which it will be proved that the various sciences, as well as Scriptural revelation, form one harmonious whole."[20] By the time he met Doyle, Drayson's beliefs had moved from orthodox Christianity toward spiritualism, but he was still trying to reconcile science and religion. In 1884, he published "The Solution of Scientific Problems by Spirits" in *Light*, the journal of the London Spiritualist Alliance, describing a recent séance at which the spirit of an astronomer had presented new data about the satellites orbiting Mars and Uranus.[21]

Doyle admired Drayson, remembering him as "a very distinguished thinker and a pioneer of psychic knowledge." Drayson introduced Doyle to the astral projections and celestial planes of theosophy through the work of Alfred Sinnett, whose *Occult World* (1881) and *Esoteric Buddhism* (1883) repackaged the elaborate teachings of its founder, the Russian émigré Helena Blavatsky, for an English audience.[22] Blavatsky promoted theosophy as the recovery of ancient wisdom, not a religion itself so much as a spiritual philosophy that fused all the world's religions together with science, transcending both Christianity and materialism. "Theosophy's interest in the formation of consciousness lent itself to evolutionary theory," Gauri Viswanathan explains, which "accounted for its attraction to people in professional fields looking for new forms of religion not founded on faith alone that would also be amenable to the tools and techniques of science."[23] When she arrived in London in 1887, Blavatsky founded a journal, provocatively titled *Lucifer*, which made the case that only theosophy could resolve the arguments ongoing in the more mainstream periodicals. "We work for true Religion and Science, in the interest of fact as against fiction and prejudice," its first issue announced that fall, emphasizing that "real Science should not be limited simply to the physical aspect of life and nature."[24] In November, Sinnett encouraged readers to explore "the higher regions of Nature" that lie beyond "the shore of materialistic thought." Those regions were nonetheless accessible by way of reason, since theosophical faith derived from "the logic of facts appealing to human intelligence." Although Sinnett railed against "ecclesiastical tyranny" that demanded "the surrender of that reason," the December *Lucifer* contained an open letter to the archbishop of Canterbury.[25] It proposed an alliance with Christianity against agnosticism and materialism, even if "professing Christians are not prepared to under-take a critical examination of their faith."[26]

Having already conducted that examination, Doyle found theosophy to be "a very well-thought-out and reasonable scheme, parts of which, nota-bly reincarnation and Kharma, seemed to offer an explanation for some of the anomalies of life."[27] Unfortunately, theosophy did not offer any empir-ical demonstrations, at least not after 1884, when the psychical researcher Richard Hodgson traveled to India to meet Blavatsky. She invited him to witness the materialization of handwritten letters out of thin air, sent by her mahatma spirit guides. Hodgson's meticulous report judged Blavatsky to be "one of the most accomplished, ingenious, and interesting impostors in history," who had staged the whole affair.[28] His damning evidence, includ-ing room diagrams and handwriting analysis, "shook my confidence very much," Doyle recalled.[29] However rationalistic, theosophy was finally too esoteric for Doyle; it placed too much faith in the individual subjectivity of the seeker. "Occultism has preached no doctrine more emphatically," asserted *Lucifer*, "than the necessity of dependence on the intuitions, and the reality of interior illumination."[30] Theosophy therefore suffered from "the defect of not being verifiable," as Andrew Lang observed, recommend-ing that its followers find themselves "a new Pythagoras, who not only remembers what occurred to him in each phase of his metempsychosis, but can bring evidence to support his memory."[31]

Lacking empirical evidence, theosophists drew analogies to empirical sciences, making concrete metaphors—higher regions, deeper waters—as fast as they could mix them. "For each sufferer from that inner cataract which shuts out from his consciousness the prospect of the invisible world," declared Sinnett, swapping oceanography for ophthalmology, "there is only one surgeon who can successfully perform the necessary operation—the man himself."[32] Drayson introduced Sinnett to Doyle, who "was impressed by his conversation" but unconvinced by his rhetoric, which "could never have met my needs for I ask for severe proof."[33] Blavatsky's own physician, William Ellis, explained that theosophists simply did not work that way: "We cannot bring proof positive to those who desire a Euclidic demon-stration." Like Sinnett, Ellis drew an analogy to natural science, arguing that theosophy advances via the same "accumulation of small details [by which] a philosopher like Darwin worked out his scheme of natural evolu-tion."[34] Nonetheless, Doyle rejected Blavatsky's charismatic authority for the same reason that the canons objected to British consular authority. A theory evolved out of the depths of individual consciousness can only be a travesty of the ordinary laws of evidence.

The proof that failed to materialize for theosophy was just what spiritualism claimed to have in hand. The movement was then four decades old, having begun in 1848 in the Burned-Over District of western New York, where the adolescent Fox sisters, Margaret and Kate, claimed that they could communicate with spirits, who responded by rapping in thin air. As spiritualism spread from America to Europe in the 1850s and 1860s, with other mediums discovering their own psychic powers while entranced in the séance circle, it accumulated more kinds of empirical evidence: tilting tables, floating handkerchiefs, sliding planchettes, slate writing, levitating mediums, spirit materializations, and ectoplasm.[35] The movement was founded on what Douglas Kerr calls the paradox of "an almost magical faith in material evidence on the part of the searcher after spirit desperate to emancipate himself from materialism."[36] In the early stages of that search, Daniel Cottom observes, spiritualism "abandoned traditional conceptions of sublimity," inviting the spirits home to shift the furniture: it therefore "vulgarized the supernatural."[37] During the 1870s, however, spiritualism adopted a more sophisticated and professional tone. Its "rhetoric and conceptual language underwent transformation," Roger Luckhurst argues, "from a predominant antagonism to science towards increasing attempts to formulate utterances inside scientific frameworks."[38] That high-level language was convincing enough to persuade a group of high-profile scientists, including the biologist Alfred Russel Wallace, the chemist William Crookes, and the physicist Balfour Stewart.

Not all scientists were convinced. "Surely no baser delusion ever obtained dominance over the weak mind of man," said John Tyndall, while Huxley called spiritualism "an additional argument against suicide," if the afterlife were indeed so full of "twaddle."[39] Spiritualism split the scientific community because it deftly turned the scientific method against itself. "It was argued time and again that one must accept the facts," Peter Lamont explains, "and that to do otherwise was unscientific." At the séance, the confidence in empirical observation collided with the commitment to scientific naturalism, producing what Lamont calls "a crisis of evidence."[40] To what extent could you believe your own eyes? To what extent could you believe someone else's testimony? How could you decide which scientists to believe? For Tyndall and Huxley, the commitment to naturalism trumped any evidence to the contrary; for Wallace, Crookes, and Stewart, all the observed evidence outweighed that commitment.

By the early 1880s, there was also enough evidence of fraud that the spiritualist community had itself split into two factions: the true believers of the London Spiritualist Alliance, who testified together in *Light*, and the skeptical investigators of the Society for Psychical Research (SPR), who tested séance phenomena in the field. The SPR, which published Hodgson's report on Blavatsky, exposed so many mediums as fakes that *Lucifer* complained it was "a society bent upon giving the lie to its own name."[41] The SPR was not itself immune to skepticism, however, especially once it started treating telepathic messages more seriously than spirit mediums. After its publication of *Phantasms of the Living* (1886), the lawyer Alexander Innes accused the SPR of "a great laxity in testing its evidence," taking testimony for truth and betraying "a bias in favour of telepathy."[42] When Balfour Stewart died just before Christmas 1887, the *Times* obituary delicately omitted the fact that he was the current president of the SPR. But psychical research still retained more credibility than spiritualism, which the *Illustrated London News* called "the modern demonology of raps under the table," while the *Cornhill Magazine* called it "blasphemous rubbish."[43]

Doyle initially shared "the usual contempt" for spiritualism, which "seemed at that time to be chaos so far as philosophy went," particularly compared with theosophy.[44] After the exposure of Blavatsky, Doyle overcame his contempt and spent much of 1886 reading about spiritualism and taking notes. By January 1887, he was conducting telepathic experiments with his friend Henry Ball and attending séances at the home of his patient Thomas Harward. While the dates and details are hazy, there is no question how quickly Doyle became convinced that both forms of communication were possible, because he said so publicly. In July, he wrote a letter to *Light*, recounting a recent séance at which a spirit had recommended a book that only Doyle knew he already had in mind. "After many months of inquiry," Doyle enthused, this experience "showed me at last that it was absolutely certain that intelligence could exist apart from the body," giving him "assurance of an after existence" that rewarded all deserving souls and refused "deathbed repentances or other nebulous conditions." Doyle praised spiritualism's liberality, as opposed to Catholicism; he closed by declaring "the truth of this central all-important fact."[45] Doyle also underscored that fact in his notebook: belief had become knowledge.[46] A month later, he wrote again to *Light*, this time "as a Spiritualist" with nothing to fear from skeptics, even Hodgson. "Spiritualism in the abstract has no 'weak points' because it is *pro tanto* truth," said Doyle; any faults emerge only in practice, when "swindlers of the lowest order" give séances a bad rap.[47]

AN EXACT SCIENCE

Waiting just offstage that summer, ready for his Christmas debut, was Sherlock Holmes. Doyle wrote *A Study in Scarlet* in March and April of 1886, offering it first to the *Cornhill Magazine*, which rejected it, and then to the house of Ward, Lock & Co., which bought the copyright but did not publish the novel for more than a year. During that time, Doyle researched, experimented, and converted. "Becoming a spiritualist so soon after creating the quintessentially rational Sherlock Holmes," biographer Andrew Lycett says, "is the central paradox of Arthur's life." Lycett immediately resolves the paradox before it can become a problem for Holmes, arguing that Doyle "regarded spiritualism as a science or, at least, a natural extension of science," just as SPR researchers did. Although he was no longer committed to naturalism, Doyle understood his beliefs to be consistent with the rational principles and empirical methods that Holmes demonstrates in *A Study in Scarlet*.[48] The *Beeton's* cover shows the same kind of laboratory where we first meet Holmes, precipitating a drop of his own blood out of a liter of water. In testing bodily fluids for evidence, the detective would certainly draw the line at ectoplasm, unlike his author. However, according to Lycett, there was no paradox from Doyle's perspective—and thus no problem from ours. If we plead contextual rationalism on the author's behalf, then we preserve the quintessential rationalism of his character.

Although he asks no further questions, Lycett does enter the research notes and the *Light* letters into evidence as proof of Doyle's early conversion, unlike previous biographers. They dodge the paradox by deferring the conversion until 1916, when Doyle formally announced in *Light* that spiritualism was "a new revelation which constitutes by far the greatest religious event since the death of Christ." He rejected the mass delusion theory, just as the bishop of Manchester did at the Church Congress; spiritualism could possibly not be "an outbreak of lunacy extending over two generations." After "thirty years of thought," he emphasized, pointing back to his *Light* subscription in 1887, he "cannot be accused of having sprung hastily to my conclusions."[49] Doyle's biographers have all since complied. In his 1931 memorial tribute, fellow spiritualist John Lamond called it "the wildest of all surmises to imagine that Arthur Conan Doyle, as the result of some sudden or erratic impulse, embraced the tenets of spiritualism." The tables are turned: it is the skeptic, not the spiritualist, who is the lunatic. But even the skeptical Hesketh Pearson agreed in 1943 that Doyle "took a long time" to arrive at his faith, "attending innumerable séances, reading hundreds of books, investigating all sorts of phenomena." Likewise, John Dickson Carr stressed in 1949 that he was "not a Spiritualist" himself, but he still defended Doyle from the objection "What would Sherlock Holmes have said?" Objection overruled: Doyle "had studied the subject for nearly thirty years before coming to a judgment," and moreover, "his judgment had never been keener or his faculties more alert." When Pierre Nordon tackled that subject in what he called "the most delicate part" of his 1967 biography, he dismissed the charge of lunacy as groundless. "It is easy to oppose a mystical or mystified Conan Doyle to the sceptical logician of the Holmesian mythology," Nordon cautioned, but "this contrast is purely imaginary." More recent biographers continue to show delicacy, downplaying Doyle's early experimental phase to avoid embarrassing Holmes. Daniel Stashower skips past the 1887 *Light* letter, noting only that "Sherlock Holmes would have made short work of it," while Russell Miller defers the letter along with the rest of Doyle's spiritualism to the end of his biography, keeping the detective in the clear.[50]

Even the contrarian Christopher Hitchens, indelicate enough to point out "the most astonishing disjunction" between author and character, soon follows the party line: "At all events, prior to 1914 Conan Doyle had shown no more than a sympathetic curiosity."[51] Lycett disrupts that timeline, but he rehearses the same conversion narrative as the other biographers, only much faster: Doyle may have taken months rather than years to reach spiritualism, but he still never had to spring there. Yet that speed is its own problem, which Lycett does not address. "The educated mind is most undeniably attempting to free itself from the heavy fetters of materialism," encouraged *Lucifer* in October 1887, but Doyle had already written to *Light* three months earlier to say that he was no longer "fettered with the prejudices of early education."[52] How did he free his mind so quickly?

The short answer: Sherlock Holmes, for whom it is time to plead con-textual irrationalism. Following Nordon, who calls Holmes "the creation of a doctor who had been soaked in the rationalist thought of the period," literary critics tend to view the detective as "the product of a period during which Conan Doyle had been substantially influenced by scientific natural-ism," which puts Holmes "at odds" with his author's spiritualism.[53] But that is not the whole story, as the record shows. Doyle was equally immersed in arguments *against* scientific naturalism and rationalist thought, especially arguments from design and for the hereafter. Because Doyle's imagination was impregnated with the spirit of pseudoscience, as Huxley would say, Holmes's conception was far from immaculate. Biographers can skirt the issue, but there is no doubt that Doyle conceived Holmes during his first enthusiastic burst of spiritualist research, which then accelerated immedi-ately after writing *A Study in Scarlet*. Soaked in ectoplasm, the detective did not arrest Doyle's religious development; he abetted it, liberating the doctor from materialism. To be convinced of spiritualism, Doyle had first to con-vince himself that it was possible to extend science that far. It is not. But it is certainly possible to invent a new method and call it a science, or better yet, a Science, whose first principle is fundamentally antiscientific. When Holmes declares that he needs only the tiniest traces of evidence, glimpsed only for a moment, to reach infallible conclusions, he undermines the sci-entific method that he apparently represents. He may look and sound like Huxley's ideal reasoner, able to follow every single link in the great chain of cause and effect, but he does so without having to fulfill Huxley's conditions of evidential weight. On the one condition of having no conditions, the Sci-ence of Deduction and Analysis can theoretically be extended forever.

Our reading of "The Book of Life" needs revision. It is not a scientific article; it is a spiritualist tract. Lawrence Frank suggests that Holmes's title is a glancing reference to the medieval Book of Nature, in which God's plan may be read, indicating that the detective rejects William Paley's natural theology. Frank then reads the article as expressing "a Darwinian worldview" of biological life, its language also echoing the views of other Victorian scientists, especially Huxley and Tyndall.[54] That interpretation is certainly possible, but it ignores the title's direct reference to Revelation, citing scripture before science. And even more than the Bible, the article's language echoes *Lucifer*. Holmes's ideal logician reasons from a single drop of water to oceans and cascades as yet unknown, just as Sinnett advised theosophists to look for the truth that lies beyond "the shore of materialistic thought." Sinnett cautioned that "to use and apply the knowledge of supermaterial laws which occult studies disclose is a life's task," but Holmes warns that his work is even more taxing.[55] "Like all other arts, the Science of Deduction and Analysis is one which can only be acquired by long and patient study," he says, "nor is life long enough to allow any mortal to attain the highest possible perfection in it" (23). Not even the housebound John Smith has time to study for the Sherlock Holmes test of thinking. Instead, seeking to unfetter his mind and think his way beyond the Atlantic to the infinite, Smith closes his eyes to "conjure up the image of a fall which shall extend from horizon to horizon," which demonstrates that "the human mind can very readily dwarf Niagara."[56] However, without that drop of water, there is no empirical evidence that the spiritual truth is out there. Only Sherlock Holmes, whose conclusions are "as infallible as so many propositions of Euclid," can deliver what Blavatsky's physician could not: demonstrations of proof positive (23). To the airy abstractions of theosophy, Sherlock Holmes adds water and precipitates spiritualism—if not yet in fully solid state, at least substantial enough for Doyle's mind to build on.

"What ineffable twaddle!" cries Watson, who possesses the characteristically English mind that rejects overelaborate deductions, as the *Contemporary Review* so appreciated.[57] The commonsensical doctor, with his scientific education, is the other authorial surrogate in play: he voices the contempt that his author initially felt for spiritualism. His role is to make Holmes convince him, as quickly as possible, that the Science of Deduction and Analysis is not just rubbish. As Edward Chamier insisted, the proper function of common sense is to ask science to explain itself: "If deduction lead where common-sense cannot follow, it has gone astray."[58] Having already startled Watson with the famous line "You have been in Afghanistan, I perceive," Holmes does so again by correctly identifying a retired sergeant of the marines from observing him across the street (18). Even with "fresh proof," Watson still harbors the same "lurking suspicion" of Holmes that Hodgson had of Blavatsky, wondering whether "the whole thing was a prearranged episode, intended to dazzle me" (25–26). Unlike Blavatsky, though, Holmes is no impostor, even if he resembles a necromancer. Upon request, he can always explain the logical steps, based on empirical observation, that lead to his result. Observing Watson's deeply tanned skin, haggard face, and stiff shoulder, Holmes reasons, "Where in the tropics could an English army

doctor have seen much hardship and got his arm injured? Clearly in Afghanistan" (24). Watson follows Holmes's line of thought, remarking that "it is
simple enough as you explain it," but the audience that matters most is his
author. Doyle was convincing himself that spiritualism, though it looked to
others like modern demonology, was just common sense.

Unlike Watson, Holmes experiences logic as a leap: "From long habit
the train of thoughts ran so swiftly through my mind that I arrived at
the conclusion without being conscious of intermediate steps" (24). He
thereby acquires the same "swift knowledge" that *Lucifer* ascribed to theosophists, "which is called intuition with certainty."[59] The Duke of Argyll
called it a higher rational order, which John Smith describes as "the power
of arriving at results intuitively and instinctively, which would cost other
men much trouble and labour."[60] Nice work, if you can get it: for Holmes,
the scientific method becomes "a kind of intuition" that transcends thought
(24). "It was easier to know it," he says to Watson, "than to explain why I
know it" (26). Holmes appropriates the power of theosophical intuition "to
enlighten the competent inquirer," as he says; what is hidden from others is
"plainly revealed" to him (23). But Holmes's kind of intuition also trumps
theosophy. He can enlighten even incompetent inquirers like Watson, slow-
ing down and backing up to explain how he got his results, while theosophy
can only keep arriving at them out of nowhere. Holmes makes revelation
seem plainly reasonable, because it is *effable*, expressible in words, which
makes theosophy sound like twaddle.

Before Holmes owns up to authoring "The Book of Life," Watson senses
these potential contradictions, calling it "the theory of some armchair
lounger who evolves all these neat little paradoxes in the seclusion of his
own study" (23). The Science of Deduction and Analysis sounds like a hoax
because, as even Blavatsky admitted, "paradox would seem to be the natural language of occultism."[61] But Holmes himself is no paradoxer. He may
translate the language of occultism into the language of empiricism, but
his own thinking never goes beyond this world: he observes, but he does
not seek. Unlike Argyll, who set no limit on this kind of following, Holmes
draws a line—or rather, his author drew it for him. He is not the lonely reasoner who John Smith imagines will one day follow the great chain of life
all the way up to a divine cause. Holmes's reasoning can extend as far as an
unknown Atlantic or Niagara, but not beyond, keeping him well within the
bounds of world geography. To meet Doyle's needs, Holmes must remain

standing on the shore of materialist thought, even as his method erodes it, so that his testimony to the nearly limitless power of pure reason carries as much weight as possible. The detective describes other people mistaking his new science for revelation, when in fact he is the one unwittingly describing Doyle's new revelation as a science. At 221B Baker Street, there are none of Mivart's paradoxes to resolve, because the 1880s arguments between scientists and apologists in the periodical press never happened. The only thing to read at breakfast is "The Book of Life."

Watson soon after vouches for his friend having "brought detection as near an exact science as it ever will be brought in this world," leaving the next world to his author (33). Even so, Watson's word may not be enough for everyone to believe that Holmes's method is scientific. "We want something more than mere theory and preaching now," says Inspector Gregson, frustrated when Holmes declines to say whom he suspects of the murders in *Scarlet*, telling Scotland Yard to wait and see (50). Gregson protests, as Watson once did, that Holmes's method seems more like revelation than reason, especially when he does not reveal his reasons. Like Zadig, he spooks the authorities: earlier in the novel, Holmes startles the constable who discovered the murder by describing that scene so accurately. "It seems to me that you knows a deal more than you should," says the officer, who has "a frightened face and suspicion in his eyes" (35). Now, "as if by magic," Holmes gets his man—his cabman, to be precise, summoned to the door of 221B. At this uncanny moment, when the detective cries out the murderer's name "with flashing eyes," Huxley's retrospective prophecy looks too close to divination for comfort. To reassure the police that his exact science is not so weird, Holmes offers to answer any questions about his chain of reasoning, having "reached the end of our little mystery" (51). Just he is about to do so, the novel interrupts him. As if by magic, we are brought as far from Baker Street as we can get in this world, westward across the Atlantic and past Niagara, all the way to the edge of the unknown: Utah.

A SUDDEN LEAP OF LOGIC

For fans of Sherlock Holmes, the long middle flashback to "The Country of the Saints" has always been the place where *A Study in Scarlet* loses the plot. Subbing for Watson, an omniscient narrator relates the American history of the London crime. To avenge the wrongful deaths of his fiancée and her father among the polygamous Mormons, the frontiersman Jefferson Hope tracks the two men responsible from Salt Lake City through Cleveland to London, where he continues the chase, now employed as a cabman, finally catching and killing them. That backstory told, the novel returns to Watson's narration of Holmes's final explanation, which covers the London murders but not the American ones. This "jump" to Utah, complained the *Hampshire Post*, is "sudden and startling," and the switch to anonymous third-person narration "jars upon the autobiographic method" of Watson's first-person account.[62] Once they got past this rocky landing in the mountain West, early reviewers generally enjoyed their visit. The *Post* admired the "remarkably well written and intensely exciting" subplot, while the *Hampshire Telegraph* praised its "weird pictures of the terrible autocracy of Brigham Young."[63] Six months after *Beeton's Christmas Annual* had sold out, the first trade edition of the novel was published; its new preface boasted, "The description of the deadly Mormon association of tyranny and vengeance, is as true in its features as it is enthralling in interest."[64]

That interest waned in the twentieth century, when fans of Sherlock Holmes began skimming through the backstory; their objection was not jumping to Utah but going there at all. These readers all took their cue from the frontiersman himself. After the flashback, Hope tells Holmes, "It don't much matter to you why I hated these men," before cutting to the London chase (78). In his 1944 edition of the novel, Christopher Morley called the flashback "a tedious interruption" and cut it down to four pages. Writing about the art of detective fiction in 1961, Jacques Barzun lumped the flashback together with all of "those intolerable middle sections which potbelly three out of four of [Doyle's] longer tales. The astute reader reads them once, at the age of twelve, and skips them forever after." No need ever to read them, suggested Loren Estleman when introducing a 1986 edition: "For those who prefer their Sherlock Holmes served up pure and without digression (and I am one), it is possible to skip over the long omniscient passage entitled 'The Country of the Saints' without losing 'the scarlet thread of murder.'" Count scholars among those purists: until the end of the century, most literary critics saw fit to emphasize the novel's "badly split narrative," which lacks "any viable transition."[65]

More recently, postcolonial critics have argued that the middle section does matter to the novel, which represents Utah as "a blank space, a land without history," where the high drama of British colonialism can be restaged allegorically in the high desert, starring new actors.[66] "Onto a blank wilderness," says Sebastian Lecourt, "Doyle's Brigham Young manages to project a model image of suburban civilization." The Mormons then make "excellent protagonists for this story of English self-globalization," in which the empire spreads across an otherwise empty map. If the Mormons are "unlikely heroes of settler ideology," that is because they are equally likely to play villains.[67] The same blank landscape invites the novel to project British imperial anxieties onto Utah, converting the pioneers into scapegoats for a variety of threats and sins, from American expansionism to Irish terrorism to English war crimes.[68] These ideological readings of the novel turn Salt Lake City into the flipside of London, "that great cesspool," as Watson says, "into which all the loungers and idlers of the Empire are irresistibly drained," along with the criminal foreigners whom Holmes rounds up (15). The apparently awkward transition between sections is thus actually a neat juxtaposition. However, when they are subsumed within a much broader history, where they assume so many other roles, the Mormons lose their own original identity. Against these readings, the characters push back, setting themselves apart from the rest of the English-speaking world. "We are the Mormons," they announce when met in the novel (57). Not even globalization can erase that religious difference, which the episode's subtitle also underscores. "The Country of the Saints" is spiritual rather than political territory, so far off the map that you can't get there from Baker Street without suddenly jumping backward.

From a nineteenth-century European perspective, Mormonism was itself a backward faith, not just primitive but atavistic, founded on false revelation no better than cheap superstition. "Homely, wild, vulgar fanaticism," *Household Words* called it in 1851, ridiculing Joseph Smith for "seeing visions in the age of railways."[69] The following year, the Mormon Church officially sanctioned the practice of polygamy, begun by Smith and continued under Brigham Young, which Victorian writers warned was a sign of "spiritual disease" and "moral rottenness."[70] These warnings were urgent because Young's missionaries were drawing so many new converts from Great Britain, promising thousands of unemployed workers and single women a fresh start.[71] During the same period, the British periodical press capitalized on sensational exposés of abduction, abuse, and worse among the Mormons, prompting the explorer Richard Burton to visit Salt Lake

City himself in 1860, with the wish "of seeing Utah as it is, not as it is said to be."[72] Burton's widely read travelogue, *The City of the Saints* (1862), took an anthropological view, describing polygamy as a custom rather than denouncing it as a sin. Later travelers often set aside the practice, emphasizing instead the social stability and economic prosperity found in Utah. "Apart from polygamy," said the Scottish agriculturalist James Barclay in 1884, "there is much in the Mormon organisation to admire and respect."[73] Doyle read Barclay's "New View of Mormonism" while revising *John Smith*, which quotes from it, and a year later he listened to another travelogue read at a Portsmouth Literary and Scientific Society meeting. Considering only "the secular aspects of Mormonism," that traveler admired "the social advancement which has come to the poor of all lands, who have come to Salt Lake to the church."[74] The Society's chairman called Mormonism "a marvellous infatuation of the human race," but Doyle was more skeptical.[75] As a prime example of "absurd" beliefs, his surrogate John Smith points to "Joe Smith with his tablets of beaten gold."[76]

A *Study in Scarlet* caters to cultural anxieties about Mormonism, recycling paranoid plot devices and reinforcing negative stereotypes. The polygamous prophet Young, who calls his wives "heifers," orders a young girl to marry within his inner circle; when she flees, his secret police of zealots hunts her down. Doyle had reason to turn against Mormonism while he was turning toward spiritualism: Victorian observers often relegated the two religions, both born in upstate New York, to the same lunatic fringe. In 1853, as the Fox sisters were growing famous, the *National Miscellany* called spiritualism "an especially American plot," pointing out that "the United States, the birth-place of Mormonism, has been fertile in these attempts to invent a fictitious supernatural evidence in favour of certain opinions."[77] The code word is "fertile," since those opinions included both the Mormon practice of polygamy and the Christian communalist doctrine of free love, embraced by radical American spiritualists. Their British counterparts disavowed such potentially scandalous behavior, trying to protect the public reputation of spiritualism.[78] Even as skeptics yoked them together, spiritualists and Mormons struggled to differentiate themselves. Each believed the other had been led into error, mistaking spirit communication for divine revelation, or vice versa. Steeped in spiritualist literature when writing *Scarlet*, Doyle viewed Mormonism as "a counterfeit form of spiritualism," as Michael Homer argues; Doyle used the novel "to expose Mormonism to other investigators and to purge it from his own mind," playing up the evils of polygamy.[79]

The hitch in this reading of the novel is that nothing could be further from Holmes's mind than marriage, especially at the moment when the narrative splits London for Utah, just as he is wonderfully poised to deliver his solution. The detective enjoys the attention so much that the novel lets him stand there for forty pages, buying time for Doyle to address a more pressing concern than polygamy: the difference between religious and retrospective prophecy. Does Holmes's professed scientific method in "The Book of Life," however true in the abstract, contain weak points in practice? The magical revelation of the murderer is clever, but will the logical explanation of the crime be convincing? To convince his readers and himself that Holmes is a true detective rather than a false prophet, Doyle turns to Mormonism, which *John Smith* had accused of fraud. The novel jumps to Utah in order to clear Holmes of the same charge, in case any suspicions are still lurking. From the Victorian point of view, the original sin of Mormonism was not polygamy but a more fundamental flaw in its theory and preaching, one that Watson would have no trouble detecting: ineffable twaddle.

When we meet them on the great desert plain, the pioneers stress that their faith could not be more effable—not only describable but also inscribable—since they "believe in those sacred writings, drawn in Egyptian letters on plates of beaten gold, which were handed unto the holy Joseph Smith" (57). The novel emphasizes a distinctive feature of Mormon doctrine: what historian Terryl Givens calls "the disintegration of that distance that separates the sacred and the profane," which offended outsiders even more than polygamy, since that separation "comes close to being the sine qua non of all Western religious faith and practice."[80] That distance has two dimensions—temporal and metaphysical—both of which collapsed when Joseph Smith started seeing visions in the age of railways. His revelation brought the divine not only up to date but also down to earth, affirming "that complete materialism which," as Burton reported, "makes the Creator of the same species as his creature." The anthropologist remained neutral, describing the belief system as it stood: "Mind and spirit, therefore, are real, objective, positive substances."[81] However, other Victorian travelers scoffed at "this new superstition," as one journalist judged it, both "intensely materialistic" and "anthropomorphic," which "teaches that God has a body, parts, and passions, precisely as we have." Although an outsider might question "the contradictoriness of their system," those paradoxes were the whole premise of the faith.[82] "It is typical of Mormon writers to insist that even God is natural rather than supernatural," Sterling McMurrin confirms in *The Theological Foundations of the Mormon Religion* (1965), "in that there is not a divine order of reality that contrasts essentially with the mundane physical universe of ordinary experience known to us through sensory data, which is the object of scientific investigation and is described by natural law."[83] In *Scarlet*, the Mormons stake their faith on that endless material plane, where sacred texts are made of heavy metal, and revelation can be hand delivered.

Spiritualism contained nearly the same "central metaphysical conflict," which Helen Sword defines as "its paradoxical proclivity to materialize the spirit world even while trying to spiritualize the material one."[84] Because those two worlds intersected only during the séance, spirit communication between them was brief and oblique, whereas Mormon revelation was direct and ongoing. "Brigham Young has said it," intones one elder in the novel, "and he has spoken with the voice of Joseph Smith, which is the voice of God" (58). The smooth relay of good information meant that Mormons could be certain of what awaits them after death, as Burton noted: "They take no leap in the dark," but rather "spring from this sublunary stage into a known, not into an unknown world."[85] Smith's doctrine of polygamy, for example, which involves not only plural but also celestial marriage, taught that all wives still belong to their husband in the afterlife. That kind of guarantee prompted another Victorian journalist to recommend drily that spiritualists "should study Mormonism," since "the Saints have long ago formulated into accepted doctrines those mysteries of the occult world which Spiritualists outside the faith are still investigating." Because Mormons accepted miracles in this world as "the most ordinary, reasonable, natural, every-day phenomena of a life of faith," he was driven to ask, "Are they all crazy together?"[86] However, miracles followed logically from the same paradoxical premise. "Religion being with them not a thing apart, but a portion and parcel of every-day life," Burton explained, "the intervention of the Lord in their material affairs becomes natural and only to be expected."[87] For that reason, when we meet them in the desert, the pioneers may not know where they are going, but they do know that "the hand of God is leading us under the person of our Prophet" (57).

"Brigham's personal position is a strange one," Charles Dilke remarked in 1868, describing the prophet's power to convert his thoughts into revelations, and then his prophecy into everyone else's reality. Seeing the need for new canals and bridges, Young "thinks about these things till they dominate in his mind—take in his brain the shape of physical creations," at which point he announces, "God has spoken," and directs his followers "to aid God's work."[88] Once the novel's pioneers arrive in Utah, where they "learned from the lips of their leader that this was the promised land," *Scarlet* illustrates this power of city planning, which seems providentially ordered, just as Chamier described. Young is such "a skilful administrator as well as a resolute chief" that Salt Lake City's "streets and squares sprang up as if by magic" (58). That magic also empowers Young to plot the individual lives of his followers. Seeing a young man, "a thought comes into his prophetic mind," William Dixon observed in 1867, and "at a moment's notice" he can send that man to become a missionary at "the ends of the earth."[89] Or, as *Scarlet* imagines, he can see a young girl and think to arrange her celestial marriage, in accordance with "the thirteenth rule in the code of the sainted Joseph Smith," which is also the word of God (64).

Presenting Smith's articles of faith as rules in a code, the novel stresses what Burton called the "severe rationalism" of the religion, the corollary of its complete materialism. "God is a mechanic," Burton heard Young preach, suggesting that the urban development of the Promised Land was both magical and mathematical.[90] "The Temple block gives form to the whole city," Dixon noted: "From each side of it starts a street, a hundred feet in width, going out on the level plain, and in straight lines into space. Streets of the same width, and parallel to these, run north and south, east and west."[91] In *Scarlet*, this grid of streets and squares arranges itself almost without human agency: "Maps were drawn and charts prepared, in which the future city was sketched out" (58). Plotting Cartesian coordinates while rejecting Cartesian dualism, Mormon theology extended those lines out from the temple and into eternity. Burton cited Young's apostle Orson Pratt, known for drawing logical deductions about the divine, and then further conclusions from there. The atoms of the Holy Spirit, Pratt reasoned, "must exist in inexhaustible quantities, which is the only possible way for any substance to be omnipresent." Burton was trained to withhold judgment about local customs, but he could not let pass these universal claims: "The analytic powers, sharpened by mundane practice, and wholly unencumbered by religious formal discipline, are allowed, in things ultra mundane, a scope, a perfect freedom, that savors of irreverence."[92]

In this world, according to the novel, the prophet allows very little freedom and absolutely no irreverence. "Do not jest at that which is sacred," readers are told upon arriving in Utah, where "to express an unorthodox opinion was a dangerous matter" (57, 62). Dissent is eliminated as if by the same magic that conjured up the city: "The man who held out against the Church vanished away" (62). When Lucy and her father anger the prophet, who rebukes them with "flashing eyes," they find that divine accounting is just as mathematically precise as divine rule (64). Given one month to bring their family up to code, by which time Lucy must choose between two polygamist suitors, she and her father awake each morning to find a countdown of "fatal numbers" marked on the ceiling, door, walls, and floors of their home, a "register" of the days remaining (67). God may be the mechanic, but the prophet sets this "formidable machinery in motion," crunching numbers and crushing spirits, thanks to his "invisible network" of vigilantes (62, 68).

A Study in Scarlet thus sensationalizes Mormon polygamy as only the most visible symptom of a deeper problem that troubled Victorian travelers and writers: the psychological pitfalls of a modern religion that was both materialistic and rationalistic. Once the distance between the sacred and the profane disintegrated, Burton observed, the difference between subjective and objective knowledge soon followed. When that happened, the position of believers became strange. They could not tell the difference between magical and logical thinking, because they did not think there was one, which put them in an endless feedback loop of believing that they knew what they believed. Burton described the resulting egotism of false prophets and zealotry of blind followers. "The mind of man," he warned, "most loves those errors and delusions into which it has become self-persuaded, and is most fanatic concerning the irrationalities and the supernaturalities to which it has bowed its own reason."[93] *Scarlet* illustrates Burton's point when we first meet Brigham Young. He is immersed in "reading a brown-backed volume," the Book of Mormon, which is the word of God, which is the voice of the prophet, who dictates terms: Lucy and John can come along as "believers in our own creed," or they can stay in the desert to die (57). The novel warns further that the feedback loop tightens, becoming more constrictive, if the mind persuades itself that it

REASONING BACKWARD, 1881–1887   59

has *not* bowed its reason to revelation. When Lucy's two suitors introduce themselves, they propose that her celestial match be a rational choice. "As I have but four wives and Brother Drebber here has seven," one elder argues, "it appears to me that my claim is the stronger one." "Nay, nay," the other protests, "the question is not how many wives we have, but how many we can keep." Lucy's father throws them out of the house, calling them "young canting rascals," but his days are already numbered (66).

Cant was all that outsiders could hear in Utah. "He talked a mass of irreverent twaddle," said Lady Duffus Hardy, listening to a young preacher in 1880, "as though he were in the secrets of the Almighty."[94] The conflation of reason and revelation made it impossible to debate questions of science and religion when visiting Salt Lake City, where the streets were straight but the logic was snarled. Struggling to understand whether "each different solar system had its own Supreme Being," the Amazon explorer William Chandless gave up: "Mormons have more readiness than exactness in argument."[95] Chandless refused even to try to follow "the certainly ingenious and acute argumentation of Orson Pratt, partly physical, partly metaphysical," which the English vicar William Conybeare also discounted as a "strange jumble of incongruous dogmas."[96] Pratt's inferences stretched so far that Young publicly rebuked him, to keep the apostle's reason in line with the prophet's revelation. So long as Pratt "has confined himself to doctrines which he understands, his arguments are convincing and unanswerable," Young proclaimed in 1865, "but, when he has indulged in hypotheses and theories, he has launched forth on an endless sea of speculation to which there is no horizon."[97] From an outsider's perspective, however, both apostle and prophet were equally prone to what Burton called the "materialistic vagaries" and "unauthorized deductions" of Mormon doctrine.[98] "In all this it is hard for us," said Dilke, "with our English hatred of casuistry and hair-splitting, to see sincerity." His complaint that Mormons "forget that they are arguing in a circle" was not just English.[99] The French naturalist Jules Rémy "never had reason to admire the force of their logic, for it is impossible for anyone of them to follow up an argument judiciously and sensibly," while the Austrian diplomat Baron von Hübner had trouble "in seizing a single intelligible thought amidst the grand phrases and the confused and illogical statements."[100] The very English *Household Words* put the case even more bluntly than Lady Duffy: "What they say, is mostly nonsense."[101]

"The Country of the Saints" thus rubbishes the Book of Mormon, presenting it as the source of even more ineffable twaddle than Watson read in "The Book of Life" and even more manifest absurdities than Doyle found in the Bible. In the novel, the prophet constructs a prison house of paradoxical language from which there is no exit, since his word is the only key code. Settling the land means unsettling the mind; the price of living in Salt Lake City is the cost of believing its creed. Utah is both a real desert and "the desert of the real," in Jean Baudrillard's terms, where the prophet's map precedes and generates the territory it claims only to describe; the actual terrain becomes "a space whose curvature is no longer that of the real, nor that of truth," where then "it is all of metaphysics that is lost."[102] When readers of *Scarlet* escape from Utah and return to London, "The Book of Life" no longer sounds so fanciful as it once did, since Holmes maps only geography—Niagara, the Atlantic, Afghanistan—that already exists without him. Though his eyes flash like a prophet's, his knowledge is plainly grounded, not revealed; his theories are something more than mere cant. The flashback neatly fits rather than badly splits the narrative: it scapegoats Mormonism for errors and delusions that would otherwise compromise Holmes's intuition, and thus Doyle's spiritualism. At the end of the novel, the Science of Deduction and Analysis is even more exact and less weird than when we left Holmes on the verge of explaining the mystery. He promises that his solution will involve only "a few very ordinary deductions," rather than either divine inspiration or infinite speculation (83).

Just before he provides that solution, Holmes compresses "The Book of Life" into a scientific abstract, eliminating the theosophical language that irritated Watson, who never has to read the whole article again, because only a single sentence remains: "The grand thing is to be able to reason backward." Having invoked Huxley, Holmes then demystifies the gift of retrospective prophecy that he shares with Zadig, explaining how a chosen few are able "to evolve from their own inner consciousness what the steps were which led up to that result." At the conclusion of *Scarlet*, Holmes catalogs all the material evidence that grounds his steps—boot prints, wheel tracks, cigar ash, bloodstains, and so on—to demonstrate that "the whole thing is a chain of logical sequences without a break or flaw." The theoretical but not quite theological claim of Holmes's article—"All life is a great chain"—has now been proved, and so the novel can stop there, with Watson promising to publish "all the facts" (83–86). Only one central all-important fact remains off the record, because it had already been documented elsewhere, in Doyle's letter to *Light* the previous summer.

AUTHORIZED DEDUCTIONS

Even with this conclusive demonstration, Watson's initial suspicion remains reasonable. "The Country of the Saints" is a prearranged episode, intended to dazzle, so that we do not question Holmes's deductions. From the start, there is something extraordinary about them. Holmes knows from Watson's "air" that he is a military man, from his "type" that he is a medical man, from his "manner" that he has injured his arm, and from his suntan that he "has just come from the tropics." Where then did this army doctor see action? "Clearly in Afghanistan," Holmes concludes, even though Afghanistan is clearly not in the tropics. Two materialistic vagaries plus one unauthorized deduction add up to what for anybody else would be a very fortunate guess. Holmes is just getting warmed up; once the game is afoot, his steps will stretch even further, in every direction. "There is much that is still obscure," he says to Watson early in the case, "though I have quite made up my mind on the main facts." Quite often, though, it seems that his mind has made up all the facts. He somehow knows from tracks in the dust that a man was talking as he walked; he infers from the expression on a corpse's face that the victim had been forced to take poison pills. From blood splashes on the floor, he concludes that the murderer must have a "florid face," being prone to nosebleeds under stress. "That was a more daring shot," admits Holmes, "though I have no doubt that I was right" (33). As it happens, he is.

And that's the problem: there is no problem. "Events proved that I had judged correctly," Holmes notes, which is an odd way to put it (85). He may warn Watson never to theorize before having all the evidence, but it is impossible for Holmes to make that mistake, because further events always prove his theory. "Everything which has occurred since then," says Holmes, pointing back to the beginning of the novel, "has served to confirm my original supposition" (50). If anything, Holmes sometimes makes the opposite mistake, thinking he must abandon a theory when new facts do not fit. But he is wrong to have any doubt. As Wilfrid Ward also held, undeniable facts always have other possible interpretations that are more agreeable to original suppositions.[103] "I should have more faith," Holmes chides himself, an aside that casts doubt on the principle that follows: "I ought to know by this time that when a fact appears to be opposed to a long train of deductions, it invariably proves to be capable of bearing some other interpretation" (49). His faith not only compels the existing facts to get on board with his reasoning but also conjures up any additional facts he might need. The Science of Deduction and Analysis is a magic act, in which objects seem to materialize out of thin air and drop into his lap: "I came into possession of the pills," explains Holmes, "the existence of which I had already surmised" (85). This is not retrospective prophecy, or even reasoning backward. This is confirmation bias so strong that it reverse engineers reality to catch up with and then run alongside Holmes's train of thought. Call it *retroactive* prophecy, a breakthrough in backtelling: the power to reconstruct not only the steps leading up to a result but also the result itself, no matter how far-fetched.

Not even Brigham Young has that much power in *Scarlet*, though he works similar magic on an apparently much grander scale. His revelations may conjure up a city out of an empty desert, but he still needs both divine intervention and road construction to help him do it. Holmes cuts God and everyone else out of the loop that runs between mind and world, closing the distance between his revelations and his explanations, until there is no difference between what he believes and what he knows. At that point, the dominion of Holmes's faith becomes clear: he has perfect freedom in things mundane, which may as well be ultramundane, since his brain creates and shapes the universe at will. His map precedes and generates not only the territory but also the whole globe, whose geography can always be reinterpreted as needed. Leading a wagon train to Utah is nothing compared to relocating the whole of Afghanistan to the tropics, or the tropics to Afghanistan—it hardly matters which, since either way, Watson has just come from there, wherever that is. To avoid falling into relativism, Mivart insisted that we are not the creators of the things we know, but Holmes is both that and the architect of the places we go. Lounging in his armchair, evolving neat little paradoxes in the seclusion of his study, he carries within himself the reasons that make everything else exist. Baker Street is both his own private Utah and his own special Afghanistan, a tropical twilight zone that covers all of Great Britain, just as Drayson predicted. When he does bustle about the streets and squares of Victorian London, seeing things with his own eyes, Holmes's observations are the projections of his own interior illumination. He gaslights everyone else's reality.

It is no secret why Holmes's backward reasoning works as if by magic. All the facts that Watson publishes are fictional, and their adventures have all been reverse engineered in the first place. "I had been reading some detective stories," said Doyle in 1900, thinking back to when he wrote *Scarlet*, "and it struck me what nonsense they were, to put it mildly, because for getting the solution of the mystery the authors always depended on some coincidence," which was "not a fair way of playing the game." For the odds to stop favoring the detective, the author would have to abandon his creation. Holmes receives two parting gifts: a "scientific education" that gives the detective "an immense fund of exact knowledge," and a "scientific system" that allows him to "reason everything out."[104] He is then left to make sense of a still mysterious but now disenchanted London, accompanied by a first-person rather than an omniscient narrator. Omniscience belongs only to Holmes, at least on his side of the Atlantic; on the other, Doyle reclaims a godlike perspective, putting the Mormon prophet in his place. Young's revelation provides merely local knowledge, whereas Holmes's reason promises total.

The only piece of information that Doyle withholds from Holmes is the Mormon backstory, which might otherwise lead the detective to lose faith in his scientific education and system. What happens in Utah must stay in Utah, even if the omniscient narrator makes a point to tell us that he knows exactly what is happening back in London. The backstory ends by returning the reader to "Dr. Watson's Journal, to which we are already under such obligations," and in which the rest of the story has been "duly recorded" (76). And not just recorded; it has already been published. The London half of the novel has its own subtitle, "Being a Reprint from the Reminiscences of John H. Watson, M.D., Late of the Army Medical Department," proving that Watson has already kept his final promise to publish all the facts (15). Holmes's origin story bends back on itself to explain its own origin, carving out a fictional nonfiction space whose curvature excludes the author. Doyle disappears from Baker Street: that "reprint" is a nice first and last touch, distancing him even further from his own fiction, which has become a hermetically sealed universe, entirely knowable through reason, ruled by probability rather than providence.

Of course, the author never really exited the novel; he just immigrated to Utah. From there, he pulls the strings back on Baker Street, playing a game that still belongs to him. "And so I had my puppets," he remembered

later, "and wrote my 'Study in Scarlet.'"[105] We might instead call them scientific toys, and retitle the novel *Science Made Easy*. Pretending to play
fair, the novel is playing so fast and loose with reason, as James Stephen
would complain, that it's hard to spot the bait and switch. The detective's
system is not science but pseudoscience, exactly as Doyle himself once
described and debunked Od photography, worth quoting again. Now it is
Holmes who "cites as facts things which are incorrect, and that in a crisp
and epigrammatic way which is delightful. From these so-called facts he
draws inferences which, even if they were facts indeed, would be illogical,
and upon these illogical inferences draws deductions which, once more,
no amount of concession would render tenable." Unlike Warner, however, Holmes enjoys unlimited concessions because his deductions are
all preauthorized. The *Hampshire Post* observed that Doyle's "principle of
composition" was to begin the story at the end, telling it backward, so that
"the problem was derived to match the key which he held in his hand." The
clues precede and generate the crime, perpetrated "under such conditions
as to harmonise with the train of subsequent events which [Doyle] had
marked out in his mind."[106] The author reverse engineers the track that his
detective can then also follow backward without going off the rails. When
Holmes's long train of deductions hooks up with Young's "great caravan
upon its journey for the West," both the detective and the prophet join
Drayson's parade of pseudoscience, which goes round and round in logical
circles, from London to Salt Lake via Afghanistan and back, wandering the
desert of the real (55).

The Science of Deduction and Analysis is not weird: it's junk. So long as
we think that Holmes is just kind of odd, we can overlook the fact that his
method is complete rubbish, as Watson soon does. All the criticism of the
novel's badly split narrative—and especially the recommendation to skip
the middle—only testifies to the strength of its unifying conception. "The
Country of the Saints" holds the novel together, papering over the enormous gap—an accumulation of manifestly absurd plot holes—that yawns
as soon as Holmes opens his mouth to reveal how he knows what he has
just revealed. Jumping suddenly across the Atlantic and then back, readers
are less likely to notice upon return that they have also landed on the far
side of logical leaps that should have fallen well short. Even the *Hampshire
Post*, knowing full well that the game had been rigged, admired Holmes's
"system of induction" and "accurate and systematic observation."[107] The

Mormon episode helped Doyle to persuade himself that spiritualism was the true faith, reachable through the exercise of pure reason, as outlined in "The Book of Life." However, because readers of *Scarlet* seek entertainment rather than enlightenment, they put their faith into Holmes much faster, without needing a detour to Utah. And so, as Holmes becomes increasingly famous, "The Country of the Saints" loses ground: it is enjoyable at first, then merely readable, then deplorable, then intolerable, and finally disposable. Knowing what to expect, we can cut to the chase; we prefer Sherlock Holmes to be served up pure. But our preference seals Doyle's bargain with himself. If we skip the middle section forever, then we permanently close the gap between reason and revelation, just as he hoped would happen in future.

The novel conceals its religious origin so well that even *Light*, knowing full well that the author was "a Spiritualist, so a little bird whispers in our ear," missed the clues to deeper meaning in the novel. "We have lately noticed so many works of fiction, shocking and otherwise, which make Spiritualism the *pièce de résistance*," said its reviewer in 1888, "that it is a new thing on the earth to find one in which the very name does not occur, which is not occult, nor ghostly, nor weird, nor creepy: but which is a really good, thrilling, well-written story, the interest of which is sustained from cover to cover."[108] Even so, spiritualism is still the novel's pièce de résistance; it just goes without saying, which is why the mystique persists. The very name of spiritualism does not occur because the author gave it a new one: Sherlock Holmes, to whom we bow and then surrender our reason.

IMMENSE SIGNIFICANCE

Other early reviews of *Scarlet*, while applauding the ingenious detective, also caught a whisper of contradiction. The *Flintshire County Herald* admired both the "foresight of Sherlock Holmes" and his "power of observation"; the *Glasgow Herald* praised "the preternatural sagacity of a scientific detective"; and the *Scotsman* called the novel "entrancing," because it "has shown how the true detective should work by observation and deduction."[109] Unlike Zadig, Holmes gets the benefit of the doubt, showing how far detectives have come since ancient Babylonia. After the Enlightenment, reason that looks like revelation is no longer spooky, however startling its results. These early reviews drafted the official story that still circulates today: Sherlock Holmes is the apotheosis of late Victorian scientism, a fantasy of human reason so advanced that it is nearly indistinguishable from magic. He is the mastermind we all wish we could be—so long as we set aside any evidence to the contrary.

Literary critics have theorized our collective investment in Holmes. On the one hand, the genre of detective fiction expresses the secular values of the disenchanted nineteenth century described by sociologist Max Weber, who saw no way out of the "iron cage" of reason to which capitalism had sentenced humanity.[110] Holmes is right at home in that cage, hammering out chains of logic, clearing up mystery, and pocketing his fee. On the other hand, detective fiction also affords some consolation, since discovering hidden clues "contests the proposition that anything can be meaningless" and thus "restores a certain immanence" to an emptied world.[111] Holmes offers his readers even more. Because he is "not just a keen observer but a visionary," his dazzling solutions have the effect of "reenchanting the world" for the rest of us, making the iron cage seem more like paradise than prison. Reading clues that only he can see, Holmes "reenacts the old theological gestures for a non-theological age, filling the world with meaning, or rather discovering the meanings with which (he claims) it is already richly saturated."[112] Those gestures were once powerful enough to convince some Victorian readers to address letters to Holmes at 221B Baker Street, asking for his help.

Those gestures are still powerful enough, Michael Saler argues, to convince some readers today to act "as if" Holmes could have written back. Calling themselves Sherlockians, his biggest fans expand upon the Victorian fantasy together by pretending—ironically but seriously—that their true detective was also a real person. The meanings he discovers in the stories enrich their world, for by illustrating how to use reason imaginatively rather than instrumentally, Holmes brings hope that "profane reality could be no less mysterious or alluring than the supernatural realm." The largest society of Sherlockians, the Baker Street Irregulars, named itself after the street urchins whom Holmes occasionally summons for help, showing that it is never too late to have a Victorian childhood. Holmes helps his fans to ironize the cage of reason, now a playroom where they conjure up the imaginary friend who threw away the key in the first place. "Clap if you believe in Sherlock Holmes," Saler proposes, and you can suspend your lifetime sentence.[113]

Literary critics, however, like to think that they know better than to pretend. The scientistic fantasy may have entranced earnest Victorians, but shell-shocked modernists started seeing through it well before skeptical postmodernists then tore it apart. In 1929, halfway between the First and Second World Wars, T. S. Eliot admired the stories, in which "the late nineteenth century is always romantic, always nostalgic, and never merely silly," although he recognized that Holmes "is not even a very good detective."[114] In 1948, three years into the atomic age, W. H. Auden knew that the stories were just a "daydream" of prewar paradise regained, but he could still admire Holmes as "the exceptional individual who is in a state of grace because he is a genius in whom scientific curiosity is raised to the status of a heroic passion."[115] Another two decades later, with hero worship going out of fashion in the 1960s, critics started patronizing the aging genius as "the eccentric knight of nineteenth-century rationalism," whose ritual function is not "to teach anything new or strange, but only to *demonstrate* . . . the comforting drama of reason."[116] Holmes's quest was both antiquated and deluded enough to require critical distance. In 1967, Pierre Nordon cautioned that "the reader is tempted to identify himself with Sherlock Holmes, as the incarnation of the spirit of his age," when "many people hoped [science] would lead to a material and spiritual improvement of the human condition."[117]

By the end of the twentieth century, literary criticism had put the Victorian detective squarely back in his own time and place. The stories "celebrated the accomplishments of science in the age of Charles Darwin," while also meeting "a need for the rendering in detective fiction of a coherent vision of the universe in a post-Darwinian moment."[118] Holmes then "operates within the last moments of a kind of European world domination and enlightenment enthusiasm," after which it is no longer possible to celebrate without feeling silly at best or guilty at worst.[119] Stephen Kern acknowledges the appeal of the fantasy even as he rejects it. "The delightfully arrogant concluding explanations by Sherlock Holmes," he says, "are mementos of a lost era that expected 'scientific' causal explanations based on 'objective' evidence and 'rational' thinking about a 'natural' order and was less inclined to question those concepts."[120] Those scare quotes are a sign of postmodern sophistication, now much preferred to enlightenment enthusiasm. Clap yourself on the back if you no longer believe in Sherlock Holmes.

These critics may debunk the scientism of the stories, but they let the pseudoscience stand. They have good reasons for doing so, as chapter 4 will explain. For now, it is enough to point out that the stories make even skeptical readers believe that Holmes is doing more and better science than humanly possible, rather than almost none, very badly. Stephen Knight argues that "the figure of Holmes was so well created and attuned to its time and audience that it has survived to the present," but surely that is a contradiction in terms.[121] The fantasy must be ahistorical, or at least not exclusively Victorian, for the figure to persist that long. Saler argues that we moderns are tempted to identify with Holmes because he transcends the gloomy spirit of our age, but neither does that explain his persistence, more than a hundred years after Weber diagnosed our disenchantment under capitalism. Will we really be forever so glum that we will always need a manic-depressive Victorian detective to cheer us up? Both these arguments presume that Holmes is a fantasy figure for whom reason is a superpower, but this chapter has made the opposite case: Holmes is a figure for whom reason is superfluous. He survives to the present because that primal fantasy is deeply gratifying, and endlessly productive, in so many future contexts.

After *A Study in Scarlet*, the detective gets busy living everyone else's dream, as the admiring client in "The Speckled Band" later confirms: "Whatever your reasons may be, you are perfectly correct" (259). Holmes's hypotheses serve as premises; his interpretations function like explanations. Watson should not be at all surprised that his new flatmate knows nothing about astronomy, Copernicus, and the solar system: "What the deuce is it to me?" Holmes asks (21). Why should he care, when the whole world revolves around him anyway? In contrast to most critics, Richard Alewyn argues that the constructed reality of detective fiction, which often defies the laws of probability, "betrays a doubt about the nature of the world" and therefore undermines "trust in reason and science."[122] However, the Holmes stories have a different effect: they bolster the paradoxical faith in material evidence that Kerr finds at the heart of spiritualism. Even if Holmes never studies the laws of nature, he never doubts them; the objects around him are ordinary, not uncanny, and the physical universe is just that. But Holmes's strict materialism is not the same thing as either empiricism or rationalism. Materialism is a worldview, not a method: insisting on hard evidence does not guarantee sound logic. By glossing the difference and then defying probability, the stories create the illusion that the best evidence is the thinnest, and that the best reasons are the faintest. They tempt us to think that there is really nothing to thinking. "If I show you too much of my method of working," Holmes says to Watson, "you will come to the conclusion that I am a very ordinary individual after all" (33). Holmes makes science look so easy that we too can just leap straight to our own conclusions, whatever they may be.

This is not scientism but a very different late Victorian fantasy, which denies science and defies reason. "The dream of the *fin de siècle*," Terry Eagleton says, "is to pass without mediation from the concrete to the cosmic, linked as the two realms are in their resistance to that analytic rationality which is the sign of social alienation." It may seem perverse to argue that the analytic and alienated detective-hero actually expresses "the period's impatience with discursive rationality," given how much he enjoys explaining his logic at the end of every story. However, the stories allow Holmes first to show off "an intuition which is radically non-discursive," bypassing conscious reasoning on the way from concrete particular to universal whole—from a drop of water to an undiscovered ocean.[123] Holmes may stop there, but his method of working encourages everyone else to go further. "The most certain path from natural science to mysticism," Friedrich Engels warned in 1878, is "the shallowest empiricism that spurns all theory and distrusts all thought."[124] Engels was appalled at how many English scientists were attending séances, but Holmes explains how and why that happens. The shallowest empiricism is the materialism he lays on so thick, making even the most far-fetched conclusion seem well grounded. "The immense significance of the curried mutton occurred to me," says Holmes in "Silver Blaze," and once that thought comes into your prophetic mind you can fill the whole universe with whatever meaning you wish to discover (348). Doyle created Holmes to resolve his dilemma: the doctor was trained in analytic rationality but still yearned for spiritual integration and universal transcendence, which that training could only obstruct. In his delightfully arrogant explanations, Holmes expresses the "contempt for all theoretical thought" for which Engels indicted all spiritualists.[125] Sublimating that contempt in his fiction, Doyle authorizes intuition, inspiration, and revelation as higher forms of reason, opening a new branch of science for religious enthusiasts, who no longer need to apologize.

Doyle thus achieved the harmony that eluded Mivart, whose paradoxes threatened the Catholic Church enough for his later work to end up on its index of forbidden readings. Those paradoxes also troubled James Stephen, who stopped just short of questioning Mivart's sanity: "The temper of mind in which a man believes in a scientific conclusion, and the temper in which he believes in any conclusion without qualification, upon evidence known to be imperfect, are so different that I doubt greatly whether they can possibly coexist."[126] He should have had just a bit more faith; one month later, *A Study in Scarlet* appeared. According to Saler, Holmes's ironic re-enchantment of the modern world did not satisfy Doyle, who then regressed to earnest premodern belief in spirits. However, as this chapter has argued, Holmes satisfied his author's scientific demands and spiritual needs so well that Doyle progressed rapidly from believing to knowing. In his view, the séance circle fully closed the generation gap, allowing him to look back on the 1880s periodical debates with bemusement, certain that he had risen above it all. At that point, as the next chapter argues, he could make even further progress—from knowing to foretelling.

CHAPTER 3

Theory and Preaching, 1887–1930

A DIFFERENT GUARANTEE

"Never for a moment abandon the use of your reason," *Light* advised in January 1887, as Doyle began attending séances at Thomas Harward's home.[1] He had already fallen away from Catholicism and settled on materialism; convinced that he was still using his reason, he now floated toward spiritualism. In the next month's *Nineteenth Century*, Huxley divided religious believers into two groups: "those who are ready to believe in any miracle so long as it is guaranteed by ecclesiastical authority, and those who are ready to believe in any miracle so long as it has some different guarantee."[2] On the authority of his fictional detective, who guarantees pseudoscience to be the real thing, Doyle was ready to believe in almost all séance phenomena. In *A Study in Scarlet*, Holmes is permitted a single metaphysical speculation, gesturing toward his author's research agenda. After enjoying a violin concert, Holmes reasons from a scientific premise—"what Darwin says about music" preceding speech on the evolutionary timeline—to the cryptic conclusion that music triggers "vague memories in our souls of those misty centuries when the world was in its childhood." To Watson, this sounds like "rather a broad idea," which is to say, more ineffable twaddle. Holmes's retort seems to plant him firmly among the evolutionary biologists: "One's ideas must be as broad as Nature if they are to interpret Nature." However, his delightful epigram turns methodological naturalism against its own premise: by that recursive logic, the definition of nature expands until it verges on the supernatural (37). Holmes always pulls up short of that explanation, sticking to the material world, but the same line of thought allowed his author to pursue mistier and mistier interpretations, as this chapter will show, until the world ends altogether.

In his letter to *Light* that summer, Doyle explained that the best way to broaden one's ideas is to make up one's mind. The spiritual seeker should cease inquiries once he finds evidence "decided enough to convince his reason without being so overwhelming as to stagger and confuse it."[3] In other words, always abandon your use of reason as soon as possible; you simply don't need all the facts, which will only hurt your head without changing your mind. Holmes makes the same case in "The Red-headed League," but he does not caution so much as threaten Watson. "You must come round to my view, for otherwise I shall keep on piling fact upon fact on you until your reason breaks down under them and acknowledges me to be right" (176). Both the detective and his author turn empiricism against its own premise: the more you know from the less you find, the sooner even the greatest mysteries can be resolved.

After reason broke down in *Scarlet*, other novels could begin the work of bringing readers around to Doyle's religious views. Just after writing to *Light*, he began *Micah Clarke* (1889), a historical novel about a young Puritan who fights in the Monmouth Rebellion of 1685, when the Catholic James II held the throne. The novel deplores the religious extremism of both parties. Its moral center is an old carpenter who advises Clarke to "take religion upon its broadest base, for the truth must be broader than aught which we can conceive." Echoing John Smith, the carpenter makes the argument from design in nature that puts religious faith "upon solid ground, without having to call to our aid aught save pure reason." Echoing Sherlock Holmes, he declares that his tenets are "as true and as capable of proof as one of those exercises of Euclid."[4] While working on that novel, Doyle also wrote *The Mystery of Cloomber* (1888), an occult thriller about the price an English soldier pays for murdering a Buddhist adept. Having broadened the base of religion in *Clarke*, Doyle pushed the limits of science in *Cloomber*, whose narrator proposes that there exist mystical powers still to be discovered. "For what is science?" he asks. "Science is the consensus of opinion of scientific men, and history has shown that it is slow to accept a truth."[5]

The record shows that Doyle was quick to reject that consensus. *Cloomber* was serialized in the *Pall Mall Gazette* during September 1888, the same month that Doyle helped to establish the Hampshire Psychical Society (HPS), of which he was vice president. Modeled on the SPR, the HPS announced that it was based in science rather than religion. Its members planned to research "supernormal" powers, such as hypnotism and telepathy, as opposed to supernatural encounters; they pledged to "conduct their inquiries by experimental methods," rather than séance circles.[6] Not everyone was convinced that the HPS had set aside supernatural explanations. One Portsmouth resident called out Doyle and his colleagues, sarcastically goading them to find Jack the Ripper by questioning his last victim: "If Dr. ———, General Harward, and the other local scientific gentlemen who pretend to be spiritualists wish to prove their claim to public confidence, perhaps they will call up the spirit of the woman Kelly."[7] The following year, Doyle endorsed spiritualism publicly but anonymously in two letters to the Portsmouth *Evening News*. In May, signing himself simply "SPIRITUALIST," he defended the movement from the attacks of not only Huxleyan agnostics but also Christian apologists: "When any new form of knowledge arises above the mental horizon of the human race there are always a certain number of well-meaning but narrow-minded men who are ready to denounce it as being opposed to Scriptural teaching."[8] In November, Doyle more nearly identified himself as "A Southsea Physician" when he wrote again to reject biblical literalism. In making his case, he cited Winwood Reade's controversial *Martyrdom of Man* (1872), a Darwinian history of civilization that renounced Christianity and endorsed a very general deism. "The broader our views the better," Doyle wrote, "for the broadest that human mind can attain to must yet be infinitely narrow when compared to that final truth which must embrace the universe."[9] Doyle was here channeling his surrogate John Smith, whose "true creed" is "infinitely broader than anything which the mind of man can conceive."[10]

The mind of Sherlock Holmes, however, is a good start. His Darwinian view of the universe in *Scarlet* is just broad enough to include the possibility of species soul memory, helping his author to bring science and religion that much closer together. By April 1890, Doyle could listen to a Portsmouth lecture on the history of witchcraft with an open mind. "Modern science," he remarked, "far from having destroyed the original idea underlying this topic, had gone a long way to confirm it."[11] Doyle himself had taken a much shorter step to confirm his own beliefs: he had just published his second detective novel.

DARING SPECULATIONS

"Let me recommend this book—one of the most remarkable ever penned," says Holmes in *The Sign of Four* (1890). He hands Reade's *Martyrdom of Man* to Watson, who flips through its "daring speculations" while day-dreaming about their attractive new client, Mary Morstan (97). In August 1889, *Lippincott's Monthly Magazine* commissioned a new work from Doyle, who decided to revisit 221B Baker Street.[12] The novel opens with Holmes injecting himself with the famous "seven-per-cent solution" of cocaine, which relieves "the dull routine of existence" (90). Here's the dilemma for a true detective who exists in a universe constructed especially for him to unravel its mysteries: being so good at your job gets old fast. "What is the use of having powers," he complains to Watson, "when one has no field upon which to exert them?" (93). The Victorian detective's night-mare resembles the dream of the postmodernist scholar who wishes "to immunize himself from the friction of reality," as Maurizio Ferraris says, by claiming that "*everything* is socially constructed."[13] Holmes does not need to make that claim; as a fictional character, he has a natural immunity to reality checks. For him, everything may seem "hopelessly prosaic and material," but still there is no rub (93). The only solution is self-medication, which he finds "transcendentally stimulating and clarifying to the mind," until his author-physician gives him a new case to raise his spirits (89).

Before Mary calls, Holmes and Watson spend the first chapter of *Sign* recapping "The Science of Deduction" for any new readers who might have missed the same discussion—under the same chapter heading—in *Scarlet*. Doyle hoped that the sequel would boost sales of the original, and so Watson dutifully plugs *Scarlet*, though Holmes did not finish and cannot recommend it. "Detection is, or ought to be, an exact science," says Holmes, but Watson has "attempted to tinge it with romanticism" (90). The detective offers two quick examples of observation and deduction, "so absurdly simple that an explanation is superfluous," to prove that his science is not "charlatanism," as Watson still suspects (91, 93). The smudges on the doctor's shoes reveal that he sent a telegram that morning; the scratches on his watch tell the life story of his deceased brother. Of this scene, Jill Galvan notes that the detective is like a psychic, handling an object and divining its owner, though "Holmes's deduction has little to do with the paranormal."[14] The deduction itself may not, but the exchange that follows suggests that Holmes's method has everything to do with Doyle's spiritualism. Convinced anew, Watson tells Holmes, "I should have had more faith in your marvelous faculty," even if Holmes doubts whether his powers "have any function upon earth," raising the question of where else they might apply (93). Providentially, Mary just then sends up her card.

Sign follows the same narrative structure as Scarlet, whose experimental form becomes a standard formula. Holmes finds clues that no one else can spot and draws conclusions that no one else can reach, which leads the police to dub him "Mr. Theorist" and Watson to worry that his friend may have lost the plot (114). "Could there be," Watson wonders, "some radical flaw in my companion's reasoning? Might he not be suffering from some huge self-deception? Was it not possible that his nimble and speculative mind had built up this wild theory upon faulty premises?" (131). Watson is right to question whether Holmes's logic is circular, confirming biases and begging questions, but he feels a bit silly for asking, since the answer is always no. "I was always oppressed with a sense of my own stupidity," he says later, "in my dealings with Sherlock Holmes" ("Red-headed League," 185). If we take him at his word, Watson is a simple narrative foil. The doctor "provides one pole of convenient stupidity that the reader is proud to avoid," while the detective "represents the ideal pole of perfect knowledge, of an entirely correct reading, toward which the reader aims."[15] Doyle himself encouraged this view, writing off Watson as Holmes's "rather stupid friend."[16]

Watson's role is rather more complicated than that, however, because stupidity is not "opposed to knowledge in any simple way, nor is it the other of thought," as the philosopher Avital Ronell defines it. She argues dialectically that stupidity "consists, rather, in the absence of a relation to knowing," an absence that nonetheless "is also a relation." Calling other people "stupid" marks a difference in kind between your way of thinking and theirs, which simply cannot comprehend what you know, no matter how much or how hard they try. The first thing Watson tells us about himself is that he has a medical degree from the University of London; the first thing Stamford tells us about Holmes is that he works in the hospital laboratory without pursuing a degree or even taking any classes. Calling a highly educated doctor stupid—and having that doctor say he feels stupid next to Holmes—allowed Doyle to write off his own education as an intellectual limitation. Watson's problem is not that he knows too little or thinks too slowly but that Holmes's mind is something to which he just cannot relate. The novel thus makes metaphysical inquiry easier: you cannot know as much as Holmes, but you can at least think differently than Watson, which is to say, not like a trained scientist. As Ronell emphasizes, "Locating the space of stupidity has been part of a repertoire binding any intelligent— or, finally, stupid—activity that seeks to establish itself and territorialize its findings."[17] There are two such spaces of stupidity in the novel: the University of London, where science is too narrow-minded, and the territory of Utah, where religion is too hardheaded. Running midway between those poles is Baker Street, where Holmes establishes himself, making him easy to find even if hard to follow. Stamford can only shrug to Watson and say, "Heaven knows what the objects of his studies are" (17).

When they meet him in the lab, Holmes announces that he has "found a re-agent which is precipitated by haemoglobin, and by nothing else." This chemical reaction will allow forensic scientists to identify bloodstains using "the Sherlock Holmes's test," as he awkwardly names it after himself (17–18). The detective has presumably just reached the end of a long process of elimination, checking off all other possible precipitants one by one. He then brings the same "method of exclusion" to the crime scene in *Scarlet* (84), where it works so well that he applies it again in *Sign*. "Eliminate all other factors," he instructs Watson, "and the one which remains must be the truth" (92). A few chapters later, the principle becomes a dictum. "How often have I said to you," he reminds Watson, "that when you have eliminated the impossible, whatever remains, *however improbable*, must be the truth?" (111). In the stories, the dictum will soon become "an old maxim," a repeated proposition so smoothly self-evident that both the italicized emphasis and the question mark are gone: "When you have excluded the impossible, whatever remains, however improbable, must be the truth" ("Beryl Coronet," 315). The scientific method—with its three steps of empirical observation, eliminative induction, and experimental verification—thus appears to ground Holmes's detective method.

This is not a fair way of playing the game; the meeting is a setup. The maxim only works under one condition: "Given a complete set of alternatives, there is no problem," Joseph Agassi explains, since "all one has to do is follow each and every one of them routinely." A science lab meets that condition, because closed experiments begin with a set list of variables that can be controlled. A crime scene does not: open investigations start with a provisional list of suspects who are never what they seem. Literary detectives, Agassi argues, must therefore supplement reason with intuition and imagination. When on the case, it is not enough to eliminate all but one of the known factors; any hidden factors must still be nosed out and turned up. Agassi concludes that Holmes represents an "unresolved conflict" between ordinary reason and "special" insight, but that ambivalence gives a free pass to his pseudoscientific method, which Agassi lets stand.[18] Even resolving the conflict in terms of "complementarity," as Jonathan Smith does, only gives Holmes more cover and greater license to skip the important final stage of investigation.[19] He should then do the work of verifying his conclusion, or at least—in Karl Popper's reformulation of the scientific method—keep trying to falsify it. A highly improbable conclusion should strongly indicate that other factors remain hidden, but Holmes is so used to improbabilities coming true that this work is no longer worth doing. With each restatement of his method, the self-described "scientific detective" becomes less and less so, until one wonders just how reliable that test was in the first place, even though it was concocted in a lab (91). The only way to verify that nothing but blood will cause that reaction is to eliminate everything else in the world, which would take forever—or an afternoon, if you are Sherlock Holmes.

Doyle's original stake in the old maxim was clear in his letter to *Light*, which recounted the same hasty process of elimination, allowing him to force the conclusion he wanted to reach. Because he had told no one about that particular book, and had not even thought about it for two days, the fact that the séance message advised him not to read it was "absolutely inexplicable on any hypothesis except that held by Spiritualists."[20] However improbable, spiritualism must be the truth. "The Sherlock Holmes's test" may work within the stories, but outside the stories it needs a new name: "the Sherlock Holmes fallacy." That phrase was coined in 1903 by the American anarchist Steven Byington, who used it to attack an opponent's poor logic and debunk his conspiracy theories, especially the one about Jesuits secretly planning the McKinley assassination. "For it was Sherlock Holmes," said Byington, "who most unblushingly formulated the claim that he could think of all possible explanations of a given set of facts, and, if only one of them would fit the further observed facts, then that one was the truth."[21] The fallacy still informs conspiracy theories today, especially the ones about who secretly planned the 9/11 attacks, as chapter 5 will discuss.

Tellingly, the first person to debunk the fallacy was not Byington but Doyle himself, well before Holmes even existed. In his short story "The Fate of the Evangeline" (1885), a young lady has gone missing at sea, alone and adrift in a boat whose anchor rope unaccountably parted; after a storm blows through, she is presumed dead. To solve the mystery, the local newspaper quotes the maxim, attributing it to Auguste Dupin, the Parisian detective whom Edgar Allan Poe created in the 1840s. On that authority, the newspaper takes the following line: because there were no sharp rocks on the sandy bottom, and because she would not have cut herself loose, and because there was no one else on board, then there must have been a flaw in the anchor rope, which just snapped. Happily, this tragic accident turns out to be fake news; the lady is not drowned at sea but married in Australia. The truth is that her forbidden lover had stolen aboard, cutting the rope to set them both free from her overbearing father. The moral of the story is that that the maxim is a fallacy; apparently something was lost in the translation from French, including the fact that Dupin never said it. Nevertheless, once Doyle converted to spiritualism, he needed its false logic to be true, and so he reassigned it to his own detective. "You remind me of Edgar Allan Poe's Dupin," Watson says early on to Holmes, who flatly dismisses the fictional detective as "a very inferior fellow." The comparison thus lifts Holmes into our reality. "I had no idea that such individuals did exist outside of stories," adds Watson, which is where the maxim will then work perfectly, for both Holmes and his author (24).

A SHOW OF REASON

When debunking Warner's theory of psychic Od, Doyle challenged the photographer to present his ideas "more logically and less dogmatically, while producing some show of reason for the faith that is in him."[22] The twenty-four Sherlock Holmes stories that Doyle produced in the *Strand Magazine* from 1891 to 1893 amount to just that: a show of reason, staged to demonstrate that his faith in spiritualism was logical rather than dogmatic.

In the opening of the first story, "A Scandal in Bohemia," Watson restates the central all-important fact of Holmes's rationalism, avowing that the detective is "the most perfect reasoning and observing machine that the world has seen" (161). The doctor's faith is now absolute: "So accustomed was I to his invariable success that the very possibility of his failing had ceased to enter into my head" (167). In story after story, what looks like sheer revelation turns out to be pure calculation. "His brilliant reasoning power would rise to the level of intuition," Watson says, "until those who were unacquainted with his methods would look askance at him as on a man whose knowledge was not that of other mortals" ("Red-headed League," 185). At the same time, the cases keep scaling back how much evidence Holmes needs to be certain of his conclusions. "It has long been an axiom of mine that the little things are infinitely the most important," says Holmes in "A Case of Identity" (194), later explaining that his method is "founded upon the observation of trifles" ("Boscombe Valley," 214).

By the fifth story, Holmes is ready to update the logician from "The Book of Life." He envisions an even more "ideal reasoner," with the power to reason not only backward but also forward. "When he had once been shown a single fact in all its bearings," such a logician would "deduce from it not only all the chain of events which led up to it but also all the results which would follow from it." The chain stretches so far that reason has come unmoored from reality; inferences now float freely within the infinite subjectivity of the reasoner, who views them as matters of fact. "We have not yet grasped the results which the reason alone can attain to," says Holmes, lounging in his armchair with eyes closed: "Problems may be solved in the study which have baffled all those who have sought a solution by the aid of their senses" ("Five Orange Pips," 224–25). Lest Holmes seem lazy, Doyle eventually provided him with a fat older brother, Mycroft, who is the ideal reasoner in all respects but one: "He will not even go out of his way to verify his own solutions" ("Greek Interpreter," 436). That flaw makes him the ideal scapegoat for his younger brother, who next to him looks like a vigorous empiricist.

The stories deliver their formula in monthly doses, each one boosting Holmes's immunity from reality. Eliminating the impossible, the detective embraces the improbable, making it seem reasonable. When he warns Watson against the mistake of theorizing too soon, he explains that "insensibly one begins to twist facts to suit theories, instead of theories to suit facts" ("Scandal," 163). Holmes has apparently been reading Tyndall's 1867 essay on magical thinking and circular reasoning, in which the physicist warned that "a favourite theory—the desire to establish or avoid a certain result—can warp even [a scientific] mind so as to destroy its power of estimating facts."[23] In practice, however, Holmes can twist the facts away. They are even more capable of bearing other interpretations in the *Strand* than they were in *A Study in Scarlet*.

The same crisp epigrams that pepper books like Konnikova's *Mastermind* also bear another interpretation: Holmes is a crackpot. He can easily force circumstantial evidence to suit his theory: "It may seem to point very straight to one thing, but if you shift your own point of view a little, you may find it pointing in an equally uncompromising manner to something entirely different." But he can also shift the meaning of direct evidence: "There is nothing more deceptive than an obvious fact" ("Boscombe Valley," 204). He excludes evidence that does not fit: "Of all the facts which were presented to us we had to pick just those which we deemed to be essential, and then piece them together in their order, so as to reconstruct this very remarkable chain of events" ("Naval Treaty," 467–68). He discovers all the evidence that his theory requires: "I only saw it because I was looking for it" ("Silver Blaze," 343). But the absence of evidence suits him equally well: "The curious incident of the dog in the night-time" is that "the dog did nothing" ("Silver Blaze," 347). On the one hand, he warns Watson "how dangerous it always is to reason from insufficient data" ("Speckled Band," 272). On the other, it is safe for him to stop gathering data whenever he likes: "It is one of those cases where the art of the reasoner should be used rather for the sifting of details than for the acquiring of fresh evidence" ("Silver Blaze," 335). The net result is that he repeatedly demonstrates confirmation bias without ever being guilty of it: "We imagined what might have happened, acted upon the supposition, and find ourselves justified" ("Silver Blaze," 344).

The detective's "we" is generous to his sidekick, to whom the Science of Deduction still looks like witchcraft. "You would certainly have been burned," Watson says, "had you lived a few centuries ago" ("Scandal," 162). Even so, the doctor soon warms to his task, recording all the different cases that follow the same routine, though never dull: "Sherlock Holmes's prophecy was soon fulfilled, and in a dramatic fashion" ("Resident Patient," 431). To emphasize that his prophecies are properly retrospective, Holmes cites the same paleontologist that Huxley did. "As Cuvier could correctly describe a whole animal by the contemplation of a single bone," he lectures, "so the observer who has thoroughly understood one link in a series of incidents should be able to accurately state all the other ones, both before and after" ("Five Orange Pips," 225). The police continue to question whether Holmes is just "flying away after theories and fancies" ("Boscombe Valley," 211), while Watson continues to vouch for his friend's "rapid deductions, as swift as intuitions, and yet always founded on a logical basis" ("Speckled Band," 258).

Doyle quit his practice just before the *Strand* series began, but he made sure that Sherlock Holmes was still founded on a medical basis. In May 1892, near the end of the first dozen stories, a magazine interviewer asked him "how on earth he had evolved, apparently out of his own inner consciousness, such an extraordinary person as his detective Sherlock Holmes." Doyle laughed at the allusion to *Scarlet*, when Holmes describes the rare power of reasoning backward, but explained that his own genius was not so original as that. The detective was "the literary embodiment, if I may so express it, of my memory of a professor of medicine at Edinburgh University."[24] Later that summer in the *Strand*, Doyle was more specific, naming Dr. Joseph Bell as "the man who suggested Sherlock Holmes to me—here is a portrait of him as he was in those days, and he is strong and hearty, and still in Edinburgh now."[25] Backed by a real-life doctor, whose image he embodies, Holmes carries more empirical weight than most literary characters enjoy. On that basis, Holmes can test the outer limits of Bell's teaching. "Round the centre of deduction and inference and observation which I have heard you inculcate," Doyle wrote to Bell that summer of 1888, "I have tried to build up a man who pushed the thing as far as it would go—further occasionally."[26] No matter how far he goes, the fictional detective will always set out from the same physical address—but not the London one he made famous. When the first dozen stories were collected in *The Adventures of Sherlock Holmes* that October, Doyle dedicated the volume to "My Old Teacher, Joseph Bell, M.D., &c., of 2, Melville Crescent, Edinburgh," which was where the original Holmes lived on.

By the end of 1891 Doyle believed that his detective had gone far enough, because "he takes my mind from better things." His mother persuaded him to let Holmes live for the full second series of stories, but by the middle of 1893 Doyle had decided that *The Memoirs of Sherlock Holmes* would be posthumous.[27] At the end of that year, in "The Final Problem," Doyle gave Holmes the archenemy he deserved—James Moriarty, a professor of astronomy, Holmes's weakest subject—and then took them both over the edge of Reichenbach Falls.

In the stories running up to that plunge, Doyle pushed the detective's reasoning further than it had ever gone before, far enough to seem out of character. Holmes begins to evolve into the lonely reasoner whom John Smith imagined would one day find evidence in nature for a new "elemental religion" that "a man may build up for himself."[28] In "The Cardboard Box," published in January 1893, Holmes solves a crime so grim that even a scientific detective must start to ask himself religious questions: "What object is served by this circle of misery and violence and fear? It must tend to some end, or else our universe is ruled by chance, which is unthinkable. But what end? There is the great standing perennial problem to which human reason is as far from an answer as ever" (901). Only nine months later, Holmes would get very close to solving that problem, thanks to a perennial. In "The Naval Treaty," Holmes stops in his tracks to admire a rose. "It was a new phase of his character to me," says Watson, surprised, "for I had never before seen him show any keen interest in natural objects" (455). In Scarlet we were told that Holmes "knows nothing of practical gardening," but now, six years later, "The Book of Life" finally gets its missing final chapter on revelation (21). Holmes muses to himself: "There is nothing in which deduction is so necessary as in religion. It can be built up as an exact science by the reasoner. Our highest assurance of the goodness of Providence seems to me to rest in the flowers. All other things, our powers, our desires, our food, are all really necessary for our existence in the first instance. But this rose is an extra." The process of elimination becomes an argument from design, convincing to the scientific detective, though he clearly knows nothing about the coevolution of flowers and bees. Holmes falls "into a reverie, with the moss-rose between his fingers," before "coming back with a start to the realities of life" (455–56). But those realities take his mind from better things, and so in "The Final Problem" he decides to retire from the city to the country. "Of late I have been tempted to look into the problems furnished by nature," he reflects, "rather than those more superficial ones for which our artificial state of society is responsible" (477). Before Holmes could enter that last phase, completing his metamorphosis into the lonely reasoner who gets religion, Doyle intervened. His diary for 1893, a year that began with him joining the SPR, records one final all-important fact: the detective was dead at last.[29]

The title of the magazine that made Holmes famous, the *Strand*, suggests the shore of materialist thought from which he can never depart. In "The Book of Life," Holmes reasons his way as far as Niagara, and no further; in "The Final Problem," his chain of logic runs out at Reichenbach, where the character takes the fall for his author. Doyle let go of Holmes but held onto the chain, so that he could extend it further himself. Immediately after "The Final Problem" appeared, Doyle wrote a new novel at high speed, *The Stark Munro Letters* (1895), recycling many passages from *John Smith*. If *John Smith* is the prequel to Sherlock Holmes, then *Stark Munro* is the sequel. *Stark Munro* is more obviously autobiographical than its source material. Its protagonist is a young medical graduate setting out in practice between 1881 and 1884, writing to an American friend every few months about his progress. If *John Smith* is digressive, *Stark Munro* is obsessive, pitting science against religion in every letter.

Munro vows to use his reason to find a way past the impasse, making the same argument from design that Holmes did, but in stronger language: "Leaving this exaggerated scientific caution on the one side, and faith on the other, as being equally indefensible, there remains the clear line of reasoning that a universe implies the existence of a universe maker, and that we may deduce from it some of His attributes, His power, His wisdom, His forethought for small wants, His providing of luxuries for His creatures."[30] Leaving aside Holmes allowed Doyle to "make a religious sensation" with *Stark Munro*, although he assured his mother that he would not mix faith and fiction again.[31] To make sure, Doyle killed both Munro and his wife in a train crash at the end of the novel—a grim accident, but paradoxically also a sign that providence, not chance, rules the universe. "It was such an end as both he and his wife would have chosen," since they died together, instantly and without pain, and "neither was left to mourn the other."[32] Doyle had good reason to be thinking beyond the unthinkable. His wife, Louisa, had recently been diagnosed with tuberculosis, from which she suffered until her death in 1906.

By 1894, Doyle had followed his fictional surrogates along a chain from scientific materialism to universal theism. Once he had eliminated those characters, only he remained to reach the ultimate truth of spiritualism, which was "infinitely the most important thing in the history of the world," as he said to the physicist Oliver Lodge, a fellow member of the SPR faith-ful.[33] While he was willing to say so privately, the now-famous author was not yet ready to proselytize publicly. He sent no further letters to *Light*, though he did contribute more than four thousand pounds—about a third of his annual income—between 1896 and 1898, to help the struggling jour-nal stay afloat.[34] Looking back in 1924, Doyle described the two decades after *Stark Munro* as another period of arrested development: "I did not lose my interest in psychic matters, but I cannot say that I increased my grasp of the religious or spiritual side of the subject." He continued reading up on the subject and attending occasional séances, but the reach of his reasoning still exceeded that grasp. Spiritualism was an all-important fact, but not yet an all-encompassing faith. For him to follow the chain of reasoning past theism to a brand-new revelation would take the coming First World War, for which he had a telling metaphor. "The smooth current of our national life," Doyle reflected, "was quietly sliding toward Niagara."[35]

BRILLIANT EDIFICES

In July 1913, Doyle wrote to Hubert Stansbury about the retired naval cap-tain's book *In Quest of Truth: A Study of Religion and Morality*, published by the freethinking Rational Press Association (RPA). Doyle introduced himself as the author of *Stark Munro*, where he had delineated "the reasons which brought me to a broad Theism" as a young man. He told Stansbury that he still held that position, although he had "since collected a good many thoughts" that might yet appear in a projected sequel, *Posthumous Papers of Stark Munro*.[36] Stansbury's book shared Doyle's premise that "the only reliable foundation of faith is objective knowledge—that is, knowl-edge acquired through the observation of facts." From there, like Tyndall, Stansbury set a limit on speculation: "All subjective knowledge which is acquired by visions, dreams, revelations, or other workings of the imag-ination, must be open to grave suspicion, although it is necessary to use the imagination, guided by the reason, to explain the facts discovered by observation." However, while Tyndall criticized all dogmatism, whether religious or scientific, Stansbury attacked the Church directly, finding no evidence for its theology and no reason for its authority. He then proceeded to eliminate religious belief entirely, reaching the opposite conclusion as

Doyle. "Nowhere have we been able to discover proof of the existence of a controlling intellect or of a creating mind," Stansbury concluded, nor were "the psychic phenomena which have been advanced in favour of spiritualism" anything more than "conjuring tricks or mental delusions."[37] Doyle wrote to steer the captain back toward theism, politely insisting that intelligent design was true and spirit communication was possible, even probable. A monthlong correspondence began, which the RPA published the following year.

Doyle was well prepared for this public debate. Stark Munro never got his sequel, but Sherlock Holmes had reappeared in 1901, when the *Strand Magazine* paid handsomely for a moorland backstory. *The Hound of the Baskervilles* is set before "The Final Problem," and so Holmes technically remained dead, but he can still defend his method when a client accuses him of "guesswork." He counters by citing Tyndall: "It is the scientific use of the imagination, but we have always some material basis on which to start our speculation" (687). However, in appealing to the physicist's authority, Holmes alters the conditions; the detective's imagination is based on materialism, not bounded by rationalism. The novel then tests his limits. Because *Hound* hinges on the question of whether the beast is supernatural, it also raises the question of whether the detective is rational. In London, studying up on the case, Holmes's use of the imagination looks like astral projection: "My body has remained in this armchair and has, I regret to observe, consumed in my absence two large pots of coffee and an incredible amount of tobacco. After you left I sent down to Stamford's for the Ordnance map of this portion of the moor, and my spirit has hovered over it all day" (683). Even when Holmes bustles down to Devonshire, he looks more like a ghost than a detective. Hiding out on the moor, keeping his eye on things, he seems to become "the very spirit of that terrible place" (726). Many critics have read him as a split figure in the novel, moving back and forth between rationalism and irrationalism, but the notion of him being split actually keeps his scientific method intact. When Lawrence Frank argues that "the detective is never only the rationalist and the empiricist," he implies that Holmes remains always a scientist, no matter what other forms of knowledge and modes of consciousness he also explores.[38] To preserve Holmes's integrity, these readings refer his "duality" or "liminality" to conflicts beyond him, whether formal or cultural. He either "embodies the conflicting genres of the novel," which contains both Gothic and realist

plots, or he "represents a marriage of distinctly oppositional epistemologi-
cal frameworks," which pit late Victorian British society against its irrational
foreign Other.[39] In neither case does the split figure simply fall apart.

More recently, both Anna Neill and Srdjan Smajić have put added
pressure on Holmes, arguing that *Hound* stresses how much his "work of
ratiocination blurs with mysticism." For Neill, Holmes is "a scientific investigator who also possesses the primitive gifts of supernormal vision." That
"supernormal" backs off the supernatural, just as the Hampshire Psychical
Society did: Neill frames Holmes's "divinatory gift" within Victorian scientific accounts of atavistic intuition and the subliminal mind.[40] Once again,
contextual rationalism saves Holmes from the question of whether his investigations were ever scientific in the first place. Smajić presses harder: Holmes
"has always been a medium of sorts, though it is not until *The Hound* that
the medium comes out of the closet." Every detective genius since Dupin
has been "a borderline occult figure whose methods often break away from
rationalist protocols," Smajić argues, but Holmes crosses the line and breaks
the rules as "a closet believer in things supernatural who had managed to
pass himself off as a materialist."[41] While he is right to question Holmes's
rationalism, Smajić goes too far. Holmes's client may have "gone over to the
supernaturalists," but the detective never does. Ruling out "the supernatural
explanation," he insists "we are bound to exhaust all other hypotheses before
falling back upon this one" (681, 684). And Holmes never does have to fall
back, which Smajić concedes in an aside: "As it happens, the mystery of the
Baskerville hound does not involve the supernatural."[42]

While Holmes must be understood in the context of Doyle's spiritualism, the detective cannot experiment with it himself. "This agency stands
flat-footed upon the ground, and there it must remain," Holmes reminds
Watson later: "The world is big enough for us. No ghosts need apply"
("Sussex Vampire," 1034). To tell the conversion story of a scientist, Doyle
needed to invent an altogether different character: Professor Challenger,
who begins his career as a zoologist in *The Lost World* (1912) and winds up
a spiritualist in *The Land of Mist* (1926).[43] The world may be big enough for
Holmes, but "Holmes isn't *big* enough" for Doyle, as he emphasized in 1926.
Compared with spiritualist thought, detective fiction may only "appeal to a
lower level of intelligence," but Holmes must remain grounded there. His
materialism is the working basis for a pseudoscientific use of the imagination, disguised as methodological naturalism.[44]

Hound thus corrects the spiritual turn that Holmes started to make before plunging over the falls; the novel walks him back to the shallowest empiricism, where he belongs. In 1903, Doyle revived Holmes for good in a new *Strand* series. In "The Empty House," Holmes pops up suddenly in London, where he explains to Watson that he climbed out of the falls, lay low for two years in Tibet, and is now ready to get back to work. Watson cannot believe his eyes, grabbing Holmes's arm for reassurance: "Well, you're not a spirit, anyhow" (486). Nor did he return a spiritualist, despite "spending some days with the head lama," though the stories continue to erode the shore of materialist thought over the next decade, without the detective ever losing his footing (488). To Watson, Holmes's rationalism has never seemed more straightforward: "Familiar as I was with my friend's methods, it was not difficult for me to follow his deductions" ("Norwood Builder," 497). And his empiricism has never seemed more stable. Holmes's "minute and laborious investigations," Watson says, "form the solid basis on which his brilliant edifices of deduction were reared" ("Abbey Grange," 643). Even so, Holmes underscores that he will never again go so far as to argue from design for providence. "If the matter is beyond humanity it is certainly beyond me," he says, maintaining as he did in *Hound* that "we must exhaust all natural explanations before we fall back on such a theory" ("Devil's Foot," 958).

In corresponding with Stansbury, however, Doyle proposed that all natural explanations must eventually lead beyond humanity; the last link in any chain of reasoning can only be "the far-off wonderful cause" of God. To Paley's argument from design, he added the argument from beauty, picking up exactly where Holmes left off: "I see all around me things which show me the presence not merely of power, but of a very singular loving kindness, often in small matters. To take an example: there is the beauty of flowers and their scent. Every utilitarian object of life could be served without that. It fulfills no function. It seems an extra thrown in out of kindness—a luxury among the necessities of life." Doyle not only ignored coevolution but also rejected natural selection, refusing to fall back on Darwinian theory: "I cannot imagine an endless orderly unfolding without purpose," because "everywhere around me I, at least, seem to see design in detail."[45] For his part, Stansbury asked whether seeming to see design might be the effect of confirmation bias. He, too, had once tried to reason himself toward theism, but eventually "found that I was arguing in a circle—as it is so easy to do." Doyle insisted that his argument "really represents my conviction and

satisfies my reason," but that was precisely the problem: his conviction pre-
ceded his reason. Stansbury pointed out that Doyle was begging rather than
answering the question: "You read my book in the light of your conviction
of a God-ruled universe, and, by dogmatically rejecting every statement
that appears to conflict with that conviction, you have failed to follow my
argument." But the circle could not be broken, and they played an endless game of leapfrog along the chain of reasoning. "You are stopping your
line of thought at the second to last link," said Doyle to Stansbury, "while
the last one would be attached to that power which I call God." Stansbury
replied, "I have passed through your position, and have reached the next
step ahead—where I am awaiting your arrival." Closing the correspondence, the RPA editors gave Stansbury the last word: "I do not recognize
any end to which the universe *is* working. What is it?"[46]

One year later, with the outbreak of the First World War, that question
became both more difficult and more important to answer, as the death
toll soared. "Millions of new clients flocked to spirit mediums in hopes of
making contact with their dead," giving spiritualism "a fresh lease on life."[47]
Doyle's friend Oliver Lodge lost his son Raymond to mortar fire in September 1915. The following year, Lodge published *Raymond, or Life and Death*, a
record of séances in which his son communicated how happy and busy he
now was in the afterlife, "helping those who are passing over in the war." The
recently departed soldiers were mustered in "Summerland," the spirit plane
closest to the earthly material plane, so close that it was almost contiguous:
Raymond "lives in a house—a house built of bricks—and there are trees
and flowers, and the ground is solid." When asked about the material of
those bricks, the spirit replied that "there are laboratories over here, and
they manufacture all sorts of things," including cigars, steaks, and whisky
sodas.[48] Skeptics scoffed, but these concrete details helped to reassure
believers like Doyle, whose large household suffered heavy losses. Doyle
had been knighted as Sir Arthur in 1902, four years before his wife, Louisa,
died, leaving their two grown children, Mary and Kingsley; after her death,
he married Jean Leckie, with whom he had three small children by the
time the war broke out. The second Lady Doyle lost her brother Malcolm
in its first month; her live-in companion, Lily Loder-Symonds, lost three
brothers in its first year. Lily found she had mediumistic powers, and the
family held séances to communicate with its dead, especially Lily's brother
Bob, until she herself fell ill and died in early 1916. Bob's spirit predicted the

course of the war, though not always accurately, leading Doyle to conclude that spirit prophecies were only probabilities.[49] Doyle's own brother Innes survived the trenches, but his son Kingsley was seriously wounded at the Somme in July 1916.

Two weeks after Kingsley returned to the front in October, Doyle wrote to *Light* for the first time since 1887. When debating Stansbury, Doyle had avoided calling himself a spiritualist, seeking common ground with the rationalist. "You do not undertake to deny absolutely the possibility of there being something which may survive death," he pointed out, "while I have never claimed it as a certainty, so there is no great gap there."[50] But now in *Light* he publicly announced his belief in spiritualism as the final answer to Stansbury's last question. Séance phenomena and spirit communications showed divine cause even more clearly than natural theology. "Further proof is superfluous," he declared, calling for "the close of the stage of investigation" and for "the period of religious construction" to begin.[51] Having satisfied his reason, it was the right moment to abandon it.

By then Doyle had nearly closed the investigations of Sherlock Holmes. There had not been a new short story since "The Dying Detective" in 1913, when Holmes again faked a near-death experience. The fourth and final novel, *The Valley of Fear* (1915), is set before Holmes and Moriarty went over the falls, allowing the archenemy to return for a curtain call. In September 1917, as Doyle entered a six-month period of religious construction—writing lectures, articles, and finally a book on *The New Revelation* (1918)—he brought Holmes up to date in the *Strand* just long enough to retire him to the country. In "His Last Bow," set two days before Britain entered the war, Holmes foils a German plot to steal military secrets and then retreats to his small farm on the South Downs, where he lives quietly, keeping bees. Perhaps he has finally studied coevolution, because instead of the argument from beauty, he makes the argument from morality: divine wrath and mercy give order and meaning to the universe. The wartime story ends with Holmes's apocalyptic forecast of "an east wind coming," after which the reconstruction of England as Summerland can begin: "But it's God's own wind none the less, and a cleaner, better, stronger land will lie in the sunshine when the storm has cleared" (980). For the first time since *A Study in Scarlet*, Doyle took the narration out of Watson's hands, adopting a third-person omniscient perspective of the two old friends. The author said goodbye to them from a distance, as the creator of their universe.

In that capacity, he wrote "Some Personalia About Mr. Sherlock Holmes" for the *Strand* at the end of 1917, reflecting on the many fan letters both he and Holmes had received over the years. The detective may be fictional, Doyle explained, but "the general lines of reasoning advocated by Holmes have a real practical application to life," echoing Holmes's assertion in *Scarlet* that his theories are "really extremely practical." Doyle cited several examples of his own detective work, including the famous cases of George Edalji and Oscar Slater, whose unjust convictions (for animal mutilation and murder, respectively) he helped to overturn. He also described smaller problems that were "very similar to some which I had invented for the exhibition of the reasoning of Mr. Holmes," though now it was the author who could explain "the links which make the chain." With the chain of reasoning weaving back and forth between the two of them, Doyle's "Personalia" article blurred the line between fiction and reality as much as Holmes's fan letters did. Even so, Doyle still refused to let Holmes himself make any link between natural and supernatural explanations: a case involving a possibly cursed ring was "upon the psychic plane, and therefore beyond his powers."[52]

But not beyond the powers of his author. With the detective out of the way, Doyle took over his reasoning, taking it all the way to the far-off end of the line. "The whole of this system," he expounded in *The New Revelation*, "from the lowest physical phenomenon of a table-rap up to the most inspired utterance of a prophet, is one complete whole, each link attached to the next one," and "when the humbler end of that chain was placed in the hand of humanity, it was in order that they might, by diligence and reason, feel their way up it until they reached the revelation which waited in the end." Doyle repeatedly anchored his argument with that chain metaphor. "The chain of evidence between the simplest cases of thought-reading at one end," he said in the same book, "and the actual manifestation of the spirit independently of the body at the other, was one unbroken chain."[53] Ending where it began, the sentence illustrates how much Doyle's spiritualist writing recycled the language of his detective fiction. "The world is full of obvious things," says Holmes in *Hound* (683), a lesson Doyle recalled in his 1916 letter to *Light*: "It is the simplest thing that catches the eye."[54] Doyle often echoed Holmes when he described spiritualists as "driven to observe facts, to reason from them," but in other places he outright plagiarized himself.[55] In *The Sign of Four*, Holmes presents "the only hypothesis which covers the facts" (120); in *The Vital Message* (1919), Doyle declared that "there is only one explanation which covers the facts."[56] Over and over again, Doyle eliminated natural explanations of séance phenomena— especially fraud, which he prided himself on being able to detect—until only the truth of spiritualism remained. To that end, he tweaked Holmes's statement of method in *Hound.* "One is bound to exclude spirit explanations until all natural ones have been exhausted," a principle that he later emphasized "cannot be too often repeated," since it was the pseudoscientific foundation of his faith.[57] At the same time, Doyle affirmed the material basis of spirit explanations. "We build from below, brick upon brick," he said in *The Wanderings of a Spiritualist* (1921), "never getting beyond the provable fact."[58] That metaphor, of course, was also drawn from his fiction. "Data! data! data!" Holmes demands in "The Copper Beeches," crying "I can't make bricks without clay" (322).

Concrete imagery added critical mass to the available evidence, which was primarily textual rather than material: the personal testimonies and public reports of spiritualists, as well as the séance messages and automatic writings of the spirits themselves. In the 1887 letter to *Light,* Doyle treated his reading about spiritualism, which included Drayson's work, as equivalent to "weighing the evidence."[59] By 1916, the evidence was even weightier, though still textual. "The evidence upon which this system rests is so enormous," Doyle averred, "that it would take a very considerable library to contain it."[60] Just as spirits made their own bricks, spiritualists manufactured their own evidence, repeating the word "fact" over and over again while quoting all those texts. The word appears dozens of times in each of Doyle's first three spiritualist books, and three hundred times in his two-volume *History of Spiritualism* (1926). Like Holmes's explanations, these statements of fact are performative rather than constative: they bring into being the reality they claim to describe. Spiritualist writing was "a mass semiotic exercise," Daniel Cottom says, "inventing a ground for meaning that ran both within and without the territory of reason."[61] Sheer repetition made the textual evidence seem fully material. "Now, arguing upon these facts, and they would appear most undoubtedly to be facts," insisted Doyle, "what possible answer can the materialist or the sceptic give?"[62] On that basis, Doyle reared up his own deductions, writing up his own contributions to the "wonderful literature" from which "this movement must gain great additional solidity."[63] Spiritualists worked mainly within that library,

cross-referencing rather than corroborating the evidence, building the collection from its cornerstone: Holmes's "Book of Life."

FEATS OF CLEAR THINKING

At the same time that Doyle undermined the distinction that the archeologist Reginald Stuart Poole made between internal and external evidence,
he scapegoated other religious groups for their even shallower empiricism
and flightier inferences. He chided both the high-minded occultism of
"our Theosophical friends, with whom we quarrel for their absence of evidence," and the close-minded fundamentalism of the Christian Evidence
Society, "since they regard a text as an argument."[64] Yet he also borrowed a
tactic from those same groups, turning the tables on scientific materialists
who "insist too much upon direct proof" by insisting that their knowledge
claims were no more substantial than his own. "What direct proof have we
of most of the great facts of Science?" he demanded, echoing *Cloomber*. He
argued that rationalists show the same faith in testimony and authority as
religious believers: "How many of us have, for example, seen the rings of
Saturn? We are assured that they are there, and we accept the assurance."[65]
No wonder that Holmes ignores Copernicus. If astronomy and other
empirical sciences are mostly just hearsay and say-so, then spiritualism
gains in comparison, because "its feet are on something more solid than
texts or traditions or intuitions."[66] From there, it is but a short step into the
uncharted waters beyond both the Atlantic and Niagara. "I am like a child
wading ankle deep in the margin of an illimitable ocean," Doyle wrote, "but
this, at least, I have very clearly realised, that the ocean is there and that
the margin is part of it."[67] Because the stage of investigation was closed, he
asked inquirers to accept his word on that, telling them to "get away from
the phenomenal side" and instead immerse themselves in "the literature of
this subject," where it is possible to "soak yourself with this grand truth."[68]

That literature is all wet, as Helen Sword explains: "Spiritualist apologists concoct ingenious responses to accusations of inconsistency or illogic,
but their explanations, shoring fragments of reason against the potential
ruins of a precarious metaphysics, often threaten to plunge believers and
skeptics alike into an intellectual abyss."[69] The abyss is much deeper than
Reichenbach Falls, from which rescue is apparently possible; it is the

maelstrom of babble from which Hitchens believed Doyle had spared Holmes. But Hitchens was wrong: Doyle pushed Holmes first and then leaped after. His spiritualist library was full of explanatory fictions that recycled not only Holmes's best lines but also his worst logic, running circles around the skeptics. Like the dog that did not bark, the spirit that did not materialize proved only that a skeptical sitter "may ruin a psychic circle," which was why "practicing Spiritualists continually get such results as are never attained by mere researchers."[70] As James Stephen would say, spiritualists were always right when they could not be tested and always wrong when they could; Stephen would also object to the impossible conditions of disproof that they imposed on skeptics. "The weight of disproof lies upon those who deny," Doyle claimed, obliging skeptics to spend all their remaining time on earth debunking every single medium as a fraud and every single witness as a dupe. But even that would never be enough, since proof of fraud today is not the same as disproof of spirits forever, a loophole often exploited by spiritualists. Nor is proof of fraud today the same as proof of fraud yesterday or tomorrow, since mediums "may be guilty of trickery when their powers fail them, and yet at other times have very genuine gifts." In fact, proof of fraud today is not even proof of fraud today—quite the reverse, if you understand that "wicked or mischievous" spirits are quite capable of "wilful deception," making even gifted mediums look guilty.[71]

Joseph Jastrow, a psychologist who specialized in optical illusions, called Doyle's lectures on spiritualism "perfect nonsense," a jab that both makes and misses the point.[72] The nonsense *is* perfect. It replicates precisely the ex post facto reasoning of Sherlock Holmes, who guarantees that his author's metaphysics are not precarious. Instead, the nonsense had the power to put skeptical materialists on edge, creating the impression that they were the ones living in imaginary universes of their own design. In 1920, the RPA invited Doyle to participate in a public debate, this time with founding member Joseph McCabe, a former Catholic priest who had lost his faith and left the church to become a freethinking writer. McCabe opened on the attack, claiming that there was too much proof of fraud to believe in the truth of spiritualism. Doyle then turned that argument against itself, casting skeptics as paranoid conspiracy theorists who see deception and delusion everywhere: "They think there is a wonderful spider's web all over the country, detectives sitting up all night planning things. (Laughter.)" The allusion is to "The Cardboard Box," in which Holmes "loved to lie in the very centre of five millions of people, with his filaments stretching out and running through them, responsive to every little rumour or suspicion of unsolved crime" (888). The audience enjoyed the joke, but McCabe did not appreciate being plunged into Doyle's fictional universe, where the facts are all twisted. "This is a complete perversion of what I said," he protested.[73]

Two months later, McCabe returned the favor. His article on "Scientific Men and Spiritualism" called Doyle's explanation of ectoplasm "a finer flight of fiction than any adventure of Sherlock Holmes."[74] In his rejoinder, Doyle laughed off the jibe—"That is very crushing!"—and flipped the script, arguing that McCabe was the one who wished to "cultivate the art of telling a story in order to produce an *ex-parte* effect."[75] McCabe was guilty of confirmation bias, because he "chooses to presuppose that such phenomena do not exist." He had lost touch with reality, because he "builds up conditions from his own imagination and puts forward explanations which are impossible on the face of them." He could not go wrong, because he "appears to think that his mere assertion, founded upon a wild guess or imaginary hypothesis, will always outweigh any records of facts." Echoing Watson, Doyle dismissed McCabe's reasoning as "merest babble with nothing solid at the back of it."[76] This ingenious response inverted the terms of debate. Rationalism then looked like insanity; materialism, like fantasy; skepticism, like credulity. Without realizing the irony, Doyle had converted McCabe into a parody of Sherlock Holmes, a charlatan who "assumes a pose of extreme accuracy. He speaks or writes in short snip-snap sentences. He will have no equivocations. All must be logical. This is the last word, the inevitable word, cold and clear. We are down to the facts at last." Point by point, the spiritualist scapegoated the rationalist for all the ludicrous pseudoscience that Holmes displays. "But when one gets behind this show of accuracy," Doyle continued, "one finds such a jumble, such prejudice, such misquotation, such an absolute refusal to conform to the same laws which he enforces upon others, and such a determination to insist that Mr. McCabe's own private opinion can ride superior over any evidence, that the general effect, after one has recovered from the surprise of it, is richly comical." Having crushed the opposition, Doyle could rest his case. "That is not Science," he concluded, "but the very antithesis of Science."[77]

McCabe tried to get the last laugh in the final pages of his *Spiritualism: A Popular History* (1920), reminding everyone who was the real storyteller. Summerland was a place too grand to be true: "Doyle, who is not a physicist, and is sublimely indifferent to the inherent difficulties, built up the golden city on an ether-basis with the facility of a master of fiction."[78] In other words, the spiritualist was designing his universe by writing his novel as he liked, which was precisely what Stephen warned would happen to any believer who tries too hard to square religious truths with scientific facts. Doyle was also a master of verisimilitude: he described Summerland as a sort of Hampstead Garden Suburb, the journalist E. T. Raymond joked, "much as if he had just returned from a week-end."[79] The literary genre of spiritualism was a heightened domestic realism: all the main elements of the nineteenth-century bourgeois novel would survive death, not only private property and material comforts but also individual personality and family histories. The only thing missing was a plot conflict, since spiritualism rewrote the many human tragedies of the First World War as a single divine comedy, with the same happy ending for everyone. Spiritualism inverted the paranoid logic of detective fiction, finding evidence everywhere that "the universe was, after all, a human-friendly place," as Thomas Laqueur says, which no longer held much mystery.[80]

"With one of our most popular and distinguished novelists as the herald of this 'new revelation,'" McCabe sniped, "the movement was bound to grow."[81] John Lamond confirmed that the author drew large crowds "wherever he went," though he was not always the main attraction. "They might be indifferent as regards the problems he was anxious to discuss with them," Lamond noted, but "they were eager to see and hear 'Sherlock Holmes.'"[82] There was also growing protest, however, that the novelist had betrayed his most popular character. "Is Conan Doyle Mad?" asked the *Sunday Express*, before giving him the benefit of the doubt, reasoning that he "could not have created Sherlock Holmes if he had not been deeply versed in the laws of evidence."[83] Other reviewers were less charitable. "Arthur Conan Doyle, in his new character, is the exact opposite of his creation," Raymond declared, complaining that the credulous spiritualist "makes cruel war on the great legend of the perfect detective."[84] The American journalist Heywood Broun also observed that "a gulf has been set up between the detective and his creator," but he viewed the infallible icon as an early waypoint on Doyle's religious quest: "Most logically a belief in spiritism grows out of a faith and fondness for Sherlock Holmes."[85]

No Holmes stories appeared between 1917 and 1921, as Doyle devoted himself to writing about Summerland instead of Baker Street. He wrote only twelve more Holmes stories in the decade before his death in 1930, largely in order to finance his lecture tours around the world. According to Doyle, the world had little need for Holmes when the star detective of the new age would be psychical rather than scientific. Whereas in 1894 he explained to the Portsmouth press "how Holmes might have deduced the writer" of Jack the Ripper's letters to the police, in 1920 he recommended in the *Strand* that "it should be possible at every great police centre to have the call upon the best clairvoyant or other medium that can be got." Doyle conceded that such evidence might not be material enough to hold up in court, but he still argued that an official deputation of spiritualists "would in itself be a strong deterrent to premeditated crime."[86] Holmes invented the profession of consulting detective, but in the end, he was too good for his own good: having led his author to the spirits, he lost his job to the psychics. When Agatha Christie went missing for eleven days in 1926, during which she was front-page news, Doyle gave one of her gloves to a psychometrist, who "at once got the name of Agatha," convincing Doyle of his power.[87] This sort of reasoning drove fans of Holmes crazy: Raymond was mad enough to identify Doyle with Watson, "the personification of common stupidity."[88] T. S. Eliot was more tactful, but he also rubbished all the letters, articles, and interviews about the new revelation. "Sir A. Conan Doyle, the eminent spiritualist of whom we read in Sunday papers," Eliot asked, "what has he to do with Holmes?"[89]

Doyle's own answer was simple: everything. After years of research, Doyle had built "a collection of psychic books," Lamond recalled, "such as I had never seen in any private library."[90] Watson is less tolerant of Holmes's document hoarding, complaining that "his papers accumulated until every corner of the room was stacked with bundles of manuscript" ("Musgrave Ritual," 386). In early 1925, Doyle made his library public, opening the Psychic Bookshop in Victoria Street, across from Westminster Abbey. That summer he added a museum in the basement, exhibiting the material evidence of his faith: spirit photographs, slate writings, fingerprints on glass, wax molds of ghostly hands, and various objects that had materialized at séances, including a Syrian jug, Turkish coins, and a Babylonian clay tablet. The tablet was a forgery, Doyle acknowledged, but he reasoned that the spirits probably found an imitation easier to transport from Baghdad than a genuine one.[91] Reviewing the museum, the London *Daily News* doubted that Doyle had solved the mystery of the afterlife, complaining that the wrong character was on the case: "Unhappily Sir Arthur did not call in Sherlock Holmes. Instead he left the problem in the hands of the amiable and credulous Dr. Watson." Doyle replied to set the record straight. The right character was already on the case, as he had been since the beginning: "[The *Daily News*] couples my name with Sherlock Holmes, and I presume that since I am the only begetter of that over-rated character I must have some strand of my nature which corresponds with him. Let me assume this. In that case I would say (and you may file the saying for reference) that of all the feats of clear thinking which Holmes ever performed by far the greatest was when he saw that a despised and ridiculed subject was in very truth a great new revelation and an epoch-making event in the world's history."[92] More than thirty years after killing Holmes because he took his author's mind from better things, Doyle publicly converted himself into his character, and vice versa, revealing that they both thought exactly alike, and that they both had the same end clearly in view.

AN END OF THE MATTER

"For thirty years," said Doyle in 1924, reflecting on all his "unconscious preparation" for the hard work of proselytism, "I have trained myself exactly for the role without the least inward suspicion of whither I was tending."[93] The core of that preparation was the detective fiction whose principle of composition and theory of method are the same: reasoning backward. Begging questions and twisting evidence, Doyle was no more conscious of living in a universe of his own design than Sherlock Holmes, nor did he have any more chance of ever getting out of it. Even the most scientific minds, Tyndall warned, have a hard time letting go of favorite theories: "I have known men to work for years under a fascination of this kind, unable to extricate themselves from its fatal influence."[94] The stage of investigation was closed, along with any possible exit. Though Doyle still bustled about on lecture tours, the wandering spiritualist had otherwise become an arm-chair lounger, evolving from his own inner consciousness the whole belief system of spiritualism. Surrounded by all those books in his study, he no longer needed to see things for himself, because he had special knowledge, as Holmes does, which facilitated matters wonderfully. That special knowl-edge of Summerland seemed purely empirical. The spirits reported back directly on the objects they observed and handled there, even if nonbelievers "protest that this world which is described to us is too material for their liking."[95] That special knowledge also seemed perfectly rational. The system was so internally consistent that Doyle could boast, "In five years of cross examination I have hardly ever made a statement which I have had even to modify after I have made it."[96] He believed in ghosts, and Holmes does not, but their experience of reason was otherwise the same; in a self-reflexive universe, textuality feels material, and circularity looks linear. The story in which Holmes rules out ghosts is the same in which he explains how to construct that universe: "When this original intellectual deduction is confirmed point by point by quite a number of independent incidents, then the subjective becomes objective" ("Sussex Vampire," 1042). Once that feedback loop gets going, the chain of reasoning spirals ever outward, and the system of belief devolves into a maelstrom. As Holmes mutters in "The Dying Detective," when he pretends to be raving with fever, "Ah, I am wandering! Strange how the brain controls the brain!" (936).

Of the last dozen stories, Lycett observes that Doyle "refrained from embellishing his Sherlockian output with any hint of spiritualism, which he realized would mean commercial suicide."[97] However, he constantly embellished his spiritualism with Sherlockian input, which led him to commit the fin de siècle's version of "intellectual suicide."[98] Leaping from the concrete to the cosmic, Doyle could persuade himself that he had proved almost anything on the basis of almost nothing. Most famously, he believed that two Yorkshire girls had taken photographs of fairies in their garden, having applied Holmes's maxim: "It was surely impossible that a little village with an amateur photographer could have the plant and the skill to turn out a fake which could not be detected by the best experts in London." The girls later confessed to what was clear to most observers, even fellow spiritualists: the fairies were paper-doll cutouts, stuck on hatpins. Doyle staked his faith on the coming of the fairies, whose existence would help to ground his larger belief system. "Having discovered this," he predicted, "the world will not find it so difficult to accept that spiritual message supported by physical facts which has already been so convincingly put before it. All this I see, but there may be much more."[99]

When looking ahead, Doyle asked the world to take his word for what he saw coming, since both further proof and further explanation were superfluous: "Having made up one's mind that it was true there was an end of the matter."[100] His mind, coupled with Sherlock Holmes's character, guaranteed the whole system, granting him the absolute religious authority that he had rejected in the first place. At the beginning of *John Smith*, envisioning a future faith based on reason, Doyle's surrogate chastises himself for being "so very dogmatic and prophetic," which he must do again toward the end.[101] Evidence, not authority, is what counts for Smith, who also knows better than to trust his own brain, as he lounges around the house speculating on the future. Thirty years later, Doyle presented himself as the prophet whom Smith refused to be. "It was borne in upon me that the knowledge which had come to me thus was not for my own consolation alone," he affirmed, "but that God had placed me in a very special position for conveying it to that world which needed it so badly."[102] Like his special knowledge, Doyle's position was paradoxical: his revelation was that he must proselytize for a faith not based on revelation.

Spiritualism's refusal of authority and hierarchy was always a potential source of chaos. If no one had authority, then everyone could claim it, as Doyle worried would happen with so many trance mediums communicating so many spirit messages to so many séance-goers. "If the whole world is to become full of minor prophets, each of them stating their own views of the religious state with no proof save their own assertion," he warned, "we should, indeed, be back in the dark ages of implicit faith."[103] To stabilize the system, he offered himself as the single authoritative voice of spiritualism, though he was careful to link his authority to the empirical chain of reasoning itself, which ascended smoothly from table-rapping to prophetic utterances. On that very highest ground, Doyle asserted his own authority simply by appealing to it.

His elevated position changed Doyle's perspective of Joseph Smith. Mormon doctrine no longer seemed so absurd as it once did to John Smith, who chuckles that "no man is too stupid or too wicked not to have a following."[104] In 1923, Doyle visited Salt Lake City and lectured on spiritualism in the Mormon Tabernacle; in *Our Second American Adventure* (1924), he treated Joseph Smith more generously than John Smith does. Rather than bad faith, Doyle suggested that the Mormon prophet was guilty of bad reasoning, done in good faith. Smith was a spirit medium who "lost all sense of proportion and misinterpreted to a great extent the evidence," believing that he was on the receiving end of a newly revealed religion. Spiritualists now knew better, as they "have been able to systematize and compare many examples of what to Smith was an isolated miracle." Mormon theology "strains us," as Doyle said, because it was "an interpolation of Joseph Smith, forging for pious ends." Doyle's tone was gentler, but his scapegoating tactic was the same here as it was in *Scarlet*. Compared with Mormonism, with its "indiscriminate adoption of supposed revelations," spiritualism was far more grounded and methodical.[105] However, his visit to the Tabernacle, where "it is a perfect joy to stand on the rostrum and feel how easily one can command one's audience," inspired Doyle; upon returning to London, he proposed building his own church for spiritualists.[106]

The established Church of England rejected the new spiritualist revelation, accusing its modern prophet of spreading false gospel. Doyle believed that spiritualism rescued the Bible from narrow-minded literalism, "re-establishing its credibility" on the basis of material evidence rather than textual interpretation, but the Church did not see it that way.[107] At the 1919 Church Congress, a London vicar warned that "Sir Arthur Conan Doyle is moving from city to city, casting out common sense and ministering to popular crazes."[108] The secretary of the English Church Union, representing the Anglo-Catholic wing, questioned Doyle's methods and rejected his beliefs.[109] Doyle countered by raising the stakes. His argument was not with the Church of England itself but with "all organised Christianity," since spiritualists were "the true representatives of those primitive Christians who themselves saw spirits and held communion with the dead saints."[110] By that analogy, Doyle was spiritualism's Saint Paul, as he enjoyed being known, a new title that authorized him to appeal even more confidently to his own authority.[111] These narcissistic tendencies troubled his friend Harry Houdini, who spent as much time debunking spiritualism as Doyle did defending it; they finally fell out when Doyle claimed to have contacted Houdini's dead mother. "Doyle thinks he is a Messiah who has come to save mankind by instructing them in the mysteries of occultism," Houdini objected publicly, "but instead of that he is misleading the public and his teachings are a menace to sanity and health."[112] But Doyle got the last word. After Houdini's death in 1926, Doyle explained in the *Strand* that the escape artist had always been a true medium, although he never realized his gift and never knew that he was being helped out of handcuffs and straitjackets by the very spirits in which he refused to believe.[113]

The same spirits were helping Doyle to embrace his new role, telling him to have more faith in his marvelous faculty and predicting that his new London tabernacle would soon be built. In 1921, shortly after Doyle's mother died, his wife began realizing her powers as first an automatic writer and then a trance medium. At first, Lady Doyle had her doubts, but the spirit of her friend Lily came through to admonish her: "It is *not* your subconscious self." At the same time, the spirit of Doyle's mother came through to apologize for not believing in spiritualism while she was alive.[114] The spirit of his son Kingsley, who had died of influenza in 1918, also came through to offer Christian tidings, but he was interrupted by the spirit of the journalist William Stead, who passed along a message from Christ himself, endorsing Doyle's mission.[115] After 1922, the family séance circle grew to include Pheneas, an ancient Mesopotamian spirit guide, who exhorted Doyle to keep up the good work, preparing for Christ's return to the earth. Doyle collected and published his spirit guide's wisdom in *Pheneas Speaks* (1927), including dark thoughts about Houdini.[116] As he worked, Doyle was receiving notes and letters from believers all over the world who praised him for teaching them. One woman in Pennsylvania thanked God for creating Doyle as the joint incarnation of Holmes and Watson.[117] His friend Lamond went so far as to predict that Doyle would one day be worshipped as a deity.[118] However, Doyle's increasingly Christianized beliefs put him at odds with the movement as a whole. In 1928, the Spiritualists' National Union rejected his proposal that the organization endorse "the original teaching and example of Jesus of Nazareth," which would have compromised its claim to be a universal religion without creed.[119]

That setback was the least of Doyle's worries. Under the Witchcraft Act of 1735, it was still illegal for anyone to claim magical powers, including mediums. Watson might laugh about Holmes being burned at the stake, but the Act was no joke to Doyle, who lobbied unsuccessfully for its repeal throughout the 1920s. Government opposition was bad enough, but Doyle also began to perceive a much deeper conspiracy against spiritualism, "a hidden hand which strikes the movement when it can," leaving behind very little "direct public evidence."[120] Good detective work may have led spiritualists to Summerland, where everyone is out to help you, but on this earth, the logic of detective fiction was still fundamentally paranoid. At the center of the spider's web was not Moriarty but the Catholic Church, with Jesuits sitting up all night planning things. On the one hand, Rome was a longtime open enemy of spiritualists, "viewing them as dangerous pretenders to sacred communion."[121] In 1917, when Father Bernard Vaughan declared that "we must sweep the country clear of these charlatans," Doyle accused his fellow Stonyhurst graduate of exhibiting "all the intolerance and the persecuting spirit of the Inquisition."[122] Another Stonyhurst graduate, Father Herbert Thurston, wrote a pamphlet titled *Modern Spiritualism* (1928), debunking Pheneas and rebuking Doyle for working "special mischief."[123] Doyle promptly published *The Roman Catholic Church: A Rejoinder* (1929), accusing Thurston of seeing "nothing good outside his own dogmatic fence."[124] When the Anglican *Church Times* declined to advertise his new book, Doyle took that to be indirect evidence of a "hidden hand trying to obstruct us," as he told an Armistice Day meeting of spiritualists. This underground conspiracy, "a kind of crypto-catholicism," involved not only the established Church but also the mainstream media; thousands of spiritualists had gathered in the Albert Hall that morning, but Doyle predicted that there would be "no allusion to it tomorrow in *The Times*."[125] As it happened, he was correct, which proved his point: the press did not bark in the nighttime.

That prediction was nothing compared with Pheneas's far more terrible prophecies about where the universe was tending. In 1924, the spirit began warning Doyle that the apocalypse was nigh. In a red leather journal, Doyle transcribed his spirit guide's "Prophesied Course of Events," scenes of horror during the end of days that would astonish Huxley and gratify Liddon: volcanic eruptions, massive earthquakes, tidal waves, raging fires, world famine, civil war, the sinking of continents, the collapse of nations, and the obliteration of cities, especially the Vatican.[126] In short, an east wind was coming, a storm even worse than the one that Holmes foresaw, so terrifying that all those descriptions were redacted in *Pheneas Speaks*, at the direction of Pheneas himself. "A detailed and verbatim account would tend to cause panic," Doyle explained in a later pamphlet.[127] What remained was the lighter side of Holmes's prophecy. Once the storm has passed, the sun will shine again on England, "the centre to which all humanity will turn," and where the elect will live happily ever after, having made the final cut.[128] The elect, Doyle noted in his journal, included all members of his family.[129] Initially, Pheneas prophesied that the apocalypse would begin in 1925, prompting Doyle to drop hints in the press that "higher powers" would soon intervene to correct the world's "shocking state of materialism."[130] When 1925 came and went as usual, he began another journal, this one untitled, in which he pasted newspaper clippings about earthquakes and windstorms around the world, just as Holmes clips articles about crimes. Doyle then cited this data in *Pheneas Speaks* to corroborate at least a few of the spirit's more local forecasts, even if the one epoch-making event had not yet arrived. "You can pack up your things," Pheneas promised: "It won't be very long now."[131]

There is no limit to this kind of following, said the Duke of Argyll, but that is only because it comes full circle, from Holmes's unsigned "Book of Life" to Doyle's untitled journal of doom. In that journal, the Science of Deduction and Analysis becomes all-powerful, as warming the climate of Afghanistan is nothing compared with raining fire on the planet. Retrospective prophecy becomes genuinely retroactive: the original séance transcripts do not contain the weather predictions that are quoted in *Pheneas Speaks*. Doyle later added those early warning signs to the book, fulfilling them after the fact.[132] When the subjective becomes objective, the objective carries no weight; the logical conclusion of reasoning backward is the end of the world. Doyle vowed not to break the same ground twice, but by the end of his life he had designed two parallel universes, one fictional and one spiritual, with the same infallible intelligence at the center of both. "When I talk on this subject," Doyle said in a 1929 Movietone News interview, "I am not talking about what I believe; I am not talking about what I think; I am talking about what I know." The newsreel preserves both the voice and the image of the author whose character led him to become a prophet. "Curiously enough," Doyle says to the camera, "my first experiences in that direction were just about the time when Sherlock Holmes was being built up in my mind."[133]

CHAPTER 4

Wonderful Literature, 1930–2020

DEATH OF THE AUTHOR

Arthur Conan Doyle died on July 7, 1930, after suffering from heart trouble for several months. His death was international front-page news. "Up to the end," the *New York Times* reported, "his enthusiasm for psychic investigation was unflagging."[1] That enthusiasm, however, no longer extended to the Society for Psychical Research, from which he had resigned six months earlier, protesting that it had become "simply an anti-spiritualist organisation."[2] The SPR had never gone over to his new revelation, sticking instead to the phenomenal side of spiritualism. "Psychical research," the physicist William Barrett said after Doyle's conversion, "may strengthen the foundations but cannot take the place of religion."[3] Doyle felt that the SPR was not even doing that much; he was still angry about its 1922 exposure of the spirit photographer William Hope, whom Doyle nonetheless continued to support. Calling for all its members to join him in resigning, Doyle accused the SPR of doing "essentially unscientific and biased work," whose aim was "obtuse negation at any cost."[4]

Fewer than a hundred members exited with him, but more than six thousand people attended the Royal Albert Hall memorial service on July 13, just as they had flocked to his lectures and debates during the previous decade.[5] At those events, Doyle invited audience members to write to him personally about their own séance experiences, documenting phenomena and recording communications. Sent from all over the world, the reports of these "tens of thousands of hard-headed observers" swelled the "enormous volume of evidence, which is recorded in hundreds of books, and thousands of manuscripts," all collected in Doyle's library. The existence of so much material was itself "a portentous fact," hard proof that even skeptics in the SPR could not negate, even if they doubted the portents themselves.[6] Doyle then recycled those testimonies in subsequent lectures, where he called for even more feedback, reinforcing his increasingly logic-proof arguments. That loop circumscribed his own authorial position, sitting in his library at the center of the spiritual universe, his infallible word holding together all those texts. Before long, inquirers approached him just as clients approach Sherlock Holmes, seeking answers and reassurances from the one person whose explanations were so total as to seem inspired. Lamond's prophecy that Doyle would one day be deified was already coming true.[7]

The thousands of followers assembled at the Albert Hall were hoping for a new portent. The organizers had placed an empty chair, reserved with his name on it, next to his widow. Would Doyle attend his own memorial service? Before long, the presiding medium, Estelle Roberts, interrupted her clairvoyant channeling of condolences to announce, "He is here," claiming she had just seen Doyle take his seat on the platform. She then passed along a private message from him to Lady Doyle, who later confirmed its evidential value.[8] The answer was final: Doyle's revelation was unflagging. "There is no question that my father will often speak to us," his son Adrian declared to the press, "just as he did before he passed over."[9] It was important to the crowd that there be no question. In contrast to theosophy, spiritualism was "a movement rather than an organization, a movement dependent upon the renewal of charismatic leadership."[10] Theosophy's bureaucratic structure enabled it "to normalize occult transmission as an institutional activity," even after Blavatsky's death in 1891, but Doyle's death left a vacuum that only his returned spirit could fill.[11]

The family may have been certain that Doyle would speak, but his channel of transmission was still an open question. Roberts was not the first medium to relay a message from Doyle. A few days before the Albert Hall service, a New Zealand medium reported that Doyle wanted his friends and family to know that they "will be able to get into touch with me shortly."[12] Shortly after the service, the spirit photographer Hope took a picture of

Doyle floating above a Yorkshire clergyman named Charles Tweedale. Interviewed at the end of the month, Lady Doyle said that her husband had not yet materialized for her, though she was otherwise in touch, and that she expected to see him soon. She asserted that she would "carry on her husband's work to the best of her ability," proselytizing for spiritualism, as would their son Denis, rather than becoming a lawyer.[13] The work was in full swing by September, when she wrote a syndicated article about a recent evidential message. A medium visiting for the weekend had contacted Doyle, who repeated something he had said previously at a private, family-only séance, which the medium could not have known. The message proved that Doyle was now "able to make his psychic presence felt."[14] The medium was Grace Cooke, who became attached to the family in the months following Doyle's death, passing along messages of love from him. On Armistice Day, she claimed to have spotted Doyle in the Albert Hall, in a parade of spirits that also included Abraham Lincoln.[15] By that time, he was communicating regularly in the home circle, offering words of praise and advice to his family, as they carried on his legacy.

The management of the literary estate fell mostly upon Adrian, who focused on selling the theatrical and film rights to Sherlock Holmes; he also vigorously defended his father's stories from copyright violations. His mother was less worried about Baker Street and more worried about Summerland, where intellectual property disputes had already arisen. In 1927, Doyle confided Pheneas's descriptions of the coming apocalypse to Sydney Fowler Wright, a science fiction author whose novel *Deluge* (1927) recounts similar events. "What I want to know," asked Doyle, "is where did you get it all?" Believing that Doyle's death ended their confidentiality agreement, Wright sent the prophecy to the *Sunday Express*; Lady Doyle sued him for violation of copyright, suppressing further publication.[16] The cultural transmission of Sherlock Holmes thus includes his family history of litigation, which the first half of this chapter explores. The Doyle estate defended the author's legacy first from overly enthusiastic followers, trespassing on his spiritual domain, and then from overly enthusiastic fans, poaching on his fictional realm. The origin of both disputes was the same question. After the death of the author, who inherited his universe? For Lady Doyle, the answer was clear: she did. However, as the second half of this chapter argues, another group of enthusiasts later staked its own claim to both universes at once: literary critics.

UNAUTHORIZED REVELATIONS

Lady Doyle's immediate problem was that death had not stopped her husband from embarking on an unscheduled whirlwind international tour. Charles Drayton Thomas, a Methodist minister and spiritualist who had also defended William Hope, faithfully promised that "Sir Arthur will continue his work for the spreading of the great cause," while Harry Price, the SPR investigator who had exposed Hope, cynically predicted that "all the mediums in the world would be falling over themselves trying to get in touch with their High Priest in order to receive the first 'message.'"[17] The race was on: while continuing to dictate messages in New Zealand, Doyle also began appearing at séances from Manchester to California to Australia. Those delighted spiritualists passed along his words not only to Lady Doyle, for which she thanked them, but also to the press, for which she did not. Within four days of Doyle's death, she was compelled to instruct the *Evening Standard* not to publish any further messages without her prior approval.[18] Adrian also tried to head off this problem of authentication and provenance, asserting the right of the family to distinguish between genuine and imitation Doyle. "We will always know when he is speaking," he told the press, "but one has to be careful because there are practical jokers on the other side, as there are here."[19]

Some of the jokers on this side were practical enough to ask for money in exchange for further messages, but most spiritualists were genuinely trying to help the family and promote the cause, not realizing that they were sowing confusion. Horace Leaf, the psychometrist who had handled Agatha Christie's glove, gave some slate writing from Doyle to the Associated Press, telling Lady Doyle that he hoped she would not object, since the publication of an authentic message would put a stop to the false ones.[20] There were simply too many, coming too fast, for them all to be believed, especially once they started contradicting one another. The American novelist Hamlin Garland found it "unthinkable" that one person's spirit "should be able to broadcast *differing* messages at the same identical moment."[21] Ridiculing spiritualism a decade later, the Catholic priest Herbert O'Neill found it "amusingly grotesque" that a message from Doyle in London could then be "denounced as humbug by 'Conan Doyle' manifesting in New York."[22] Even the skeptical Price experimented with contacting the spirit of his former adversary, who did speak to him at a séance, though Price speculated that the medium might instead be channeling "emanations from the brain of the *living* Doyle which had in some way become crystallised."[23]

After three months of chaos, the spirit of Doyle came through in the family circle to reclaim control of his own identity, declaring that he would not communicate through outsiders. The automatic writer for that séance was a family friend, the mother of the American violinist Florizel von Reuter. It may have been her hand holding the pen, but the spirit insisted that it was really he, Doyle, writing the words.[24] Despite this say-so, proving the spirit's identity on top of his reality continued to be difficult, even with no medium involved. In a 1931 *Liberty* magazine article, Lady Doyle presented a handwritten spirit message from her husband that Hope had captured directly on a photographic plate. The magazine also invited an outside expert to analyze the evidence. After comparing the message with a sample of Doyle's known handwriting, which revealed differences, and examining the plate under ultraviolent light, which revealed erasures, the expert concluded that the message was a "simulation."[25] He made no further inferences, but the implication was clear: despite Adrian's confidence, the family might not always know when Doyle was speaking.

To ensure that it would at least always know best, the family gave the Science of Deduction and Analysis a new practical application—to the afterlife. "There are tests which my mother knows," Adrian emphasized, "such as little mannerisms of speech which cannot be impersonated and which will tell us it is my father himself who is speaking."[26] On the one hand, "little mannerisms" could be tested objectively: Doyle's language contained empirical traces of his individuality. On the other hand, only Lady Doyle could perceive those traces, which were themselves only a subset of many other "such" clues, which only she knew how to interpret, or even find. Her impression of his expressions was all that mattered, which meant that her unique subjectivity outweighed both scientific objectivity and expert authority. She was not listening or looking for particular signs of Doyle's individuality so much as feeling for a familiar sense of his whole character. "When the same dear human personality comes through" to talk with her, Lady Doyle explained to the *Daily Sketch* in 1932, "then I *know* it is him indeed."[27] Only she could test for that personality, because she herself was the perfect instrument. "Never in all the wonderful years we were together did I fail to feel a thrill when he was near me," she said after his death, which now allowed him to make his psychic presence felt. Her "knowledge of his presence" was intuitive rather than rational, holistic rather than analytical; it was therefore also infallible.[28] When it came to reading her husband, she was Sherlock Holmes: "A wife knows more of the true character of a man than anyone else on earth. It is the little daily things which speak."[29]

Lady Doyle's personality test improved on her husband's own method of authenticating "the alleged posthumous writing of great authors," especially Charles Dickens. Dickens died in 1870, halfway through writing *The Mystery of Edwin Drood*; three years later, a medium in Vermont channeled his spirit and completed the novel. Doyle's literary-critical judgment of the work was impressionistic: "It seems to me to be like Dickens," he concluded, "but Dickens gone flat." Even so, there were "small points of style which could hardly be imitated," a phrase later echoed by Adrian. Moreover, the lifeless style was itself proof of afterlife, given that the author's spirit was now working from a great distance, through an imperfect medium. "The most that we can hope for," Doyle cautioned, "is something which is strongly reminiscent of the deceased writer."[30] In his own last book, *The Edge of the Unknown* (1930), Doyle added that he and the von Reuters had contacted the spirit of Dickens, who repudiated the Vermont medium and challenged Doyle to finish *Drood*, letting drop that Edwin is still alive and in hiding.[31]

As for the spirit of Doyle, no one on earth had more authority to decide what was strongly reminiscent of the living man than his widow. Her sense of his continued sparkling presence granted her the exclusive right not only to receive but also to interpret his ongoing revelations. Coming from her, those interpretations carried the full weight of final explanations. In the *Liberty* article, she explained why Doyle might be having trouble writing more than a few lines on the plate: either the message was too personal, or the method was too new. In any event, "the wonderful evidence of the signature" itself proved that "there is no death—only transition."[32] On those grounds, she could cite even more "wonderful evidence" without having to supply it, since those messages were "of too private and sacred a nature for publication."[33] By that logic, she could explain away all the difficulties that outsiders had with spirit communication. To protect a sensitive medium from rude skeptics, good spirits often switched off her powers; at the same time, those skeptics often attracted bad spirits, who caused the medium to make mistakes and even commit fraud.[34] Rehearsing the same circular arguments, Lady Doyle took over her husband's starring role at the center of the spiritualist universe. That role included his consulting duties: the press coverage of his return prompted people from all over the world to write to her, seeking guidance and solace. The *Liberty* article, in which she prays and his spirit praises, gave a timely boost to her authority.[35] Nino Pecararo, an Italian medium whom Doyle had once defended from Houdini, had just confessed in April to being a fraud, claiming that he had once deceived the Doyles together.[36] The hoax was front-page news at home and abroad; she immediately wrote to deny the account, and instructed her lawyer to serve writs for libel.[37]

Lady Doyle's special position was a double bind. How could she discount unauthorized messages without debunking spiritualism itself? How could she promote her husband's new revelation while also prohibiting his followers from channeling him? Her criticism of well-meaning spiritualists had an unintended consequence that exposed the weakness of her position: they simply reported that they had received additional messages from Doyle, authorizing communication and licensing publication. Lady Doyle publicly announced in January 1931 that only her own messages from Doyle were genuine, which offended Charles Tweedale. He had continued to contact Doyle after their photograph together; on the spirit's instruction and with the widow's permission, he had sent some of those messages to various newspapers. Now feeling that Lady Doyle had spurned him, he wrote twice in January to inform her that Doyle's spirit had come through to tell him to tell her to make amends. Asking her to endorse his work in her next article, Tweedale mentioned that he also held further messages from Doyle, some of which were highly controversial, though he had no plans to release them—at least, not yet. That aside apparently did the trick. Lady Doyle recertified the clergyman three months later in the *News Chronicle*, after which he stayed on message.[38]

The ongoing threat, however, was how easily Doyle's communications from beyond could drift off message. During the spring of 1931, Lady Doyle exchanged letters with T. A. R. Purchas, a spiritualist in Johannesburg, whose *Spiritual Adventures of a Business Man* (1929) had been published by Doyle's Psychic Press. Purchas claimed that Doyle had recently come through in a séance to apologize for having caused offense on his last trip to South Africa in 1928. While in Bloemfontein, Doyle had criticized an Afrikaans inscription on the Women's Monument there, which commemorates the deaths of women and children in British concentration camps during the Boer War. Purchas reported the belated apology to his local press, after which Doyle's spirit visited their circle to laugh approvingly that the news had reached as far as the *Yorkshire Post*. Not amused, Lady Doyle demanded that Purchas retract the apology, which her husband would never have made, and publicly repudiated the messages to his circle. Purchas replied that only Doyle himself could demand a retraction, which he had not yet done, and demanded that she retract her repudiation. The correspondence closed on bad terms, with Purchas accusing her of giving spiritualism a bad name, and Lady Doyle protesting the abuse of her husband's good name.[39]

Apologizing for a political misunderstanding was one thing; calling the whole of spiritualism a theological error was quite another. Early in 1931, an esoteric theosophical society in Paris, the Polaires, wrote to Lady Doyle, hoping to contact Doyle himself. She agreed to a series of séances in London with Grace Cooke, who had become her husband's "private line of communication."[40] At first, Doyle communicated indirectly, relaying messages through Grace's spirit guide, "White Eagle." Those messages endorsed the work of the Polaires and the wisdom of their guiding power, the Oracle of Astral Force. On his birthday in May, Doyle finally spoke through Grace in his own voice, announcing a brand-new revelation to replace the old new one: "I see now that some of the phenomena in Spiritualism is attributable to *astral* projection and *astral* memories."[41] Delighted, the Polaires published an account of the sittings, suggesting that the great spiritualist had posthumously converted to theosophy. Alarmed, Lady Doyle asked Grace and her manager husband Ivan whether this spirit could be an imposter; Ivan advised her to keep an open mind.[42] The Cookes proposed to continue their séances without Lady Doyle, seeking proof that this spirit was in fact her husband. Over the next year, they received dozens of messages from Doyle correcting "the mistakes of the Spiritualists," who were too narrowly obsessed with the next life to expand their consciousness in this one: "It is unnecessary for man to pass through physical death to contact all the planes of spirit life."[43] Lady Doyle was increasingly doubtful. It took another two years for Ivan to convince her to let him publish the séance records as a book; she finally agreed on the condition that he would not attribute the teachings definitely to Doyle. Ivan played nice on the title page, which credits a spirit "Believed to Have Been Known on Earth as Arthur Conan Doyle," and then played coy in the book itself, asking readers to make their own literary-critical judgments. "Will men find in the phrasing, in the style, in the trick of narrative," he prompted, "something of the former A. C. D.?"[44]

Only well after Lady Doyle's death in 1940 did the Cookes dare to authenticate the work themselves, republishing it as *The Return of Arthur Conan Doyle* (1956). Its preface announced "the new revelation of Spiritualism that he made," having realized after death that his beliefs "needed revision."[45] They were smart to delay publication: even as her health declined in the late 1930s, Lady Doyle continued to fight any such unauthorized revision or false attribution. In 1935, spiritualists on a plane flying over New York City reported that Doyle had told them to reassure his wife, saying "I am looking after her interests."[46] In her view, such messages were worse than fake; they were inferior in quality, damaging his reputation and devaluing his body of work. "It is deplorable," she complained in a spiritualist magazine the next month, "that his name should be attached to the many useless platitudes that are given out as purporting to come from him." Her statement made it clear that she was perfectly capable of looking after her own interests, both spiritual and legal.[47]

After she died, however, the center of her husband's universe could not hold. Her sons were more interested in literary rights than spiritualist claims, and her daughter, Jean, had already launched a successful career in the Royal Air Force. At that point, entropy took over. Reports of Doyle appearing at séances dropped off: once there was no objection to contacting him, there was less reason to do so, as the presumption of his authority evaporated. At the 1944 trial of Helen Duncan, the last medium to be imprisoned for violating the Witchcraft Act before it was finally repealed in 1951, one witness reported that Duncan had induced Doyle to materialize. But the spirit appeared just once, and only for ten seconds, and even then, "the figure was rather fibrous."[48]

UNLICENSED ADAPTATIONS

When Lady Doyle died on June 27, 1940, the *New York Times* observed that she had both advanced her husband's cause and defended his property. "In no circumstances," she was quoted as saying, "would I allow any of the characters created by Sir Arthur to be used by anybody else."[49] At least not without a licensing fee: during the 1930s, thanks largely to Adrian, the family had consolidated its control of stage, radio, and film productions. In 1937, when a German studio released *Der Mann, der Sherlock Holmes War* (The man who was Sherlock Holmes) without permission, the family sued, even though the film was a parody about two detectives only pretending to be Holmes and Watson, rather than a story about the characters themselves.[50] 20th Century-Fox purchased the rights to Holmes for two authorized movies in 1939, starring Basil Rathbone and Nigel Bruce, after which the rights went to Universal. The series continued with another dozen movies produced between 1942 and 1946, all of which credit Doyle as the original author. Even the German movie finally gives credit where credit is due, though retroactively, through a last metafictional twist. At the end of the movie, the character of Doyle shows up in court, cheerfully pardons the two impostors, and then negotiates a deal for the rights to their story, which he intends to write himself. His proposed title: *Der Mann, der Sherlock Holmes War.*

Credit was not always forthcoming. Six months before his mother died, Denis was surprised not to hear his father's name mentioned at all during a dinner in New York City hosted by the Baker Street Irregulars (BSI), Holmes's first fan club. The writer Christopher Morley founded the club in 1934; by its 1940 dinner, the members were deep into their "Great Game" of treating Holmes and Watson as real people and reading the fiction as actual history. As part of that game, the BSI had begun producing a body of mock scholarship—Sherlockiana—that fixed key dates, located street addresses, traced genealogies, checked backgrounds, and, most importantly, analyzed inconsistencies of plot and character. (Most famously, Watson is called both John and James in the stories.) The Sherlockians thus adopted Holmes's own intellectual values, as Stephen Knight points out, "especially those of trivial research and tidy unitarian structures that organically justify the narrow concern with a single subject."[51] They also adapted Doyle's fictional universe, filling it with new meaning and claiming it as their own, which brought them into the same conflict with the family as the spiritualists.

The pretense of Holmes's reality dates from the early 1890s. J. M. Barrie interviewed the detective at his author's house for *The Speaker*, after which the *National Observer* interviewed him on Baker Street, where he accused Doyle of misrepresenting him without permission.[52] The more advanced game of Sherlockiana dates from 1912, when Ronald Knox published

"Studies in the Literature of Sherlock Holmes" in the Oxford *Blue Book*. At the time, Knox was a newly ordained Anglican chaplain, though he soon converted to Roman Catholicism and became a well-known author. As an apologist, Knox was an early adapter of Holmes. His novel *Sanctions* (1924) cited the detective's argument from design in "The Naval Treaty" and quoted "The Devil's Foot" to explain that when God watches you, just as when Holmes does, you may expect to see no one. As a priest, however, Knox was no friend of spiritualists, although he did allow that Doyle was "more of an intellectualist than the rest of them." He stated his main objection in *Caliban in Grub Street* (1930): "I should be more inclined to believe the spirits if the spirits were not so careful to tell me exactly what I want to hear."[53] Doyle probably did not read that book, as it was published just before he died, but he would likely have included Knox within his crypto-Catholic conspiracy theory.

Knox's "Studies in the Literature" is not a pastiche of the detective; it is a parody of the German higher criticism that questioned the authority of the Church. As the crime writer Dorothy Sayers appreciated, Knox aimed to show that "one could disintegrate a modern classic as speciously as a certain school of critics have endeavoured to disintegrate the Bible."[54] The mock-serious essay questions the authenticity of the stories, noting various errors and contradictions, including problems of both internal chronology and historical influence. It entertains the possibility of a "Deutero-Watson" who authors a subset of the stories; it recovers the "primitive type" of a Holmes story, giving each stage of the investigation its own classical Greek term.[55] (The client's initial presentation is the *exegesis kata ton diokonta*.) Cited throughout is a fictional cohort of Continental scholars, including "Backnecke," "Ratzegger," and "Piff-Pouff," who have apparently devoted their careers to this highly specialized field of pedantic exegesis. Doyle appears only briefly, to explain that Watson's mysterious name change was just an editorial slip, but the scholars ignore him and continue their heated debates.

Inspired by Knox's essay, the Irregulars ignored Doyle throughout the 1930s, publishing Sherlockian papers and monographs, which they archly termed "The Higher Criticism." Reviewing three early contributions to the field, the *Times Literary Supplement* dubbed it "Sherlockholmitos."[56] By the time Denis attended the 1940 BSI dinner, his father was mentioned only rarely, and then only as Watson's literary agent. The demotion of the author created room at the top for the detective, whose status rose from fictional character to historical personage to spiritual figure. German criticism was hostile to fundamentalism, but Sherlockian criticism encouraged it, or at least a puckish version of it. The Victorian cultural critic Matthew Arnold predicted that literature would one day replace religion as a source of universal meaning and personal consolation, but he did not foresee that crime fiction rather than classical poetry would be the new scripture. The Irregulars based their belief on what they termed "The Sacred Writings" of the stories, which document the reality of the detective. The Sacred Writings include only the four novels and fifty-six stories; Doyle's other writings about Holmes are "The Apocrypha." The library of Sherlockiana preserves all the early evidence gathered by the faithful. The Boston archeologist H. W. Bell visited London to reconstruct the site of 221B Baker Street for his *Sherlock Holmes and Dr. Watson: The Chronology of Their Adventures* (1932). Another disciple was Vincent Starrett, author of *The Private Life of Sherlock Holmes* (1933), in which he argued that Holmes's existence was "more than a matter of mere faith," citing various testimonies.[57] Taken to an extreme, the Great Game trumped even the Higher Criticism. "I am a Fundamentalist," declared Bernard Darwin in 1948, seeing no need to reconcile the uncertain chronology of the stories: "The evidence of the dates troubles me no more than the incontestable evidence of the rocks troubles those who believe that the world was created in a precise order in the course of six days."[58] His anti-scientific testimony came with a wink: Bernard was Charles Darwin's grandson.

Sherlockian belief may be ironic, as Michael Saler argues, but the faith is earnest. Matthew Arnold would now enjoy reading the archive of BSI correspondence, which documents how Holmes not only re-enchanted but also redeemed the capitalistic modern world for these educated but dispirited urban professionals, reeling from the 1929 crash and worrying about the rise of Hitler. "Depressions may come and go—I fancy he will go on forever," Starrett said in 1933.[59] Edgar Smith, a General Motors executive who was the BSI's chief organizer during its first two decades, contrasted his day job "selling automotive transportation to the heathen" with the "love pure and simple" he felt for Holmes.[60] The BSI often described its "esoteric organization" in playfully ecclesiastical terms.[61] Writing to Smith in 1947, Morley reflected on "the humble origins of the fathers of the Church" in the previous decade; recounting the same period, another early Irregular described "the Mother Church in New York" being visited by "an unexpected angel from a most unusual source, General Motors."[62] That angel Smith hailed BSI members as "the truly elect," discouraged "lay" interpretation, and decried any emendation of the canon as "sacrilege."[63] When the mystery writer Rex Stout proposed in 1941 that Watson was a woman, Smith introduced his essay as "a heterodox doctrine that challenges the very foundation of our faith."[64]

Denis was in town for the 1940 dinner because he was on an American lecture tour, spreading the cause of spiritualism. Part of his surprise was the discovery that his father had also founded another faith: a brand-new literary humanism to go with a now-dated religious revelation, which together rejected materialism in all its forms, from scientific principles to corporate values. The origin of both systems was Sherlock Holmes: teasing the connection, Starrett called the detective a "most fascinating ectoplasmic emanation."[65] Denis was not at first troubled that Doyle was getting no credit for that emanation. On behalf of his father, he signed a copy of *221B: Studies in Sherlock Holmes* (1940), the first major BSI collection of its own scholarship. "Let us talk of the realities that do not change," Starrett urged in the introduction: "Let us talk again of Sherlock Holmes."[66] Writing about the dinner to his mother, Denis explained the subtext. Talking again and again about the reality of the character but never about the life of the author was in fact a great honor to them both.[67]

The family's opinion of the BSI changed, however, after someone else did start talking about the life of the author. In 1943, Hesketh Pearson published *Conan Doyle: His Life and Art*, the first biography of Doyle since Lamond's 1931 tribute. Lady Doyle had commissioned Lamond specially, but Pearson worked independently, having received permission to consult and quote from private papers and unpublished works. In the acknowledgments, Pearson thanked Denis and Adrian for granting him full access, even "though I am not what is commonly called a 'spiritualist.'"[68] The biography relegated Doyle's spiritualism to the last chapter, but that was not what angered the sons when the book was published. To explain the popularity of Doyle's art, Pearson explored the truth of a remark he once made at a spiritualist luncheon: "I am the man in the street."[69] Taking that line as his epigraph, Pearson argued that the author was a representative everyman rather than an individual genius. Furthermore, when discussing possible models for Holmes, Pearson credited Joseph Bell, as well as

Zadig and Dupin, but not Doyle himself, whom Pearson at one point called "singularly unobservant," more like Watson.[70] Outraged, Adrian publicly denounced the biography in the *Times*, declaring once and for all, "The fact is that my father himself was Sherlock Holmes."[71]

Adrian was repeating a point his mother had made in her afterword to Lamond's book, though she used more materialist terms: "My husband truly had a Sherlock Holmes brain himself."[72] Thanks to this organ transplant, the fictional Holmes gave intellectual weight to Doyle's spiritual beliefs. For ten years after his death, Lady Doyle fought to preserve her husband's identification with those beliefs; after her death, for another ten years, Adrian fought to preserve his father's identification with that character. To defend their image rights, mother and son employed the same tactics. She wrote to the press, repudiating all unauthorized mediums and messages; he published letters denouncing Pearson and calling the biography a fake. She ordered séance circles to cease and desist, forbidding further communication; he threatened Pearson's publisher with a lawsuit if they went ahead with a reprint. She corrected misrepresentations of her husband, writing her own syndicated articles about him; he challenged misrepresentations of his father, writing his own short memoir, *The True Conan Doyle* (1945), insisting that Doyle, not Bell, was "the epitome of Holmes."[73] Adrian sent his book to the press and prominent public figures, including King George VI, but that was still not enough to set the record straight. He finally did what his mother had done in the first place, commissioning a friendly biographer, John Dickson Carr, the American mystery writer. "Who *was* Sherlock Holmes?" Carr asked in his *Life of Sir Arthur Conan Doyle* (1949), but only after assuring readers that this was "a question to which the answer will be self-evident."[74]

The tactics were the same, but the motives were different. Lady Doyle was protecting the family's interest in Doyle's religion of the future, while her sons were protecting the family's stake in his backlist of fiction. After the death of its author, which law would apply first to the Baker Street universe: copyright or entropy? For Denis and Adrian, identifying their father with his immortal character was the best way to hold together that universe, prohibiting any adaptation of the stories without the proper permissions and licensing fees. For the Irregulars and other Sherlockians, decoupling the author from his character was the best way to expand that universe, encouraging wild spins and original takes on the stories, rewriting Holmes as they liked. The family history of litigation repeated itself as farce; trying to restrain Sherlockians proved even more futile than trying to shepherd spiritualists. The brothers could squash further printings of *The Misadventures of Sherlock Holmes* (1944), Ellery Queen's anthology of parodies and pastiches, and they could prevent Edgar Smith from publishing a complete edition of the original stories, the last of which were still under copyright, but they could not stop fans everywhere from forming local "scion" societies of the BSI, or from contributing Higher Criticism to its new *Baker Street Journal*, founded in 1946. From their perspective, the Great Game was like playing whack-a-mole, but the brothers could not see that they were working against their own future interests. "Having a vast and passionate fan base creating a number of derivative works," one law professor has recently argued, "does not inevitably hurt the market for the original work." Quite the opposite: "a robust fandom" sustains the original work, preserving its value and making further capitalization possible.[75] The intellectual property may have belonged to the heirs, but Sherlockians were angel investors of creative energy in its development, asking for nothing in return other than permission to keep playing their game.

A VAST SUBSTRUCTURE

What Edgar Smith cheerfully called "a widespread devotional cult" has flourished on the internet, where a global fan base continually updates the Holmes universe, which expands infinitely in every direction, from straight pastiche to slash, steampunk, and crossover fiction. While he objected in 1953 to "the Holmes Cult in America," Adrian did glimpse that future, though he still believed he could master that universe.[76] Working with Carr, he produced twelve new Holmes stories, collected as *The Exploits of Sherlock Holmes* (1954), which were not only fully authorized but also carefully authenticated. First, each exploit was based on a case that Watson mentions but does not write up himself, tying these pastiches directly to the originals, which counteracted entropy. Second, Adrian's biographical note stressed that he wrote on "the very desk on which his father wrote," where he was also "surrounded by the same objects that his father handled."[77] Posthumous work may be inferior to the living man, but psychometric writing is the next best thing: the author's touch still tingles.

In 1969, Adrian gave a television interview in which he called the BSI "a religious cult," whose members want "to prove that Watson was a lesbian, or that Holmes was in fact Moriarty," as opposed to "normal sane people who love the books for what they are."[78] He died the following year, never allowing that those two groups might overlap, or that it could be healthy for them both to play together in the imaginary world of the books, where Saler suggests they recover both a sense of wonder and a sense of community missing from their modern one. Saler does not go so far as to suggest that the Great Game will ever become a religion itself, but other scholars have observed that Sherlockian fandom on the internet "has developed some of the characteristics of institutionalised religion," including both sectarianism and eschatology.[79] In 2012, when Moriarty framed Holmes for all the crimes committed on the BBC's *Sherlock*, making the detective look like a fraud, the hashtag #ibelieveinsherlock spread widely on social media, leaping across software platforms and then back into the show itself the following season. The hashtag was a message of literary faith, at once personal and universal, that Matthew Arnold would applaud.

It would be theoretically possible to extend Saler's line of thought toward a utopian ending for this book. The grassroots fandom of Sherlockians recalls the grassroots movement of spiritualists, with the same literary figure at the core of both belief systems. They both rose up against the same kind of enemy: institutional authority, whether church or estate, each with its own brand of dogma. They both share a history of legal persecution, whether by Acts of Parliament, charges of fraud, writs of libel, or notices of infringement. And they both survive and even flourish on the internet. The spiritualist organizations to which Doyle once belonged all host websites today; the Spiritualists' National Union even celebrates him online as its Honorary President-in-Spirit.[80] Spiritualism has also diversified its interests, evolving during the 1970s into a variety of New Age groups, esoteric societies, and faith healing movements. Among them is the White Eagle Lodge, founded by the Cookes and now led by Grace's grandson; its website sells an updated edition of the original spirit communications, retitled *Arthur Conan Doyle's Book of the Beyond* (2003).[81] The Great Game has an even happier ending for Sherlockians. After decades of litigation, the United States Court of Appeals for the Seventh Circuit ruled in 2014 that the character may be immortal, but the copyright on all but the last ten stories has expired. Even those stories will be public domain by 2023, after which Conan Doyle Estate Ltd. will have to stop licensing the character and instead start marketing the author, "determined to make him famous once more," as its website advertises.[82] In future, Doyle may finally get what he always wanted: to be known for something beyond his detective.

However, Saler's line of thought represses the danger of believing too deeply in Holmes, so deeply that you come to identify with him. Even when fandom becomes obsessive, approaching something "akin to a religion promulgated by zealots," its core belief in Holmes himself is still ironic.[83] Sherlockians may follow the detective on social media, but they do not follow his logic in real life. True believers in Holmes do exist today, but they occupy other parts of the internet, fact-free zones where the detective helps less-than-ideal reasoners convert what they believe into what they know, just as he helped Doyle to do. They form online communities just as fans of *Sherlock* do, but they did not evolve from the Baker Street Irregulars. Instead, they have more in common with the one person who gave Doyle more credit than even the family could accept.

Born in 1894, Pope Hill became a professor of mathematics at the University of Georgia, where he had received his undergraduate degree in agricultural science. After office hours, he moonlighted as a Sherlockian. In 1947, Hill self-published the first part of his eighty-thousand-word manuscript, *Dating Sherlock Holmes*, which argued that Doyle deliberately planted logical and factual errors in the stories, as a secret intelligence test for his most observant readers. Reading those errors as clues, Hill traced a "vast substructure" of hidden meaning, a pattern that suggested the existence of a master key to interpreting the stories. This unpublished document, buried somewhere in the Doyle family papers, would contain the true solutions— masked by the official ones—to all of the cases. Predicting that the key would turn up soon, Hill explained that he was publishing his manuscript now in order to prove later that he had already "deduced the existence of a secret document."[84] Five years later, still missing the key, Hill published more of his theory, retitled *The Sherlock Holmes Hoax*, restating his claim scientifically. He calculated that the probability of the hidden substructure arising purely by chance, rather than by design, was one in four to the sixtieth power, a number "more than a million times as great as the total number of snowflakes that would fall on the whole earth in a million years."[85]

All this sounds very tongue-in-cheek, written in the spirit of the BSI's Higher Criticism, but Hill was earnest enough that he wrote to Doyle's heirs, asking for their help in recovering the master key, which he thought might be in a safe deposit box. Denis declined to comment, which Hill took for assent, while Adrian dismissed him as an embarrassment.[86] The BSI was even less friendly, refusing to publish his manuscript, which it publicly denounced as "heresy," since it broke the rules of the Game by reintroducing the author to his stories. The BSI's rejection prompted Hill to self-publish his theory, after which Smith called him "our pontifical bullartist."[87]

They should have known that Hill and his theory would not just go away. He was a researcher driven enough to have once tested the law of probability itself. In 1933, he conducted an experiment, filling a can with an equal number of pennies dated 1919 and 1920, drawing out one penny, recording its date, returning the penny, shaking the can, and then drawing again. He did so one hundred thousand times, which took a full year; the date 1920 just barely edged out 1919, by a score of 50,145 to 49,855.[88] Having weighed the odds by hand before calculating them in literature, Hill was certain he was on "the highroad to proper interpretation," which is to say, interpretation that proceeds logically from the solid basis of empirical science.[89] Hill's intellectual path, from agricultural research to probability theory to literary criticism, ran along the same road. In fact, however, his interpretation proceeded improperly from the mistaken assumption that it was proceeding rationally. In 1955, the *Baker Street Journal* finally agreed to publish an abstract of Hill's theory, in which he explained his method: "It was not until I became an armchair detective," he said, "that I discovered that Conan Doyle had put clues in."[90] His first step was thus to imagine himself as Sherlock Holmes, at which moment all the random editorial errors became meaningful, and he could start seeing the authorial design he was looking for. This is next-level confirmation bias. Hill's capital mistake was not just theorizing before having all the evidence but theorizing first that there was evidence to be had, after which it was impossible not to detect hidden substructures of meaning and to reconstruct master keys to interpretation.

The fundamental belief in yourself as Sherlock Holmes is harmless to others, so long as you confine your theorizing to the characters and stories, as Hill did. Chapter 5 will demonstrate that it is much riskier to theorize about the next world, which may lead both yourself and others astray in this one, as Houdini warned. And theorizing about this world is more dangerous still, especially once the internet makes it possible for bad faith to travel around the world even faster than Doyle's good spirit. Good faith may lead to bad science, but the science gets much worse when the faith is bad to begin with. If Sherlock Holmes has the power to re-enchant our world, does he also have the power to hex it?

But first, before answering that question and reaching the end of this book: a sudden jump to Utah, and another backstory.

A PREARRANGED EPISODE

The backstory of this book is a metanarrative, because Sherlock Holmes is also a central figure in the conflicted history of literary criticism, a field that has long struggled to demarcate itself from both pseudoscience and mysticism. Recounting that history requires a shift in perspective, as in *A Study in Scarlet,* though this time from third person to first.

Sitting here in my office in the English Department of Utah State University, I deeply identify with Pope Hill. Let me explain how that has come to be—although for those who prefer their Holmes served up pure and without digression, as Estleman recommends, it is possible to skip the rest of this chapter without losing the thread of argument.

Professional scholars can be touchy about Sherlockiana, "a game about seriousness" that parodies their own work, making them look like armchair loungers.[91] The Great Game reveals "how easy it is for an unscrupulous pseudo-scholarship to extract fantastic and misleading conclusions from a literary text," Dorothy Sayers said in 1946, "by a series of omissions, emendations and distortions of context."[92] In self-defense, we professionals have three possible countermoves to make against the amateurs. First, we can scapegoat them. If Sherlockiana is "the most tedious pseudo-scholarship in the history of letters," then our real scholarship looks far more exciting.[93] Better yet, we can ignore them. "They're in the MLA Bibliography," alongside our own monographs and articles, "but we don't have to cite them."[94] And best of all—our finishing move—we can study them. So long as they represent a "traditional" stage of "transmedia fandom," Sherlockians cannot embarrass the scholars for whom they are just historical footnotes, safely archived within the academic field they once mocked from a distance.[95]

As if.

Even after studying Sherlockiana in the first half of this chapter, I feel just as unscrupulous as when I began this book. What could be more misleading than to conclude, after distorting the context, that Holmes is an old friend of spiritualism and the right hand of pseudoscience? Even worse, to make that case, I have broken a fundamental principle of literary criticism, which dates from the same year that Sayers debunked its fantastical claims. In 1946, W. K. Wimsatt and M. C. Beardsley warned their fellow New Critics away from the "intentional fallacy." They argued that the original intention and conscious design of an author have nothing to do with the meaning of the work itself, which the critic must take on its own terms. This idea was already old news to the Baker Street Irregulars, who did not need the permission of English professors to pretend that Doyle had never existed. Pope Hill did disrupt the Great Game long enough that one Irregular felt compelled to reassure another, "I don't see how in the world he can prove anything with Doyle dead."[96] But even if Doyle weren't dead, it wouldn't have mattered to the New Critics, who also ignored the stated intentions of living authors.

Now, I have not been arguing that Doyle *intentionally* designed Holmes as a secret weapon against rationalism and materialism, only that the character helped to meet the author's needs and resolve his conflicts, but even that narrower case doesn't hold up long. In 1967, Roland Barthes announced "The Death of the Author," whose psychology and biography no longer matter either: literary texts do not harbor any deep secrets or private meanings. Barthes felt the New Critics were still too authoritative, since their own interpretations and conclusions simply substituted for any original intentions. For him and other poststructuralists, all readers together inherit the text, thus reconceived as "a multi-dimensional space in which a variety of writings, none of them original, blend and clash."[97] Readers play freely within that space, actively writing and rewriting the text, generating new and provisional meanings rather than reconstructing first or final ones. The Sherlockians were again way ahead of literary critics: another name for the Great Game was "The Writings About the Writings," in which Watson could very well be a lesbian, and Holmes may as well be Moriarty. When Adrian objected to those writings, appealing once more to his father's memory, he illustrated the critical point that Michel Foucault made the same year, following Barthes: "The author is therefore the ideological figure by which one marks the manner in which we fear the proliferation of meaning."[98]

Both the New Critics and the French poststructuralists tried to make criticism seem more empirical, distancing literary interpretation from its theological origins in biblical exegesis and hermeneutics. Wimsatt and Beardsley viewed the text as a stand-alone, solid object. "Judging a poem is like judging a pudding or a machine," they insisted, requiring only "that it work." Literary critics can disregard authorial intention for the same reason that natural scientists disregard the argument from design: they have no need of that hypothesis. "It is only because an artifact works that we infer the intention of an artificer," who thus becomes irrelevant. Wimsatt and Beardsley's ironic last line at once deifies and debunks the author: "Critical inquiries are not settled by consulting the oracle."[99] For Barthes, the text is much less solid, though still material; it is more like a "tissue of quotations" to be "disentangled," much as one would follow "the thread of a stocking." Even so, he agreed with the New Critics that interpretation must be "an anti-theological activity," since to remove the author is "to refuse God."[100] While Foucault also agreed, he argued that God was not yet dead. He noted that Barthes's idea of writing as endless free space "seems to transpose the empirical characteristics of the author into a transcendental anonymity," a move that still retains "the religious principle of the hidden meaning."[101] In contrast, Foucault considered himself "un empiriste aveugle" (a blind empiricist), feeling his way through the historical archive without looking for any secrets. He aimed to reconstruct cultural discourses of power and knowledge from residual fragments and local facts, an inductive method he likened to archeology and genealogy.[102]

Foucault died in 1984, five years before I began graduate school, where I learned to read poststructuralist theory and write cultural criticism, the dominant model of Victorian studies in his wake. Three decades have passed, but it still feels awkward, even embarrassing, to be writing a book about Sherlock Holmes in which his author appears throughout. Trying to get in touch again with any author, let alone Doyle, looks far too much like mysticism and not nearly enough like empiricism. Invoking Doyle himself makes things even worse. His spiritualism calls attention to the theological jugglery of this book, as well as its circular logic, false objectivity, and shallow empiricism. I have repeated all the same pseudoscientific errors that I have recounted Doyle making, especially confirmation bias; my last chapter is actually where I began, and where I am still determined to end. In backtelling my argument, I am perfectly willing to treat both texts and testimonies as material evidence, twisting the so-called facts and making overelaborate deductions, piling quotation after quotation on you until your reason breaks down under them and acknowledges me to be perfectly right. Swiveling in my office chair, I am surrounded by the library of wonderful literature that I have gathered, hundreds of books and articles on the same subject. The bibliography of this book is a portentous fact. All that specialized knowledge facilitates matters wonderfully, though occasionally I do have to bustle about and see things with my own eyes. I once visited the University of Texas at Austin, for example, to play with Doyle's Ouija board.

Knox foresaw in his own "Studies in the Literature of Sherlock Holmes" what would happen as soon as critics stopped consulting the oracle: they would have to start playing detective. "If there is anything pleasant in criticism," he proposed, "it is finding out what we aren't meant to find out." The target of Knox's satire was broader than German biblical scholarship; it also included the emerging profession of English literary studies, which by 1912 had already slung the author, though not dead yet, onto the cart. "It is the method," Knox observed of any historical criticism that reconstructs sources, "by which we treat as significant what the author did not mean to be significant." The critic interrogates the text, searching for clues to meaning far beyond any original intent. "We delight to extort economic evidence from Aristophanes," Knox mused, "because Aristophanes knew nothing of economics." The critic must bully the text into giving up secrets that even its author does not know, secrets that are themselves puzzles containing deeper secrets. "We try to extract cryptograms from Shakespeare," he added, "because we are inwardly certain that Shakespeare never put them there."[103] Knox was describing the idea of fun that most literary critics, whatever their differences, have shared ever since. It is the method that we now call "suspicious" reading, whose pleasures date back to "our earliest methods for deepening our object of study, for making literature opaque."[104] Once we all decided to become armchair detectives, we started discovering even more hidden clues than Hill did; he was still fixated on the author, whereas we are now inwardly certain that larger cultural forces are at work in the background. After all, as Knox knew, we aren't playing just any old detective: "There is, however, a special fascination in applying this method to Sherlock Holmes, because it is, in a sense, Holmes's own method."[105]

In other words, critical inquiries must now be settled by consulting the one detective who might as well be an oracle, since he comes straight from the séance, trailing strands of ectoplasm. Knox's essay calls Holmes's method into question, poking holes in his "ludicrously bad logic" and poking fun at his retrospective prophecies, which are always self-fulfilling. When Holmes chastises himself for doubting his deductions, even when the facts don't fit, Knox's question becomes pointed: "What sublimer confession of faith could any realist make?"[106] Having refused God, the critic is entirely at liberty to mix empirical reasoning and magical thinking, blurring the line between subjective interpretation and objective explanation. Barthes famously concluded that "the birth of the reader must be at the cost of the death of the Author," but Knox had already accounted for another price to be paid in future: the rise of the pseudoscientist.[107]

While biblical scholarship was established enough to withstand satire, the younger and still untenured discipline of literary studies was insecure about its status in the academy, where hard science was the gold standard. "A scientific basis dignifies our profession," declared H. C. G. Brandt at the first Modern Language Association meeting in 1883, while acknowledging that "there is a great deal of prejudice still on this score against our department, strongest, perhaps, against the study of English."[108] At the same time that Knox mocked historical criticism, the medievalist Frederick Tupper warned that a parallel branch of study—textual criticism—was also becoming ludicrous. The goal of textual criticism was to reconstruct a lost original manuscript, reasoning backward on the basis of surviving fragments, other copies, and later versions. In Tupper's opinion, however, "the critic has been too prone to hint doubts, hesitate suspicions and airily assume the existence of corruptions—in order to display his art as diviner." Once critics assume that a text is missing or hiding something, they succumb to "the oracular mood" that encourages confirmation bias: "premature conjecture" licenses their "arrant guesswork." To stop his colleagues from doing "this sort of detective work," Tupper directed them "to balance probabilities and to give due weight to every shred of evidence," thereby maintaining "complete freedom from preconceived theories."[109] In that 1910 article on "Textual Criticism as a Pseudo-Science," Tupper did not name names, but he eventually did finger the original culprit, the moody detective whose theories are always preconceived. A 1927 book review, in which Tupper chastised historical critics for trying equally hard to be "ingenious detectives," is titled "Chaucer and Sherlock."[110]

Sherlock Holmes thus emerges in the history of literary criticism as its scapegoat, blamed for the bad faith and worse science that would otherwise ruin the profession. To shore it up, T. S. Eliot argued in the 1920s for a different approach, neither historical nor textual. The new basis of interpretation was instead "the scientific mind" of the highly educated critic, sticking to "practical conclusions" that "halt at the frontier of metaphysics or mysticism."[111] Eliot had no patience with literary appreciation; its dreamy vagaries attracted both amateurs and impostors. In contrast, his method of interpretation was so objective that it was "not interpretation at all, but merely putting the reader in possession of facts which he would otherwise have missed." By converting his critical ideas into empirical facts, however, Eliot risked playing Holmes to the reader's Watson, who might reasonably complain that those facts seem to exist only in the critic's mind, scientific as it may be, making them practically impossible for anyone else *not* to miss. Eliot knew how easily interpretation could fall down the rabbit hole of subjectivity, where "instead of insight, you get a fiction," and so he scapegoated the detective in his 1929 review of the collected stories.[112] He observed that "Holmes's reality is a reality of its own kind," a cosmic outpost so far beyond the frontier of metaphysics or mysticism that it never matters that he is "not even a very good detective," who exhibits many signs of "mental decay."[113] In contrast, critics like Eliot clearly "see the limits of our particular ignorance," as he said later that year. While they do "collaborate" with the sciences, they also "know where to stop" before literary interpretation becomes self-deluded pseudoscience.[114]

Eliot inspired the New Criticism to adopt the professionalized model of the research sciences, even as the New Critics also set their higher moral claims against the "technocratic tendencies" of those sciences.[115] This ambivalence evolved into paradox. Because they believed that "the matter of poetry is ontologically distinct from that of science," those critics opened a loophole to another reality of its own kind, where poems are like puddings.[116] By the late 1950s, Eliot worried that they were "pursuing criticism as if it was a science, which it can never be." Not knowing where to stop, going well "beyond the frontier of literary criticism," New Critics would end up playing Sherlock Holmes. Eliot called their work a "kind of detection" in which they "unravel all the threads and follow all the clues," while remaining "unconscious of the fact" that "they invented the puzzle for the pleasure of discovering the solution." Unlike Holmes, however, their problem was not mental decay. New Critics were such good detectives, Eliot concluded, that they "may even come to seem, in retrospect, too brilliant."[117]

Ten years later, after poststructuralism finished off the author, the New Critics just seemed naïve. Criticism could still proceed as if it were empirical, unraveling threads with Barthes and collecting scraps with Foucault, but it knew better than to believe that literature is an object, or that interpretation has a ground, or that any kind of reality is real. There is only language, and then more language: the "linguistic turn" that Jacques Derrida carved in the late 1960s compelled critics to distance themselves even further from Sherlock Holmes. As we saw in chapter 2, they caricatured him as an idealized Victorian empiricist, who believes that his scientific explanations are neutral accounts of objective reality. Of course, actual Victorian empiricists were never so naïve as to think that. They well understood "the necessary impossibility" of their task, but Holmes eliminates that impossibility, since whatever he says immediately goes for everyone else.[118] "Nothing clears up a case," he affirms, "so much as stating it to another person" ("Silver Blaze," 336). Holmes's solutions require only that he find the right words, not the right clues. Poststructuralists faulted the detective for not being sufficiently self-aware to know that he constructs not only the case but also the reality that he claims to describe. "A rigorous knowledge must beware of all forms of empiricism," Pierre Macherey declared in 1966, "for the objects of any rational investigation have no prior existence but are thought into being."[119]

To assist in their investigations, new schools of suspicious readers in the 1970s decided to partner with warier detectives, who more favorably reflected their own intellectual values. Fredric Jameson and the American Marxists tagged along with Raymond Chandler's streetwise Marlowe, whose beat takes him "outwards into the space of the world," where he is "obliged to move from one kind of social reality to another incessantly." Those social realities are so fluid, so full of shifting agreements, varying stories, and changing lies, that Marlowe doesn't bother trying to find the actual truth. Instead, he spends his time trying to avoid being framed, long enough to find the right lie, the one on which everyone can agree.[120] Across the Atlantic, Jacques Lacan and the French psychoanalysts shadowed Poe's Dupin, whose purely cerebral method consists of a "torrent of logical impasses, eristic enigmas, paradoxes and even jests," as he spends his time restating the case out loud, from different perspectives, over and over again, until the paradoxes resolve.

Holmes states the case only once and only from his perspective, which makes his explanations seem arbitrary; Dupin's running commentary flows from "the very foundation of intersubjectivity," where minds meet and meld. Poststructuralists base everything on that fluid foundation, including social reality, which allows Marlowe to build and rest his cases there, too.[121] Going down the mean streets where everyone else lives, the hardboiled detective "no longer inhabits the atmosphere of pure thought," whereas Holmes goes on living in his own little bubble.[122]

Yet Holmes was too useful a scapegoat to be allowed to retire permanently, especially as critics became increasingly suspicious of stories. In 1980, Catherine Belsey published *Critical Practice*, her influential introduction to cultural constructivism, which analyzes the ideological function of literature. The text constructs the personal identities, social relations, moral values, and political norms that it appears merely to reflect, making its cultural context look perfectly natural. The job of the critic is to deconstruct the text, analyzing its biases and blind spots, showing how often it reverses and contradicts itself. But the text of *Critical Practice* contains its own contradictions. On the one hand, Belsey opposes her method to empiricism: if our individual subjectivity is wholly constructed, then our knowledge of objective reality is equally contingent. On the other hand, she labels her method "a scientific practice," though one that "is not a process of recognition but work to produce meaning." That sounds more like pseudoscience, as Belsey concedes: "This new critical practice could tumble back into subjectivism, into an individualistic quest for increasing ingenuities of meaning-production."[123] To keep herself out of Eliot's rabbit hole, Belsey, too, makes an example of the detective, who takes the fall for her. "The project of the Sherlock Holmes stories is to dispel magic and mystery, to make everything explicit, accountable, subject to scientific analysis," she says, but they also "display the limits of their own project," since the detective exhibits both patriarchal biases and political blind spots.[124] Holmes's so-called scientific theories are just a lot of bad faith preaching. But Holmes's project is awfully close to Belsey's own practice, whose goal is to dispel the mystifications of literature, to make its meanings explicit and accountable, subject to analysis. Distancing and debunking Holmes's false objectivity makes constructivism seem more scientific.

After Belsey, critics continued interrogating "the ideological work performed by positivistic science," which reverse engineers bourgeois norms as facts, rationalizing patriarchy, capitalism, and empire.[125] In these arguments, Holmes figures as the mastermind at the center of a broader conspiracy: he is "the literary personification of an elaborate cultural apparatus by which persons were given their true and legitimate identities by someone else."[126] Charged with fraud, he is found guilty of being "a flamboyant liar in the realm of factuality, spinning elaborate *fabula* that act as definitive reconstructions of past events."[127] Holmes remains a scapegoat, however, because constructivism always verges on pseudoscience itself, especially as its interpretations become more and more elaborate, its deconstructions more and more flamboyant. By the mid-1980s, it was clear that literary criticism had already put itself into an impossible bind, along with the rest of the humanities. Hayden White's observation then still applies now: humanistic disciplines "feign to aspire to the status of sciences without any hope of achieving the kind of procedures developed in the physical sciences for the resolution of conflicting interpretations."[128] Under these conditions, calling Holmes a fake allows literary critics to stave off a professional panic attack, self-diagnosed as the "tacit methodological desperation" that comes from the "inherent shakiness" of any "stabilizing interpretive frame."[129] Derrida's linguistic turn has generated the dizzying infinite regress of anti-foundationalism: texts have contexts, but those contexts are texts too, which have their own contexts, and so on. The same logic led the Duke of Argyll from the physical sciences toward metaphysics; just as he hoped, there is no limit to this kind of following.

Desperate times induce nostalgia for happier days, which means that even an overconfident Victorian detective still retains some appeal for critics missing a foundation. He just needs to be brought back down to earth. In 1980, the semiotician Carlo Ginzburg yoked his analysis of cultural sign systems to Holmes's method; they both employ the same "conjectural paradigm," reading little clues to larger meanings. Ginzburg literally grounds interpretation, since his paradigm goes all the way back to "the gesture which is the oldest, perhaps, of the intellectual history of the human race: the hunter crouched in the mud, examining a quarry's tracks."[130] He then retraces that history through a series of knowledge workers: from hunters to oracles, detectives, psychoanalysts, textual scholars, and now all semioticians, including literary and cultural critics. As the quarry evolves from animals into abstractions, however, the ground erodes enough that interpretation starts to get shaky again: "Is rigor compatible with the conjectural paradigm?" asks Ginzburg. His ambivalent answer keeps interrupting itself: the method has an "elastic rigor (to use a contradictory phrase)" and remains "rooted in the senses (though it goes beyond them)." But not too far beyond. Ginzburg draws a line before the conjectural paradigm becomes either fanciful or mystical, insisting that it "has nothing to do with the extrasensory intuition of various nineteenth- and twentieth-century irrationalisms."[131] To ground his method, Ginzburg must muddy its origin: the postmodern death of the author makes it possible to bury and forget the spiritualist who created Holmes in the first place.

Ginzburg's essay became the cornerstone of *The Sign of Three* (1983), Umberto Eco and Thomas Sebeok's collected apologetics for semiotics. The book pleads contextual rationalism for the Victorian detective: his logic may not be deduction, but it is certainly abduction, defined by the nineteenth-century logician Charles Peirce as "inference to the best explanation." The problem with this apology is that Holmes never bothers to share and compare his abductions with other people's reasoning, as Peirce insists must be done, nor does he bother to verify his explanations.[132] A fictional detective practicing abduction is therefore "one whom the reader can only admire, not emulate," but that does not stop the semioticians, who selectively read the stories to avoid Holmes's worst explanations.[133] The detective's first assured steps are far more important to them than his doubtful final results. Despite Holmes's "failure to test the hypotheses which he obtained," which makes his conclusions "logically inadequate if not invalid," his method nonetheless demonstrates for them "a systematic and consistent orientation."[134] So long as he is crouched down, studying clues in the mud, he can float whatever theories he wants, permitting critics to do the same when hunched over the text. But that empirical posturing also describes various nineteenth- and twentieth-century irrationalisms, whose orientation was nothing if not highly systematic and consistent, always pointing directly from the concrete to the cosmic. To defend his own conjectures, Eco spins the failure to reality-test as a moral victory. Because Holmes is so good at "inventing only for the sake of elegance," he demonstrates "the courage of challenging without further tests the basic fallibilism that governs human knowledge."[135] By that logic, verification is a sign of intellectual weakness: the best explanation is the most elegant invention, and the truth is for cowards.

Even so, when constructivists now compare themselves to Holmes, they stress the stage of investigation when empirical evidence is being gathered, putting off the moment when irrational conclusions must be verified. The analogy can go only so far: "Like a particularly insightful literary critic," Holmes "navigates his way to a solution not by what is familiar and easily comprehensible, but by focusing on what doesn't make sense."[136] So long as we are concerned with finding only *a* solution, rather than *the* solution, then fictions can still serve as insights. For example, Yumna Siddiqi describes herself as "the detective who investigates culture by reading clues and reconfiguring the literary and historical facts of the case into an intelligible whole," which again is not the same as the verifiable truth. Like Ginzburg, she follows in the first few steps of Holmes's method: "I attempt to keep my nose to the texts and make conjectures." Before she gets too close to the detective, however, Siddiqi dumps him: "It may be wise to follow the advice (if not always the practice) of Sherlock Holmes and avoid jumping to conclusions in the absence of evidence."[137] Critical practice looks comparatively restrained, and therefore stable, which tempts even the most radical deconstructionists of language to emulate Holmes. "After Derrida, purely empirical critical approaches seem naive," says Richard Klein, because "there is no objective reading possible, no scientific truth to be observed." However, even Derrida "always starts with the words for things," which is the shallowest possible empiricism that still stops him from tumbling into "pure subjectivism." From there, the detective work of criticism begins: "On the same elegant heuristic principle, Sherlock Holmes writes a treatise on tobacco ash in which he indicates everything that can be learned about a smoker from the least flick of his extinguished ember."[138] Once again a model of intellectual elegance, Holmes helps to reassure the interpretive humanities that its scholarly monographs and articles are not just blowing smoke.

That's not just smoke, sniff the New Empiricists: that's incense. The most recent wave of criticism includes a variety of approaches, from surface readers to digital humanists to cognitive critics. Aspiring to the status of sciences, they all reject constructivism, whose critical practice is still too close to being "a theological exercise."[139] They warn, as Tupper did, that playing detective gives rise to the oracular mood, in which suspicious readers enjoy "disdaining the obvious in order to probe the infinite mysteries of the unsaid." They worry, as Eliot did, that scholarship has become a mind

game, an endless loop of "puzzle-making and puzzle-solving."[140] To avoid
that pitfall, they advise their colleagues to keep their noses to the text without making any conjectures at all. For example, surface readers observe, but
they do not seek: "What lies in plain sight is worthy of attention but often
eludes observation—especially by deeply suspicious detectives who look
past the surface in order to root out what is underneath it." The goal is not
to construct ingenious interpretations but rather "to produce undistorted,
complete descriptions," or, as Eliot would say, to put the reader in possession of all the facts.[141] Some surface readers record their own affective or
phenomenological experience of reading the text; others detail the literal
and denotative meanings of its language. Brandt's wish seems finally to
come true: a scientific basis dignifies the profession.

But it is not so easy to quit the detective. Literary criticism's ongoing fascination with Holmes—a mix of attraction and repulsion—still
characterizes surface reading. The standard introduction to the method
encourages readers to emulate Poe's Dupin, because he is a much less suspicious detective than Holmes. "The Purloined Letter" (1844), in which
Dupin notices the document that has been sitting in plain sight all along,
"continues to teach us" to pay close attention without urging narrow suspicion.[142] This description of the story, however, is anything but undistorted
and complete. The blackmailer has disguised the compromising letter as an
ordinary one; it takes a deeply suspicious mind to look past the surface and
detect the lie. Identifying with Dupin only makes things worse for surface
reading: you're still playing Sherlock Holmes; you just don't know it. Even
when you do, Holmes will still compromise your method. For example,
Elaine Freedgood unpacks the literal meanings of literary objects, taking
them as they are rather than as symbols or metaphors. A pudding in a poem
is just a pudding, for example, not a clue to deeper figurative meaning. This
approach rejects the conventions of detective fiction, because there is no
suspicion be aired or mystery to be solved. Even so, Freedgood chooses
"The Blue Carbuncle" to illustrate her method. When Holmes describes
the unknown owner of a lost hat, he is like "a 'reader' who almost always
possesses the necessary empirical information to tease out the precisely
right meanings in each case." The scare quotes around "reader" ironize the
analogy so that Holmes, "no matter how silly" his explanations, can still
figure as a model critic.[143] But the detective will always make empirical criticism look silly. In that scene, he deduces the owner's high brainpower from

his large hat size, which is nonsense enough, but he also tries on the hat, which "settled upon the bridge of his nose" (247). His head is much too small—and so he fails his own pseudoscientific intelligence test. There is no need to worry, as he is right about the owner anyway, but the deduction produces a contradiction. How can he be so smart when, by his own reasoning, he must not be so smart? The scene illustrates the circular logic of paradox that the critic also rehearses: figuratively speaking, Holmes is a "reader" like herself, who takes everything literally, except for Holmes himself.

Other kinds of New Empiricists claim that "the field of literary studies is weakened by its refusal to engage with empirical methods," but their methods also have weaknesses.[144] These critics tend to keep "a strange silence concerning standard critiques of the 'neutrality' of observation," which invites questions about how far their theories are preconceived.[145] After all, even the refusal of an interpretive frame is just another even shakier interpretive frame. Circular logic is a special problem for digital humanists, like those in Franco Moretti's Stanford Literary Lab. Experimenting with Google n-grams, they search the whole corpus of digitized texts for large-scale formal patterns and generic trends in literary history. The goal is objectivity, but as Maurice Lee points out, such experiments are conducted "under conditions of mass information in which seemingly unlikely coincidences are highly probable and easily targeted by bias-confirming searches."[146] In other words, Google is the perfect way for literary critics to get in the oracular mood, which makes them look like bad detectives rather than good scientists. To demarcate his work from pseudoscience, Moretti begins by scapegoating Sherlock Holmes. Hoping to restore a "reasonably testable foundation" to criticism, he proposes to shuttle between literature and sociology, synthesizing interpretation and explanation. To assess whether this is "a reasonable project and not just a little personal utopia," he tests his method on the Sherlock Holmes stories, just as Belsey did, although he finds the detective guilty of bad science rather than bad faith. Enjoying "perfect self-referentiality," Holmes "mimes the univocality of scientific language" and "furnishes only the sensation of scientific knowledge."[147] He makes us feel like we are feeling our way along a chain of reasoning, when in fact we are empty-handed.

Although Moretti's project then seems reasonable in comparison, his own statement of method mimes Holmes, conflating deduction with induction: "Deducing from the *form* of an object the *forces* that have been at work: this is the most elegant definition ever of what literary sociology should be."[148] There goes that adjective "elegant" again, making it no surprise that Moretti's project often strikes others—and at times, even himself—as being pure invention. As one reviewer puts it, circular logic and confirmation bias ensure that Moretti is "never at a loss for the nifty Holmesian explanation."[149] Those fallacies also ensure that he can never let go of Holmes, his uncanny double, though his digital method of "distant reading" keeps the detective at arm's length. Distant reading views all of literary history as a Darwinian "slaughterhouse" of competing genres and forms; in reconstructing that history, Moretti revisits the stories several times over the course of his work, mapping, charting, and diagramming them, until they lose all their mystery. In the resulting taxonomy of plot devices, Doyle's "unintelligible" clues are a useful adaptation, turning Holmes into the only "Superman" who can read them.[150] Having debunked the utopia of Baker Street, Moretti can safely describe his own Literary Lab experiments as "detective work, focusing on clues," without worrying whether the number on his door is 221B.[151] But if distant reading requires that you tout your "little pact with the devil," in order to demarcate digital projects from theological exercises, then you're still blowing smoke: it's just brimstone.[152]

To move literary studies "closer to the sciences in theory, method, and governing ethos," some English professors have gone so far as to collaborate with evolutionary biologists and psychologists.[153] Darwinian cognitive critics argue that human beings have evolved from muddy hunters, who track animals low to the ground, into highly sophisticated mind readers, who track other people's thoughts, especially their thoughts about our thoughts about them. This survival skill, called Theory of Mind, helps us to answer a basic question: Are they friend or foe? To practice that skill and keep us fit, the argument goes, we have also evolved into sophisticated writers of literature, thinking up characters who teach readers to think about thinking. While the premise is scientific, the chain of reasoning contains so many admittedly unverifiable inferences that it's no use denying that the logic is Sherlockian. And so, cognitive critics make a virtue out of necessity, presenting Holmes as their best example of reasoning so evolved that it is perfectly backward. Detective fiction explores "the furthest limits of our metarepresentational ability," as marked by "the Sherlock-Holmesian grandstanding" that reconstructs every nuance of the criminal mind.[154] We can admire but never emulate that skill; the most famous mind readers in literature, "such as Sherlock Holmes, are more like gods than humans." As soon as Holmes crosses that frontier into mysticism, of course, the evolutionary argument turns against its own premise. If literary characters are "the greatest practical-reasoning schemes ever invented," then what does it say about human beings that our greatest fictional thinker—the one who survived Moretti's slaughterhouse of literature—is so bad at reasoning?[155] To answer that question, one Darwinian critic argues that we have evolved "a little Sherlock Holmes in our brain," who helps us to navigate our world. However, because that cognitive function is to "fabricate the most confident and complete explanatory stories from the most ambiguous clues," the critic must also concede that if Holmes were a real person, "he would be a dangerously incompetent boob."[156] A neat little paradox has evolved. If the theory of a Sherlockian brain is true, then it must also be a complete fabrication, a story that our mind tells itself to explain itself. Strange how the brain controls the brain!

Eliot was right: pursuing criticism as if it were a science is no cure for methodological desperation. The alternative is to shake up the empirical sciences, undermining their professional basis and putting them on equal footing with literary studies. In the late 1980s, following the logic of philosopher Thomas Kuhn, humanities disciplines began "converging to call into question the rationality, verifiability, and systematic nature of science."[157] The resulting interdisciplinary school of Science and Technology Studies, founded by Bruno Latour, argues that scientific knowledge is not objective. Because doing science is a social activity conducted within a professional network, its methods are culturally constructed, and its facts are therefore as provisional as its theories. To deconstruct the scientific disciplines, Latour enlisted the fictional detective who had already wreaked havoc in the humanities. In *Aramis, or the Love of Technology* (1996), part roman à clef and part manifesto, Latour casts himself as "a laboratory Sherlock," who pursues "the methods of detective novels" so closely that he calls his intern "my dear Watson."[158] Latour relishes the role of detective because it precipitates the oracular mood, allowing him "to indulge in empirical metaphysics," as he later called his actor-network theory.[159] The theory requires that we treat as real any subjective belief that motivates people to act; unlike the shared single universe of traditional metaphysics, many realities exist, with each person living out a different one. By that relativistic logic, a fictional detective is as good as an empirical fact. Whether you are acting as if you were Sherlock Holmes or as if you were nothing like him, he motivates your actions and thus creates your own personal reality, uniquely true for you. Criticism's fascination with Holmes brings him to life; once again, the Baker Street Irregulars were way ahead of the game. Of course, Latour's theory is the only one that is true for everyone, which is as it should be; his belief about beliefs retroactively makes him Holmes in the first place. Real scientists have objected that Latour's detective work "leaves no ground whatsoever for distinguishing reliable knowledge from superstition."[160] Mission accomplished: now they know how it feels to be a humanist.

I said that I deeply identify with Pope Hill: his reality is also true for me. The high road of interpretation circles endlessly around the same intellectual abyss for both of us. There is one difference: he kept the faith in Sherlock Holmes, but I cannot. I would love to take Holmes for my "model of liberal professionalism," as has recently been suggested, but that would mean having to believe that he "tries to avoid confirmation bias" and "often succeeds," even as the stories "make clear that this is a difficult habit of mind to maintain."[161] Only confirmation bias could lead to that interpretation of the stories, which so consistently reward confirmation bias. As ever, there is no way to write criticism about the detective without his method undermining your own. The only countermove is to sideline Doyle, which at least keeps his spiritualism out of the interpretive frame. The death of the author permits critics to keep passing over what Doyle believed to be his life's work, but that is not a fair way of playing the game. Nor is it playing fair to skip past Utah in *A Study in Scarlet*, as if the religious context of Holmes's origin story doesn't much matter either. The truth may be inconvenient, but the return of the author in this book reveals a central all-important fact about the universe of literary criticism. It revolves around a fictional detective, just like Baker Street and Summerland, spinning the same ineffable twaddle.

CHAPTER 5

Negation at Any Cost, 2001–2020

THOUGHT CREATIONS

The spirit guide Pheneas's prophecy that the world would end in flames did not come true in 1925, but a few years later there was a smaller signal fire. In August 1929, the thatched roof of Doyle's country retreat ignited; the local brigade arrived just in time to save the cottage, but not without considerable loss of property. The cause was a mystery until the end of the month, when the spirit of Doyle's first wife, Louisa, came through in a circle of Lady Doyle's friends to explain. The negative psychic energy of the Sherlock Holmes stories had contaminated the furniture, which needed to be destroyed before the cottage could host any more séances. For the sake of the family, good spirits had torched those bad characters; rather than arson, this was an exorcism.[1]

The idea that literary figures could exert a moral influence was familiar, but the idea that they might also enjoy a spiritual existence was new. Not even the theosophical Ivan Cooke was willing to go that far, although he was willing to speculate. At a 1931 séance with Grace, the spirit of Doyle himself came through to caution that some mediums have the unconscious power to create "thought-forms," which materialize and communicate as if they were independent spirits, but which are actually manifestations of the subconscious self. They are not under the control of the medium; in fact,

they now act like spirit guides for the medium. Wondering if this phenomenon could be true, Cooke pointed to one piece of circumstantial evidence:
"There was once a thought-creation which has inspired a complete literature, [and] has become in personified form a household word. This
thought-creation may have largely modified the police system and practice
of several continents, and, incidentally must have profoundly altered and
changed the circumstance of the man from whose consciousness it sprang.
Its name? Yes, of course; 'Sherlock Holmes.'" Although Cooke reserved
judgment about the possible existence of thought-forms, he was certain
that an "idea-character" like Holmes has the power to change the real world,
just as if he were an actual being.[2]

    But there really are no other characters like Holmes. When philosophers
discuss the metaphysical nature of fictional entities and objects—including
whether such entities and objects can be said to exist at all—they are always
on the same page. "Their knowledge of literary works," says Terry Eagleton,
"seems to consist entirely of the Sherlock Holmes stories."[3] Because Holmes
is as close to being real as a character can get, he helps philosophers to test
different theories: possibilism (Holmes exists in a possible universe, where
he is a fact, but not in our own universe, where he is a fiction); creationism (Holmes exists in our universe, because he is a fact in Doyle's fiction,
which is a fact in our universe); and antirealism (Holmes does not exist,
anywhere, ever). The entry on "Fictional Entities" in the *Stanford Encyclopedia of Philosophy* mentions Holmes's name almost one hundred times;
sheer repetition makes his presence carry at least as much weight as the
scholars listed in its bibliography.[4] Holmes is popular in other branches
of philosophy as well, where he troubles the distinction between subjectivity and objectivity. When materialist Daniel Dennett probes the nature
of consciousness—asking whether it exists at all—he refers the question
to Holmes. "When Sherlock seems real," he asks, "does this require him
and his world to be rendered somewhere, in—let's call it—*fictoplasm*?" Of
course not, he answers: "There is no need for a medium of fictoplasm to
render fiction effective."[5] The medium of consciousness is just a fiction, too,
according to Dennett, even if it seems real to us; it is not a place where our
subjective experiences happen, as Cartesian dualism posits, but rather a
subjective experience itself. Strange how the brain controls the brain!

    As an object of study, Holmes is rendered inert. Because we are think-
ing *about* him, rather than *like* him, his pseudoscience cannot influence

either our minds or our lives. As a rhetorical figure, however, he becomes active. Saying that we are thinking like Holmes, or even just thinking that we are thinking like him, brings us straight to the edge of an intellectual precipice. The Duke of Argyll was right that the "imposing character" of an explanation is no guarantee of its truth; Holmes imposes his magical thinking on any argument that invokes him to support its logical claims.[6] Both spiritualists and theosophists used extended empirical metaphors— from forging chains to exploring oceans to performing elective cataract surgery—to make mysticism seem more scientific. Sherlock Holmes is the meta-metaphor for those metaphors: he stands for all the science that now can go without saying or doing. Citing his authority is therefore the fastest and most efficient way to persuade yourself and convince others that your reasons, whatever they may be, are perfectly correct. Scapegoating Holmes is a more roundabout move, executed deftly by the literary critics in chapter 4, but the net effect is the same: calling his theories chimerical makes your own seem more practical. But thinking that you are a better thinker than a fictional detective only realigns you with Holmes, since he thinks exactly the same thing about Dupin, "by no means such a phenomenon as Poe appeared to imagine" (*Scarlet*, 24).

Holmes is a far superior fellow, imposing himself even on the author who imagined him. The character enabled Doyle to rationalize his faith within a belief system with one core principle: it is not a belief system. Calling itself a field of scientific knowledge, spiritualism "would not respond to reason," as Daniel Cottom says, "because it claimed to represent reason."[7] John Tyndall put it more bluntly: "Science is perfectly powerless in the presence of this frame of mind."[8] In the case of the author, good faith may have led to bad science, which then reinforced that faith, but there were no sinister or even ulterior motives, and Doyle stood to gain nothing. Quite the opposite: his good faith effort to bring hope to other people took a toll on Doyle's finances, reputation, and health. Skeptics may have felt that spiritualism was a waste of people's time and energy, taking their minds from better things, but the movement made no political demands, other than lobbying against the Witchcraft Act, and requested no funding. All it asked was to be taken seriously.

Nonetheless, the totalizing belief system had unintended conse-quences. Some of them were purely subjective and largely contained: McCabe's frustration with Doyle's logic, for example, or Doyle's suspicion of the Catholic Church, or his family's conviction that the world would soon end. Even Doyle's falling-out with Houdini did no harm beyond their friendship. But Houdini feared further consequences, far more negative because also objective, damaging lives as well as minds. To prove that Doyle was a public menace, he collected news stories of people whose spiritualist beliefs had led to endangering themselves or others. In 1922, during the same week that Doyle was lecturing on the beauties of Summerland in Carnegie Hall, a young New Jersey housewife, Maude Fancher, killed both her infant son and herself by drinking Lysol. She had converted to spiritualism shortly after her marriage, though her husband was not a believer. Her note explained her reasons for committing murder-suicide: she knew that she and her child would be happy together in the next world, and that her struggling husband would be free to find better employment in this one. She also promised to return as a spirit guide, helping him to start a new family. To stop others from following the logic of spiritualism toward a death wish, Doyle put out a statement, emphasizing that suicides are separated from loved ones in the afterlife, where they also do penance. "If this poor woman had been better instructed," he asserted, "she would never have ventured on such a deed."[9] But even an editorial that absolved Doyle of responsibility also acknowledged his influence: "She Could Quote Sir Arthur."[10]

After Doyle's death, his spiritual universe expanded, as mediums everywhere could quote him ever more freely, but Houdini's worst fears did not come true. The movement did not harm either public education or the common good, even if Christian apologists warned that it undermined their faith: one called Doyle's *New Revelation* "the cruellest work of fiction he ever wrote."[11] Doyle's fictional universe also kept expanding, despite the family's efforts to put the whole thing under contract, insisting that nobody could quote Sherlock Holmes for free. Nonetheless, playful Sherlockians reapplied his pseudoscientific method to the stories themselves, and professional critics then applied that method to all of literature. Throughout the twentieth century, any ill effects were thus safely confined to fan clubs and English departments. The detective has now entered the public domain, however, and so the next question is whether he can influence the real world enough to become a public menace.

As this final chapter argues, that menace grows once the idea-character of Sherlock Holmes goes to work on the internet, where cruel fictions do widespread damage. The danger is not the character itself—fan sites and fan fictions promote the same innocent idea of fun as the original Baker Street Irregulars, who delighted in hand-drawn diagrams and mimeographed pastiches—but rather our *idea* of the character as an ideal thinker. The internet extends the reach of that idea and amplifies its influence, encouraging and enabling pseudoscientific theories that confirm biases, poison minds, and end lives. In 1887, the bishop of Durham warned that the self-declared doctrine of infallibility leads to both the "stultification of reason" and the "denial of history," and his warning seems especially urgent today.[12] It is one thing for Doyle to paraphrase Holmes when debating intelligent design with Stansbury; it is another for creationist websites to cite Holmes repeatedly when lobbying for intelligent design to be taught in public schools. It is one thing for Doyle to detect the hidden hand of crypto-Catholicism in the London *Times*; it is another for 9/11 Truth forums to quote Holmes frequently when spreading hateful anti-Semitic and Islamophobic conspiracy theories around the world. "The general lines of reasoning advocated by Holmes have a real practical application to life," Doyle said in 1917, but he could not have predicted what follows.[13]

THE STULTIFICATION OF REASON

The stated aim of the intelligent design (ID) movement is to challenge Darwin's theory of evolution; its ultimate ambition is to make room in the physical universe, and thus in public school science classrooms, for divine cause. The movement is therefore "an upgraded form of the religious fundamentalist creationism long familiar in America," whose proponents are "crusaders, just as inspired as, but much more effective than, the old literalists, whose pseudo-science was easily recognized as ludicrous."[14] ID claims to have found a friend in science, as the president of the 1887 Church Congress hoped religion would one day do. The special friend of ID is Sherlock Holmes, invoked repeatedly to validate its pseudoscientific methods and verify its crypto-theological conclusions. The appeal to his fictional authority goes all the way back to Doyle's friend and spiritualist mentor Alfred Drayson. Defending his astronomical theory in 1894, Drayson publicly counted the author among his supporters and claimed the character's method as his own. The British Astronomical Association was skeptical, doubting "whether Mr. Sherlock Holmes would necessarily offer a valid proof that the proper motions of the fixed stars are due to a 'secondary rotation' of the earth."[15] Despite that early professional caution, Holmes has since become so famous that the scientific community can no longer afford to let him keep working only for the creationist enemy. But once scientists also start appealing to his authority, the consulting detective turns double agent, playing both sides against each other.

In their *Intelligent Design Uncensored* (2010), William Dembski and Jonathan Witt argue that certain biological forms are intricate enough that they could not have evolved incrementally through the unguided process of natural selection, as Darwin holds. The bacterial flagellum, for example, is a microscopic rotary engine built of proteins so tightly interlocked that the absence of any one of them would cause the whole mechanism to fail. The flagellum is therefore what Michael Behe calls "irreducibly complex," defying any step-by-step explanation of its evolutionary development.[16] One must therefore consider the alternative explanation, Dembski and Witt propose, that the flagellum was designed by an intelligent agent, from whose consciousness it sprung full-blown into existence. To confirm their reasoning, they turn to the expert: "In a classic Sherlock Holmes detective story, *Silver Blaze*, Holmes realizes that the key to the mystery is not the presence of something but the absence of it: nobody heard the guard dog bark. Similarly, in the case of the bacterial flagellum motor, an important clue to its origin is the absence of something after a long, assiduous search by numerous well-trained, highly motivated evolutionists—a detailed Darwinian pathway from simple ancestor to complex motor."[17] They stretch the detective's inference even further than he does; Holmes does not conclude that a supernatural being intervened to muzzle the dog, only that it already knew the human culprit. However, as Elliott Sober points out, ID proponents stop just short of Christian apologetics, which preserves the illusion of scientific method. They insist that their own inference—to an unknown "intelligence," not a religious deity—is a "comparatively modest claim" relative to creationism.[18] That distinction is clever, but not convincing. Behe is a professor of biology at Lehigh University, but the department publicly rejects his views: "It is our collective position that intelligent design has no basis in science, has not been tested experimentally, and should not be regarded as scientific."[19]

The inference to intelligence is the argument from ignorance, a logical fallacy that even Holmes knows to avoid. The inability of scientists to explain certain phenomena—whether the rotors of the bacterial flagellum or the footsteps of a gigantic hound—does not mean that it is time for scientists to give up on natural explanations and fall back on supernatural ones. It just means that they need more time to research. Nonetheless, ID proponents have invoked Holmes to make that argument since the 1980s, when they started attacking the evidence for Darwinian evolution. In *Evolution: A Theory in Crisis* (1985), Michael Denton argues that "even if we were to construe with the eye of faith some 'evidence' in the pattern of diversity for the Darwinian model of evolution this could only be seen, at best, as indirect or circumstantial." To emphasize that his opponents are the ones making leaps of faith, Denton closes his discussion of comparative anatomy with a literary allusion: "Readers familiar with Conan Doyle's Sherlock Holmes stories will recall the views of the great detective: 'Circumstantial evidence is a very tricky thing,' answered Holmes thoughtfully; 'it may seem to point very straight to one thing, but if you shift your own point of view a little, you may find it pointing in an equally uncompromising manner to something entirely different.'"[20] Denton himself had yet to point to ID, but his book inspired the movement, which has continued to borrow the same quotation to challenge both biological and paleontological evidence. In the ID textbook *Of Pandas and People* (1993), Mark Hartwig and Stephen Meyer criticize evolutionary biologists for passing off their inferences as facts and refusing to admit that other inferences—such as design—deserve equal time in the classroom. To convince schoolteachers, Hartwig and Meyer quote as above "the insightful warning of fictional detective Sherlock Holmes," called on here to teach a lesson in epistemology.[21] If shifting our point of view so that the available evidence points to design means that we must disagree with Darwin, then we do so on the good authority of Holmes. On that same authority, Charles Thaxton concludes his review of "A New Design Argument" in 1998 with the same old line about circumstantial evidence, still cited frequently on ID websites and forums, along with the dog that did not bark.[22]

That next argument from design—Dembski's theory of "specified complexity"—goes beyond looking for holes in evolutionary theory. Instead, it claims to offer logical and empirical proof of its own inference. Dembski employs a three-step "explanatory filter" for detecting design. If natural laws cannot account for a complex event, *and* its purely chance occurrence is highly improbable, *and* its complexity conforms to a useful or meaningful pattern, then an intelligence must have designed it. The filter gives Behe's biochemical argument a mathematical twist: the irreducible complexity of the bacterial flagellum is not only scientifically inexplicable but also statistically improbable. No known law of nature would necessitate the gradual assembly of all those different proteins into that mechanism, and yet it is practically impossible that they would come together, all at once, to meet its precise specifications. Eliminating both necessity and chance leaves design as the only possible explanation. Nonetheless, the theory of specified complexity is only a new twist on the argument from ignorance: the argument from incredulity. It may be hard to believe that the flagellum could have evolved in precisely this way, but that doesn't mean it didn't happen. Doyle made the same fallacious argument against Stansbury: "I cannot imagine an endless orderly unfolding without purpose."[23]

Once again, Holmes helps to disguise the logical fallacy. "To attribute specified complexity, and thereby design, to a biological system is to engage in an eliminative deduction," explains Dembski, "a form of reasoning used throughout the sciences." And yet, his own form of that reasoning comes from literature: "Provided the proposition, together with its competitors, form a mutually exclusive and exhaustive class, eliminating all the competitors entails that the proposition is true. (Recall Sherlock Holmes's famous dictum: 'When you have eliminated the impossible, whatever remains, however improbable, must be the truth.')" Holmes's dictum allows Dembski to submit forensic evidence for his claim about the origin of the flagellum, while the clueless evolutionary scientists continue to search in vain: "Specific complexity is a reliable empirical marker of intelligence in the same way that fingerprints are a reliable empirical marker of a person's presence."[24] However, Dembski's theory leads to infinite regress. If the flagellum is both complex and improbable, then its designer must be at least equally if not more so, which means that the designer in turn has a designer, and so on. David Berlinski tries to interrupt this vicious circle by recycling the dictum in *The Devil's Delusion: Atheism and Its Scientific Pretensions* (2008). "The demand that explanations mention only events no more improbable than the events they explain is in any case intolerably abstemious," he insists, before citing again what "Sherlock Holmes observed to Watson" about eliminating the impossible, a line now quoted online as often as the rule of circumstantial evidence.[25]

Even if ID proponents avoid mentioning divine cause, these are all "God of the gaps" arguments: anything that science cannot explain leaves wiggle room for creationism. Holmes is friendly to such arguments because his chain of reasoning encourages the leap of faith. Stephen Kendrick quotes the dictum several times in *Holy Clues: The Gospel According to Sherlock Holmes* (1999), in which the Universalist Church minister explains that the stories teach us "to trace the spiritual fingerprints left behind by a mysterious God."[26] Because Kendrick is perfectly upfront about his religious beliefs, his book contains no hidden agenda, makes no scientific claim, and thus exhibits no confirmation bias. In contrast, ID proponents identify with Sherlock Holmes in order to conceal their biases, presenting themselves as scientists doing the same "historical detective work" as evolutionary biologists, anatomists, geneticists, and paleontologists: observing present effects, inferring past causes, and testing possible hypotheses until only the best explanation remains.[27] "Historical scientists proceed in the same manner as the fictional Sherlock Holmes," argues Meyer in *Signature in the Cell: DNA and the Evidence for Intelligent Design* (2009), stating that he "consciously followed this method of reasoning" as he investigated the biochemical origin of life.[28] High school students will enjoy learning that method as much as they enjoy reading the fiction, suggests Patrick Clancy in *Teaching the Controversy* (2008): "It is this search for 'whodunit' that makes Sherlock Holmes books and stories so perennially popular."[29]

Stretched this far, the analogy also allows ID proponents to explain why their work gets better results. Because evolutionary scientists refuse to search for an intelligent "who," looking instead for an unintelligent "what," they miss or misread all the evidence of design in nature that Dembski's filter detects. Scientific methods can prove "that an intelligence did something," says Edward Sisson, a lawyer who participated in the Kansas State Board of Education evolution hearings in 2005, even if those methods do not reveal its identity or explain its motive: "Everyone who has read or watched a Sherlock Holmes story knows this."[30] In other words, scientists who rule out design a priori are not only poor detectives but also poor readers of detective fiction, committed to the absurd premise that crimes can somehow happen without criminals to commit them. "Seems like an odd sort of rule, doesn't it?" asks Chuck Colson, a conservative Christian radio commentator: "What would Sherlock Holmes say? I don't know, but I can guess. He'd probably agree with William Dembski."[31] Dembski himself presses the point: "Not just forensic science, but the whole field of detection is inconceivable without the design inference. Indeed, the mystery genre would be dead without it."[32] His doubters might point out that criminal plots do not spring from super-natural minds, but ID apologists have an answer to that objection. Denyse O'Leary explains: "The line of reasoning of eliminating the impossible and accepting the improbable worked well for Sherlock Holmes in the famous detective stories. After all, Sir Arthur Conan Doyle had already built in an improbable solution for Holmes to find. Although Holmes didn't know it, his cases were a product of intelligent design. But the Darwinist, by the very nature of what he believes, rules out an intelligent designer as the 'author' of nature. He knows by faith that there is no such author. He may end up stuck with improbabilities, and no place to go."[33] Like Denton, O'Leary turns the tables on scientists, who now stand accused of faith-based reasoning so illog-ical that they believe stories do not need authors to write them. The appeal to fictional authority is complete: the fact that Holmes is a character in a story, not an actual scientist, is now the strongest point in his favor. For that reason, another apologist rests his case by endorsing the detective without whom the design inference would be dead: "I encourage everyone to see reason at work in the stories about Sherlock Holmes."[34] If you are stuck with reality, they are the best and only place to go.

Apologists may hail Dembski as "intelligent design's Sherlock Holmes," but for scientists, Dembski illustrates the pitfalls of reasoning like an infal-lible fictional detective.[35] The theory of specified complexity rehearses the same circular logic as Paley's watch argument and the Duke of Argyll's theory of instrumentality: it presumes the existence of the maker that it claims to detect. O'Leary reveals as much when she extends her analogy, advising scientists to "put their faith in intelligent design" as a basis for inquiry, "because then they might reasonably believe that someone left them clues—in much the same way that Arthur Conan Doyle always left clues for his great detective Sherlock Holmes to find."[36] The argument from design, then, depends on first imagining that you are an armchair detective in a story, at which point it will become clear that an author is dropping hints that he is pulling strings. Like Holmes, you will immediately find clues everywhere you look; you will also not ask why you are the only one who can see them. Unlike Holmes, however, your reasoning will take you behind the scenes of the story itself, at which point you start looking more like Pope Hill, reading the deepest meanings into the tiniest accidents, especially once you start calculating the probability that any of this could have happened by chance.

"When you cannot prove that people are wrong, but only that they are absurd," advised Huxley, "the best course is to let them alone."[37] The Baker Street Irregulars simply ignored Hill, but the scientific community cannot afford to ignore the ID movement. In 1887, Darwin's theory of human evolution through natural selection was gaining traction with many Victorians, but all of the corroborating evidence since then has still not been enough to convince most Americans. Only 22 percent believe that human evolution is an unguided process, according to a 2019 Gallup poll, while 40 percent believe that God created humans in their present form within the last ten thousand years.[38] Public education is under siege: even after *Kitzmiller v. Dover*, the 2005 court case that barred ID from the classroom, the movement continued to lobby for state legislation that would require schools to teach "false critiques and controversies promoted by creationists."[39] To defend the biological theory of evolution, as well as the constitutional separation of church and state, scientists have made the case for Darwin in the courts of both law and public opinion.

When doing so, they often fall into the trap of quoting Sherlock Holmes themselves. They have a good reason: his expert opinion is also a celebrity endorsement. But it is a losing rhetorical strategy, because the detective sided first with intelligent design; he is no friend to scientists, whose arguments start breaking down almost as soon as he shows up. For example, on the opening day of the *Kitzmiller* trial, biologist Kenneth Miller debunked the ID argument from ignorance. He emphasized that unsolved mysteries, far from invalidating methodological naturalism, instead drive further experimentation that advances scientific knowledge: "What attracts scientists to research is the lure of the unknown. There is nothing more dreadful than to wake up one morning and think that all the fundamental problems in your field have been solved. On the day that I think all fundamental problems in cell biology have been resolved, I will retire to Sussex and keep bees, as Sherlock Holmes once said."[40] Miller went on to discuss another such puzzle for biologists—the bonding of amino acids—but his analogy is itself a puzzle for Sherlockians. Holmes *does* in fact retire to the country, which is what Miller implies a real scientist could never do; what's worse, Holmes starts appreciating nature only once he quits solving mysteries, which makes his testimony here immaterial.

Nonetheless, eight trial days later, the plaintiffs called another biologist to the stand, who also then called on Holmes. Kevin Padian argued that the universe might appear to be designed for humans, but that good scientists have to question appearances and challenge assumptions, just as Copernicus once did: "For all the world, it looks like, you know, to us normal people, that the sun goes around the Earth. And for most people, it wouldn't make a difference whether the sun went around the Earth or it went around the moon, as Sherlock Holmes famously said to Watson." Once again, the analogy to Holmes collapses under cross-examination: Padian misreads the scene from *A Study in Scarlet*. Holmes does not say the Copernican revolution makes no difference to most people; he says that "it would not make a pennyworth of difference to me or to my work" (21). Though he calls himself a scientific detective, Holmes devalues the work of researchers like Padian, who want "to discover things that will make a difference to our understanding of the natural world."[41] Only in retirement does Holmes start puttering around outdoors, making one small contribution to biology: his *Practical Handbook of Bee Culture, with Some Observations upon the Segregation of the Queen*, which he ironically deprecates as "the *magnum opus* of my latter years!" (978).

The analogy to Holmes did not slip enough to cause trouble in the *Kitzmiller* courtroom, where the judge sided with the biologists and threw ID out of the classroom. Even so, science writers who extend the analogy always end up having to backpedal, which eventually means throwing Doyle under the bus. Massimo Pigliucci, a philosopher who specializes in debunking pseudoscience, often refers admiringly to Holmes: "A scientist is not really different from a modern, technically savvy version of Sir Arthur Conan Doyle's Sherlock Holmes," who is himself "the quintessential fictional icon of logical rigor."[42] He does allow that the famous dictum must be qualified each time it is quoted, since it works only when "there is a limited number of options, and they are mutually exclusive," and even then only if the detective is "well aware that he needs good information before it becomes possible to arrive at a reasonable inference." Because those conditions do not apply to the stories, however, Pigliucci preserves Holmes's iconic image by scapegoating Doyle, whose credulity makes the detective look savvy. "Then again, Holmes's creator was not above making major blunders when it came to science and pseudoscience," he notes after quoting the dictum, as if those blunders have nothing to do with Holmes.[43]

Disavowing Doyle's beliefs allows Pigliucci to keep the faith in Holmes's logical method, fictional as it may be. The whole history of spiritualism must be minimized and then put off indefinitely: "Incidentally, it is ironic that Holmes's creator, Sir Arthur Conan Doyle, believed in spirits and poltergeists—but that's another story."[44]

It is impossible, however, to eliminate that story so that only Holmes remains. The biologist Richard Dawkins invokes the figure of a "late-coming detective" throughout *The Greatest Show on Earth: The Evidence for Evolution* (2009). He makes the same case for retrospective prophecy that Huxley did: "Given that, in most cases, we don't live long enough to watch evolution happen before our eyes, we shall revisit the metaphor of the detective coming upon the scene of the crime after the event and making inferences." ID proponents are more like bumbling sidekicks than master detectives; the evidence for evolution found in plate tectonics is so obvious that "even Dr Watson couldn't miss it." Halfway through the book, having identified himself with Holmes to the point of quoting his signature line, "Elementary, my dear Watson," Dawkins gives himself a reality check. He fact-checks the quotation, conceding in a footnote that Holmes is doubly unreal, not just fictional but also mythical: "Alas, Holmes never said it . . . but the allusion works because everybody thinks he did." The footnote corrects the misquotation, which allows Dawkins to leave it in place, since everybody now knows that he knows better than to think that Holmes really said it. The larger question, which cannot be settled in a footnote, is whether Holmes's method also works only because everybody thinks it does, and whether Dawkins knows better than to think so, too. At the end of the book, Dawkins undercuts the metaphor of the late-coming detective, going well out of his way to mention the pseudoscientific cosmological theories of "Conan Doyle's Professor Challenger, a fictional character even more preposterous than Sherlock Holmes."[45] The parting shot proves that Dawkins knows Holmes is fanciful, which allows him to leave the qualified metaphor in place, but only because there is even more ineffable twaddle surrounding a different character, in another story.

Like Dawkins, philosopher Michael Ruse often debates creationists; unlike Dawkins, who advocates atheism, Ruse believes that science and religion can be reconciled. He is therefore more comfortable quoting the famous dictum, so long as he can adjust its context. He explains that Paley's watchmaker analogy is actually quite sound, given that the theory of evolution was not yet an option. Paley followed Holmes's process of elimination to a theological conclusion because it was the only one available at the time. "In the alternative's absence," explains Ruse, "the Holmesian point applies."[46] In other words, the less science you know, the better the method works. Even so, Ruse also quotes the dictum to explain how Darwin followed the same process of elimination to his alternative conclusion. However, the Holmesian point then applies only if a different detective makes it: G. K. Chesterton's sleuthing Roman Catholic priest, Father Brown. "Brown was a better guide here," Ruse adds immediately after quoting Holmes, "for he knew that there is always some possibility of a rival explanation."[47] Ruse emphasizes the priest's caution, but his religion is what makes him reluctant to leap to conclusions. When solving mysteries, Father Brown takes special care not to abandon his use of reason; believing too quickly in miracles not only weakens his judgment but also cheapens his faith. "You attacked reason," he says after unmasking a false priest in his first story: "It's bad theology."[48] Precisely because Father Brown does not rule out the supernatural explanation, he applies the dictum more judiciously than the detective who accepts any other alternative, no matter how unreasonable.

The fact that Ruse would rather enlist a fictional priest to defend the theory of evolution—even one who takes shots at Darwin, as Father Brown occasionally does—says everything about the credibility of Sherlock Holmes. It also suggests how far scientists and their advocates have fallen into what Dembski calls, with apparent satisfaction, "the spiraling rhetorical nightmare faced by neo-Darwinism."[49] Rather than playing tug-of-war over Holmes, trying to pull him back onto their side, scientists would do better to let him go—and then go on the attack, turning the detective metaphor against the ID proponents who rely so heavily on it. The oft-quoted "Silver Blaze," in which a horse trainer turns up dead, is a beautiful illustration of how and why the design inference fails. The dog that did not bark in the nighttime ends up leading Holmes astray, precisely because he assumes there must be design; he suspects the wrong person when he should not be suspecting any person. The death was only accidental: a startled horse kicked the trainer in the head. Holmes makes the same mistake in "The Lion's Mane" (1926), in which the culprit turns out to be not a jealous lover but a poisonous jellyfish: the death was entirely random. In those stories, Holmes does resemble Dembski, who also takes appearances at face value;

they both see design because they are already looking for it, when in fact these are chance events. The difference is that Holmes eventually realizes that his assumption has led him astray; he solves the mystery by readmitting accidental natural causes, not by falling back on supernatural explanations. More broadly, scientists might encourage everyone to see the circular logic at work in all the stories, pointing out that ID proponents follow the same backtelling principle of composition as Doyle, prearranging their conclusion, and then reasoning toward it.

It is also telling that ID proponents rarely quote the one story in which Sherlock Holmes explicitly makes their argument for them: "The Naval Treaty," in which he stops to smell the roses that seem designed to stop him in his tracks. The gap has shrunk since then, from a flower to a flagellum, but the same divine providence is there to fill it. The problem for ID here is that Holmes goes too far, past the point of plausible deniability; letting slip the creationist agenda of the movement, he blows its pseudoscientific cover. Kendrick, on the other hand, who has nothing to hide, begins *Holy Clues* with the same scene. Doyle also recalled that scene in his debate with Hubert Stansbury, which concluded with a prophecy. "Some day the whole world will be divided between your position and mine," Doyle predicted, though the Gallup poll now indicates that this is not an equal split. Their debate devolved into a spiraling rhetorical nightmare, a blur of mixed metaphors, until Doyle finally warned Stansbury that symbolism can be dangerous: "It gives a false sense of knowing something when we don't really."[50] That pleasurable feeling is exactly why the ID movement loves to quote Sherlock Holmes, and why scientists take his name in vain.

THE DENIAL OF HISTORY

From the denial of Darwinian evolution to the denial of more recent human history is just a short step, because it follows the same circular logic of spiritualism. Twenty-first-century television adaptations have brought the Victorian detective up to date. At the same time, Holmes has given his blessing to the broader spread of pseudoscientific claims and fallacious arguments that now infect all zones of public discourse. "A habit of nursing illusions in religion," as Joseph McCabe warned after debating Doyle, "will not refuse its hospitality to illusions in politics and economics."[51]

The Holmes stories have always welcomed readers dreaming of escape from social conflict and political violence. Although Doyle began the series "during a time of terrorist incidents that resonate with our current sensibility," he chose "not to address contemporary political bombings," especially the Irish Fenian dynamite campaign from 1881 to 1885.[52] Scotland Yard founded its Special Branch in 1883 to investigate possible terrorist plots, but Holmes seems to have been invented in 1887 to eliminate the possibility of such plots altogether. For a brief early moment in *Scarlet*, when Holmes finds the word RACHE (German for "revenge") scrawled in blood at the crime scene, the novel alludes to contemporary European politics. But Holmes immediately discounts that reading: the clue is "a blind intended to put the police upon a wrong track, by suggesting Socialism and secret societies" (33). Instead, the revenge plot is a private matter, a lover's vow rather than a terrorist's oath, which sets the pattern for all the cases to follow. "Once subjected to [Holmes's] scientific gaze," says Ronald Thomas, "what might have appeared to be a political crime turns out time and again to be a mere domestic intrigue or personal betrayal."[53] As Watson observes, Holmes's knowledge of politics is "feeble," and so they never discuss the current events and contemporary debates described in chapter 1. For Victorian readers of *Scarlet* reeling from the news of Bloody Sunday, which renewed their fears of Fenians and anarchists, it was a relief to be served a quiet breakfast on Baker Street.

For modern readers, it is even more of a relief to travel back to the "always romantic, always nostalgic" nineteenth century of the stories that T. S. Eliot appreciated.[54] During the atomic age, gaslit Victorian London was a safe haven. "To re-read the sixty adventures that comprise the Baker Street saga is to evoke snug echoes of a vanished era," said one Irregular in 1967, "totally unshadowed by the bomb."[55] Fifty years later, in the shadow of 9/11, the stories provide the same homeland security. Mark Gatiss, co-creator of the BBC's modernized *Sherlock* (2010–17), is never without his copy of the complete original Holmes: "It's a great comfort to me; a world in which German spies have bombs under their cloaks and submarine plans are stolen in the fog is a nice place to be when you fear that a dirty bomb might go off at Liverpool Street any day."[56] In updating the stories, Gatiss made the same choice to substitute individual for political motives. The television series "repeatedly features acts of terror that are all too familiar in contemporary society," Ellen Harrington argues, "but these are all enabled and sometimes staged by Moriarty." By replacing the Bush administration's "Axis of Evil" with just one evil mastermind, *Sherlock* suggests "that there is an underlying order to criminal enterprise that defies fears of anarchic, urban violence and global terrorism, and that Sherlock can duel Moriarty to stop it."[57] The original stories offer the same reassurance. Although "The Final Problem" introduces Moriarty as "the Napoleon of crime" only to eliminate him, he returns as "the controlling brain of the underworld" in *The Valley of Fear* (471, 769). Modernizing the stories produces "a kind of Victorian nostalgia," as the new episodes "allow viewers to escape from contemporary, post-9/11 fears," especially the fear that the war on terror will be endless.[58] When the series premiered, viewers could still hope that eliminating Osama bin Laden would be a final solution. Moriarty would be the next best thing.

Updating the Victorian detective creates a philosophical paradox. A present-day story must go all the way back to 1887 and then rewrite history, scrubbing all traces of the old fictional Holmes on which the new real-life one is still based. The Irregulars finally get their wish: in that parallel universe, Doyle never did write the stories, and yet Holmes exists without him. The three Universal films in the early 1940s that match the detective against the Third Reich—*Sherlock Holmes and the Secret Weapon* (1942), *Sherlock Holmes and the Voice of Terror* (1942), and *Sherlock Holmes in Washington* (1943)—wink at the paradox without resolving it. In *Secret Weapon*, when Holmes (Basil Rathbone) gives his address to his newly assigned military driver, she stops him with a smile: "I know, 221B." The joke is the first in a long string that "disarms any criticism of implausibility."[59] The Universal Holmes is just that: he is "ageless, invincible and unchanging," as the title card to each film says, transcending history even as he enlists in the Second World War. *Sherlock* takes a different approach to history. When Watson (Martin Freeman) decides to Google his strange new roommate, the search turns up practically no results. In our universe, there would be tens of millions of hits, but *Sherlock* begins with a "clean slate," as Ashley Polasek describes "this fictional world in which none of the multitude of Sherlock Holmes referents that have built up within modern culture over the past century exist."[60] In *Sherlock*'s universe, not even Holmes's brother knows his address yet—Mycroft (Gatiss) has to double-check his notebook—and thus one of the meta-plots of the series is Holmes rapidly becoming an "internet phenomenon," as Inspector Lestrade (Rupert Graves) sneers.[61]

Holmes's personal history in the series soon catches up and meshes with the current reality of the audience: he has fans staking out his known address in both worlds.

For Polasek, the clean slate allows *Sherlock*'s writers to play freely, just as Barthes would encourage; Gatiss and his co-creator Steven Moffat can adapt and update the original stories as they like, giving Holmes a smartphone and Watson a laptop. For Balaka Basu, on the other hand, what appears to be modernization is actually "a reification of the retrograde and the nostalgic, which suggests that the past *is* actually the present." Holmes and Watson may play with shiny new toys, but their politics are still fusty, exhibiting the same old biases and blind spots that Catherine Belsey critiqued in the original stories. The Gherkin and the London Eye in *Sherlock*'s opening credits—shiny new monuments to capitalism and tourism—perfectly represent its neoliberal worldview, whose complacency is a great comfort. "This is a Britain that may well have never experienced the welfare state or the social revolutions of the 20th century," says Basu: "It is only imaginable as a Victorian dream of the future."[62] The stories were already a dream of the Victorian present, in which there is no morning news of Bloody Sunday or any other recent conflict to report, but *Sherlock* also glosses over all the news of the world since then. The Universal films gave Holmes life during wartime, but they did not meddle with history; their plots ran parallel to the events ongoing in the world outside the theater. The BBC series, on the other hand, reboots not only the stories but also the timeline of history itself, making a single change in the present—the detective is now an Apple fanboy—that wipes out much of the past. The Sherlockian butterfly effect works backward, setting off a chain reaction of historical revisionism. If Holmes is real, and the Universal movies were never made, did the Second World War ever happen?

Well, yes—sort of. The leap forward from Victorian to modern London has given Holmes even greater powers of retrospective prophecy. In the second season, Holmes overhears a whisper of "the Coventry lot" and infers that the British government, knowing of a terrorist plot, would rather let it succeed than compromise the intelligence source. His inference depends on "a story, probably not true," about Winston Churchill: "In the Second World War, the Allies knew that Coventry was going to get bombed because they'd broken the German code, but they didn't want the Germans to know that they'd broken the code, so they let it happen anyway." Historians have long since debunked that conspiracy theory, but even so, Holmes bases his reasoning on it: "The plane will blow up. Coventry all over again. The wheel turns. Nothing is ever new."[63] Circular logic turns back the clock and revises history from there; something that never happened is nonetheless happening all over again. If nothing is ever new for Holmes, that is only because *Sherlock* never let much history happen in the first place, which makes it possible for him now to tell any old story he likes. Once you have eliminated the historical, whatever remains, however mythical, must be the truth.

Sherlock treats more recent history even more lightly. The first scene of the series takes place in the dreaming mind of Watson, who has returned from the war in Afghanistan and now apparently suffers from post-traumatic stress disorder. From the nightmare of a firefight, we awaken with him; he opens his laptop and stares at a blank screen titled "The Personal Blog of Dr. John H. Watson." In the next scene, his therapist encourages him: "Writing a blog about everything that happens to you will honestly help you." Watson sighs and says, "Nothing happens to me." Very soon, Sherlock Holmes will happen to him, not only removing his writer's block but also reversing his doctor's diagnosis: Watson suffers from ennui, not trauma. The therapist "got it the wrong way around," says Mycroft, observing that the adrenaline high of detective work has cured Watson's psychosomatic hand tremor, as it will shortly cure his limp: "You're not haunted by the war, Dr. Watson. You miss it. Welcome back." For this brief early moment, *Sherlock* suggests that the series will modernize Holmes so as to mobilize him in the post-9/11 war on terror, patrolling the home front of London just as he once did in the Universal films. "When you walk with Sherlock Holmes," says Mycroft, "you see the battlefield."[64]

Sherlock, however, gets it the other way around. Waking with Watson makes it hard to recognize that we are still dreaming, but the series welcomes us into Holmes's reality, where we are not at all haunted by the war on terror. Early in the first episode, during a police press conference about a recent outbreak of suicides in London, our cultural trauma disappears as fast as Watson's PTSD. "How can suicides be linked?" asks one reporter. "You can't have serial suicides!" exclaims another. "If they are suicides, what are you investigating?" asks a third. After 9/11, these questions sound odd to viewers at home; the journalists are somehow unable to imagine that suicides can be coordinated, or ongoing, or murderous. The official police story is equally out of touch with our reality. "Obviously this is a frightening time for people," says Lestrade, "but all anyone has to do is to exercise reasonable precautions. We are all as safe as we want to be." Holmes's humor seems even more out of touch. Later in the episode, he minimizes the invasion of Afghanistan—a "ridiculous" thing for Watson to have done—and then jokes about what declaring war "does for the traffic." His knowledge of politics is indeed so feeble that 9/11 never crosses his mind—and thus never happened for anyone else. In this universe, as Lestrade later informs us, Interpol's Most Wanted list has been topped since 1982 by a kidnapper named Ricoletti, rather than bin Laden.[65]

Defeating Moriarty allows Holmes to stop global terrorism because *Sherlock* has already done so for him, emptying the universe of social and political conflict. Twenty-first-century London feels more like the Victorian dream of a happier-ever-after Summerland. "Quiet, calm, peaceful," says Holmes, looking out the window of 221B: "Isn't it hateful?" Immunized from the friction of history, the detective is much safer than he wants to be. His perverse wish is the screenwriter's command: a neighboring house immediately explodes. Even so, London remains a nice place to be, because once again "the police are unable to say if there is any suspicion of terrorist involvement." The only suspect, a dead MI6 clerk, has "no known terrorist affiliations or sympathies," and neither does anyone else, including Moriarty.[66] Without actual terrorists, the war on terror seems terribly dull, no matter which side you are on. At the end of the first season, Moriarty (Andrew Scott) tosses the missile defense system plans into a swimming pool, calling them "boring"; at the beginning of the second, Holmes also calls news of a suspected terrorist bomb "boring." He does disguise himself as a Karachi terrorist in that episode, but only so as to rescue Irene Adler (Lara Pulver) from the cell, not to eliminate the cell itself, which poses no larger or further threat to *Sherlock*'s universe. The third season begins with London's terror alert at critical, but the threat is North Korean rather than Middle Eastern. Holmes still finds the whole plot "boring," perhaps because he deduces its necessary anticlimax: when it comes to defusing dirty bombs on the Underground, "there's always an off switch."[67] That switch is flipped the moment that Watson opens his laptop, after which we stop seeing the battlefield. Our real history of 9/11 now belongs entirely to his bad dream, and he can start blogging revisions.

THE WALL OF CRAZY

A habit of nursing illusions in London does not refuse to travel abroad; the closer that Sherlock Holmes gets to Ground Zero, the less evidence there is that 9/11 actually happened. The CBS television series *Elementary* (2012–19) relocates the detective to New York City, raising expectations that Holmes has come to America to fight the war on terror. "I've decided to resume my work as a consultant here in New York," says Holmes (Jonny Lee Miller) in the opening scene of the pilot episode, which then cuts to the title card of the city's skyline, an image that cannot help but recall the missing World Trade Center. Expectation mounts when we learn that NYPD Captain Gregson (Aidan Quinn) first met Holmes just after 9/11, when in London observing Scotland Yard's counterterrorism bureau: "Holmes mostly worked homicides, but our paths still crossed a few times."[68] Despite these teasers, Holmes never does cross paths with terrorists, who are even more conspicuously absent in *Elementary* than they are in *Sherlock*. "When it comes to aviation, air accidents, I'm something of an expert," Holmes boasts in the sixth episode, "Flight Risk." A single-engine plane has crashed on Rockaway Beach, a small-scale version of 9/11 that neatly illustrates how the show diminishes its historical impact. As "a specialist in the field of deductive reasoning," Holmes applies his method to "the complex chain of events that can turn a triumph of human innovation into a smoldering pile of wreckage in seconds," adding "I can't think of a more compelling application than that." Rather than a terrorist cell, the investigation uncovers only a local drug ring, which under the circumstances is something of an anticlimax.[69] The same logic applies to the rest of the series. A bioterror attack on a police precinct turns out to be false cover for a robbery; a truck explosion blamed first on terrorists and then on the government turns out to be the endgame of a real-estate war over a new skyscraper construction. The Twin Towers may be gone, but the city itself is totally unshadowed by 9/11.

Holmes's knowledge of politics is even feebler in *Elementary* than in *Sherlock*; he cannot think of terrorism at all, even when the evidence points directly to it. In "Flight Risk," he explains that he fears flying because of "the amount I see when I board an aircraft," leading us to imagine him consulting for the Transportation Security Administration. Instead of profiling suspicious passengers, however, he evaluates the crew's mental health, screening the pilot for signs of alcoholism or the mechanic for signs of depression. The historical event of 9/11 is simply never part of the complex chain that Holmes unravels. When Moriarty finally appears at the end of the first season, Holmes wonders what his archenemy "is up to in New York," but there is no reason for residents to worry, because Moriarty has even fewer terrorist affiliations or sympathies than in *Sherlock*. Rather than attacking America, Moriarty masterminds a billion-dollar currency bet that rides on provoking hostilities between Greece and the Republic of Macedonia—again, a rather anticlimactic plot, which Watson (Lucy Liu) jokes is "all very fascinating in an NPR kind of way."[70] The soothing voice of public radio dispels any post-9/11 fear of flying, along with all the rest of our emotional baggage.

With a clear mind and clean slate, Holmes is free to start spinning whatever new theory he likes. In the original stories, Holmes does not detect Moriarty's presence so much as conjure him up: "Without a shred of empirical evidence, he senses Moriarty lurking at the center of London's criminal webs."[71] But neither is there any evidence of a web, since the conspiracy covers "undiscovered crimes in which I have not been personally consulted," as Holmes says in "The Final Problem," which together make up only part of "all that is undetected in this great city" (471). In other words, of all his feats of detection, by far the greatest is when Holmes discovers what even he cannot detect. Conspiracy theory is the purest form of reasoning backward: your mind simply goes ahead and frames everyone, after which all the clues point to a cover-up, especially all the clues that aren't there. When debating spiritualism with McCabe, Doyle compared skeptics to "detectives sitting up all night planning things," presuming the secret designs they claim to discover, but he himself followed the same totalizing logic toward both the hidden hand of crypto-Catholicism and the choir invisible of Summerland.[72] Those two complementary conspiracies—one malevolent, one benevolent—continued to feed each other after his death. In 1932, his spirit came through at a séance to warn the Marylebone Spiritualist Association that "a great force opposing us" was hatching a sinister new plot: "You must watch and protect your mediums in the next two months."[73]

Both *Sherlock* and *Elementary* indulge Holmes's late-night habit of planning things—the dark side of being an armchair lounger. In *Sherlock*'s "The Hounds of Baskerville," Holmes investigates a conspiracy theory about an underground animal research lab; in "The Reichenbach Fall," Moriarty turns the tables by pretending to be an actor hired by Holmes to pretend to be Moriarty, so that Watson and others will believe that Holmes "made up a master villain" to make himself look like a master detective. "That's your weakness," taunts Moriarty, as his anti-conspiracy-theory theory circulates in the media, and Holmes finds himself disgraced as a fraud: "You always want everything to be clever." What Moriarty does not know is that Holmes's clever theories always prove correct; the lab is in fact conducting genetic experiments, and Moriarty is in fact a master villain. Likewise, in *Elementary*'s "The Red Team," although Holmes pooh-poohs conspiracy theories in general as "pure sophistry," he finds that the particular theory in question—about a secret counterterrorism war game run amok—is true, and that the United States government really is trying to cover up a flaw in national security. Even when he wants to, Holmes cannot debunk conspiracy theories, because his own thought process replicates their paranoid logic, which then rewrites the universe. The Coventry myth will come true as soon as he states it to another person. *Elementary*'s Moriarty taunts Holmes just as he did in *Sherlock*: "You look at a thing so closely, you start to see things that aren't there. You know you do."[74] What Moriarty does not know is that the things Holmes starts to see will always wind up being there. The detective, not his archenemy, is the controlling brain of the underworld.

Although "The Hounds of Baskerville" turns on the mystery of a vanishing rabbit, *Elementary* is more concerned than *Sherlock* about the potential for Holmes to follow conspiracy theories down the rabbit hole of his own imagination. "The Red Team" opens with Holmes staring at what a worried Watson calls the detective's "wall of crazy," where he pins fragmentary evidence of Moriarty's movements and tries to connect the dots. To reassure Watson, Holmes takes a break to pursue his hobby, although it still seems far from healthy: "My hobby is conspiracy theorists. I adore them, as one would a barmy uncle or a pet that can't stop walking into walls." As if to prove that he is not so barmy as they are, Holmes goes online to "visit swirl theory.com and discuss conspiracy theories," egging on the other members in their obsessions and seeding his own wild rumors: the CIA inventing crack cocaine, or Scientologists infiltrating the Supreme Court. Those rumors end up in the cataloged binders of "Zapruder," the website's moderator, whose files are "worth a laugh," until he turns up dead. Zapruder appears to have accidentally hanged himself during a bout of autoerotic strangulation, but Holmes looks closely enough to see something else there. What ensues is a meta-plot, in which the detective investigates the death of his own likeminded double, a conspiracy theorist whose fantasies turn out to be more than just masturbatory. On the other hand, Zapruder remains barmy enough to serve also as a scapegoat, whose murder therefore acquits Holmes of autosuggestion. If Holmes can solve the case, proving that he is clever, not crazy, then he can go back to staring at his wall without Watson worrying about him.

He does solve the case, because he cannot do otherwise, but his kind of detective work sets a bad example for all the conspiracy theorists watching at home. The 9/11 Truth movement returns the favor and adores Holmes, making him its mascot. "Truthers" and "9/11 skeptics" cite him again and again to create an alternate universe in which they can treat lightly the threat of terrorism so as to take seriously other fancied plots, no matter how improbable. Playing detective creates the illusion of empirical method and logical discourse. Debunking anti-Jesuit conspiracy theories in 1903, Steven Byington had to uncover and identify the Sherlock Holmes fallacy, but now it just lies in plain sight.

The title of Paul Rea's *Mounting Evidence: Why We Need a New Investigation into 9/11* (2011) makes the rhetorical strategy especially obvious. Rea immediately elaborates: "Although this rendering reflects serious sleuthing, what you'll find here is less a research treatise than a detective mystery in the spirit of Sherlock Holmes. The inquiry goes where the evidence leads it." Suspicious of both research reports and official treatises, from which he wants to distance himself so as to critique them, Rea locates his own work within a more "reader friendly" genre, a move that softens up the factual ground, making the historical record easier to revise. The more Rea channels the spirit of Sherlock Holmes, the more material his case will seem. Wondering why so many passengers on United 93 were able to make cell-phone calls at high altitude, Rea reasons that a cell-phone repeater must have been planted onboard, to help construct what he calls the "instant legend" of the flight: "If we entertain the 'special device' hypothesis, we do so in the spirit of Sir Arthur Conan Doyle and his famous creation, Sherlock Holmes: 'When you have eliminated the impossible, whatever remains, however improbable, must be the truth.'"[75] The famous dictum ensures that the inquiry does not go where the evidence leads it; it goes wherever the truther wants it to go. "The whole point of conspiracy theory is that nothing is impossible," Francis Wheen emphasizes: "What remains is everything,

and so everything must be true."[76] It is much more probable that some passengers were able to connect calls, despite the altitude, than that the calls
were scripted or faked, but the question of altitude alone is enough to turn
that probability into an impossibility, so as to turn an improbability into a
truth. Rea self-published his book online with iUniverse, a company name
that suggests precisely the conflation of subjectivity and objectivity, the
outward and infinite projection of individual ego, enabled by Holmes.

Just as ID creationists do, 9/11 truthers and skeptics repeatedly "eliminate the impossible" to authorize their logic; the sheer number of different
remaining truths demonstrates the fallacy. One quotes the dictum to conclude that Wall Street and the CIA colluded to profit from insider trading
before the attack; another accuses the mainstream media of serving as
agents of the state.[77] In a BBC interview, James Fetzer cites Holmes's line
to point "in the direction of a deeper and darker complicity by officials"
in the United States government; in a YouTube video, "9/11 Experiments:
Eliminate the Impossible," Jonathan Cole argues that the Twin Towers
were brought down by controlled demolition.[78] One blogger agrees with
Cole, insisting that "hard scientific and engineering realities cannot be
evaded," and so the dictum must be applied; another blogger applies the
dictum differently to argue that American Airlines Flight 11 never flew, and
so "the Bush conspiracy theory of some 19 Arab hijackers is thus dead in
the water."[79] Describing his recent conversion to the Truth movement, one
anonymous blogger urges readers to "accept the compelling logic of Conan
Doyle's Sherlock Holmes," applying the dictum to conclude that 9/11 must
have been an "inside job," though the list of possible suspects is still long.[80]

While Holmes may enjoy lurking and trolling in *Elementary*, in the real
world he is highly visible in online forums such as *911 Blogger* or *Let's Roll*.
If truthers aren't eliminating the impossible, they are chasing dogs that do
not bark. With "Silver Blaze" in mind, the inquiry goes everywhere the
absence of evidence leads it. The Secret Service did not immediately whisk
President Bush out of the elementary school classroom, and so they already
knew he was not a target; or, none of the airline pilots entered the standard
hijack code into their transponders, and so there were no hijackers; or, the
tenants of World Trade Center 7, many of them government agencies, did
not request an investigation into the building's collapse, and so there is a
massive cover-up.[81] "This all reminds me of the famous Sherlock Holmes
'curious incident of the dog in the night-time,'" concludes a pseudonymous

blogger, "as lots of things that should have happened didn't, and evidence that should be widespread isn't."[82] Watson may stare at a blank laptop screen in *Sherlock* because nothing happens to him, but conspiracy theorists need no better reason to start blogging.

"Thus you come to realize that Sherlock Holmes is not quite as fictional as you might think," says one 9/11 skeptic, recommending the detective as a "learning tool that can be applied in many ways."[83] Quotation is one way; pastiche is another. The whole Truth movement is a collaborative Sherlockian fan fiction: its multidimensional space even contains Victorian vignettes, in which Holmes solves the mystery of 9/11 from his armchair on Baker Street. "But my God, Holmes," says Watson in one, "the possibility that Israeli Mossad agents would hijack our airplanes and crash them into New York skyscrapers may be your greatest flight of fanciful conjecture so far, but I'm willing to hear your theory."[84] The use of Sherlockian pastiche for propaganda is not new; from the same armchair in 1918, Holmes defended spiritualists in the pages of *Light*, since "the one thing essential is to find out the truth."[85] A century later, pastiche is not quite as fictional as you might think, even as history itself becomes more so. The film *Captain Sherlock Solves 9/11* (2011) begins with the famous dictum on a title card before following the investigation of a retired pilot who believes that the Canadian government helped to hijack the planes remotely, using military gyroscopic sensors.[86] The role-playing becomes so immersive that the investigators themselves become fictions. Says Hugh Cort of Paul L. Williams, his partner in research, "Paul is Sherlock Holmes, and I am the humble Dr. Watson, his faithful sidekick, assisting him as best I can."[87] But in the age of the internet there is no reason to be so very humble, or even to be Watson. "With just a little common sense and a few clicks of a mouse," the online manifesto *Stranger Than Fiction* suggests, "Google and Yahoo now enable anyone with an ounce of curiosity to become a Sherlock Holmes."[88]

That invitation has been open since 1895. Shortly after Holmes plunged into the Reichenbach Falls, the journalist William Stead—whose spirit later passed Christ's message to Doyle—called for the detective's fans to take his place. Believing that a London doctor had been wrongfully convicted of forgery, Stead issued a booklet: *Wanted: A Sherlock Holmes!* (1895). Laying out his case, he asked the public for help, especially from anyone with an "abnormal appetite" for reading Holmes. "Under his skilful tuition there ought to be some hundreds, if not thousands of men and women who believe themselves qualified to act as Amateur Detectives," Stead reasoned, before making his appeal: "Where is our Sherlock Holmes?"[89] Thanks to the internet, with its bias-confirming searches under conditions of mass information, he is now everywhere. Soon after the 2013 Boston Marathon bombings, the *Los Angeles Times* reported that "thousands of people have taken to the internet to play Sherlock Holmes," but these "legions of Web sleuths cast suspicion on at least four innocent people, spread innumerable bad tips and heightened the sense of panic and paranoia."[90] Once upon a time, back in chapter 1, the measured pace of print publication and periodical circulation constrained imaginative atrocity-mongers like Canon MacColl. These days, however, online social media "allows for the rapid dissemination of unsubstantiated rumors and conspiracy theories that often elicit rapid, large, but naive social responses."[91] In other words, the correspondence can no longer be closed.

"I hear of Sherlock everywhere," says the original Mycroft to Watson, "since you became his chronicler" ("Greek Interpreter," 437). The same thing can be said to 9/11 truthers: when they walk with Sherlock Holmes, they blog the conspiracy. That conspiracy is deep enough to involve even screen adaptations of the Victorian detective who inspired the Truth movement in the first place. Reviewing the Coventry episode of *Sherlock*, the *Red Dirt Report* begins to "suspect the BBC and the writers are allowing us to see hints of what the elite are really up to." The episode itself is a clue to the larger mystery of current events: "To think that a *Sherlock* episode coincides with these [Guantanamo Bay] trials and the CIA claiming they foiled a plot to blow up a US-bound jetliner is evidence to this writer that the US and allied governments are not giving up their totalitarian behavior anytime soon."[92] Even if there is a 9/11 news blackout on Holmes's iPhone, *Sherlock* becomes reality TV. On the big screen, the media conspiracy looms even larger. The *American Free Press* connects the same dots after watching Moriarty conduct "a series of false-flag bombings" in the 2011 film *Sherlock Holmes: A Game of Shadows.* "In the real world, a tragic war against Iran seems one false-flag operation away," and so the film "asks the average person to consider the fact, not the theory, of criminal rule behind the throne—what some dare call conspiracy."[93] Some might even dare to connect one last dot, suggesting that the government has been behind the media conspiracy all along. Three years before *Sherlock* premiered, the Department of Homeland Security made its own pitch to bring Holmes up to date: "To thwart another September 11, analysts must meld the ency-clopedic eye of Google-age technology with Sherlock Holmes's inductive genius."[94] Nothing is ever new: this is the same Victorian dream of the future, in which we are all as safe as we want to be.

THE END OF A HOLMES STORY

"I know well that I have it in me to make my name famous," says Holmes after revealing himself as the author of "The Book of Life," which Watson has just slapped back down on the breakfast table (25). If fame is the plan, then writing an anonymous article in the third person about "a logician" seems like an odd first move. But the detective is playing a long game. The impersonal perspective suggests both critical detachment and scientific objectivity, though not strongly enough to convince Watson on first read-ing. It may also seem odd that Holmes marks the article and leaves it out for his new friend to find, but this, too, is part of the plan. He is testing to see if the Science of Deduction and Analysis will go viral; once Watson becomes his chronicler, it does, leaping from the Baker Street universe into our own. This book has told the story of that cultural transmission, from Doyle as patient zero to the theories swirling around Ground Zero. Confined to the stories, Holmes can do no harm, but released into public, he jeopardizes sanity and health, as Houdini would say, because he gives a false sense of knowing something when we don't really. An alternative title for this book—finished just as internet conspiracy theories and Sherlock Holmes quotations began swirling around the 2020 US presidential elec-tion—would be *Why Not to Think Like a Fictional Detective.*

Other possible case studies of Sherlockian reasoning remain on the table. ID creationism and 9/11 Truth conspiracy theory are the two exam-ples most closely linked to the original stories and their author, but there is no limit to this kind of following, which leads to the darkest parts of the internet. Wherever history is being revised, you will find Holmes: *The Gas Chamber of Sherlock Holmes: An Attempt at a Literary Analysis of the Holocaust Gassing Claim* (2000) is an anti-foundationalist text for deniers. Wherever reality is being distorted, you will find Holmes. "Not to get too meta," says Mike Cernovich, who blogged conspiracy theories about Hil-lary Clinton in 2016, "but one of the ways that I analyze the world is I pay more attention to—from Sherlock Holmes—the dog that didn't bark, right?"[95] Getting very meta, Cernovich connects alt-right fake news to the literary theory he read in college. "If everything is a narrative, then we need alternatives to the dominant narrative," he explains, adding, "I don't seem like a guy who reads Lacan, do I?"[96] Actually, he does. French poststructuralism and detective fiction belong together on the same syllabus, as chapter 4 argued, because their plotlines are so tightly intertwined. Bruno Latour foresaw the rise of the Sherlockian alt-right: soon after 9/11, he worried that constructivist critical theories were eroding the public trust in both scientific and historical facts, enabling conspiracy theories that apply the same detective logic. "In both cases, you have to learn to become suspicious of everything people say," Latour noted, and "in both cases again it is the same appeal to powerful agents hidden in the dark acting always consistently, continuously, relentlessly."[97] Latour's actor-network theory makes a different appeal—literary texts are social gatherings rather than crime scenes—but the Sherlockian reasoning that drives conspiracy theory has only grown more powerful. "Read Sherlock Holmes," Cernovich recently tweeted to his followers, certain that the detective "will be studied 100 years from now still."[98]

Even so, there are signs that the alt-logic of conspiracy theory is being recognized for what it is. After President Donald Trump fired FBI director James Comey and then tweeted that there might be secret tapes of their conversations, one *Huffington Post* contributor snapped, "Where his whopper cannot be sustained—such as the suggestion that President Obama wasn't born in the U.S. or that there are Comey 'tapes'—he just makes like Sherlock Holmes and announces he has solved the case."[99] After Trump called for the Justice Department to investigate the author of an anonymous *New York Times* editorial, the talk show host Seth Meyers expressed disbelief: "He sounds like Sherlock Holmes after a concussion."[100] From Baker Street to the Oval Office may seem like a stretch, but Joseph McCabe warned a century ago that the health of a democracy depends on the sanity of its citizens. Letting spiritualism alone is therefore bad public policy. "If we have no wish to undo the democratisation of power," McCabe said after rebuking Doyle, "let us hurry on with the democratisation of that moderate degree of mental culture which is known as common sense."[101]

The hurry is that we are running out of time—and moderate degrees. Pheneas promised that the world would soon boil over, as Canon Liddon described, and Holmes is now helping to make that happen. His power of reasoning backward not only revises the past and distorts the present but also erases the future: wherever climate science is being denied—and fossil fuel is being promoted—you will find him. Attacking the conclusions of the United Nations Intergovernmental Panel on Climate Change (IPCC), the libertarian Heartland Institute quotes Holmes on making the "capital mistake" of theorizing without data: "It applies perfectly to today's global warming debate, especially where the IPCC's scary conclusions and forecasts are involved."[102] Another Heartland article cites the dog that didn't bark to argue that grandstanding Democrats who don't draft bills are "merely using fear of catastrophic climate change to get the support of low-information voters."[103] A commentator at the Cato Institute cites the same dog to explain that all the recent years in which no hurricanes made landfall might add up to evidence that greenhouse gases are in fact good for the weather.[104] And of course you hear the famous dictum everywhere, as climate skeptics try to eliminate the scientific consensus on global warming. For example, one adviser to the Committee for a Constructive Tomorrow takes the dictum as his epigraph before arguing that the scientific consensus is just "doomsday dogma."[105] Once, Holmes helped to cast religion as science; now, he helps to cast science as religion. Environmental scientists can try to turn the tables—publicizing research that "looks at the evidence just as Sherlock Holmes would" and concluding that the case for global warming is "elementary, dear Watson"—but they are only making the same capital mistake as the evolutionary biologists.[106] Science is powerless to change a Sherlockian mind, and so let us eliminate Holmes from our thinking, before nothing on earth remains.

"It is sheer power of mind that does the trick," Christopher Hitchens concluded.[107] After reading Holmes's magazine article even more suspiciously than Watson, we can confirm that Hitchens was right, but for the wrong reasons. Before closing "The Book of Life" and returning it to Doyle's spiritualist library, let's check out its sequel, written between his first and second American lecture tours. In 1922, Princess Marie Louise asked leading authors of the day to contribute one volume apiece to the library of Queen Mary's Dolls' House, a 1:12 scale miniaturization of an Edwardian royal residence, designed, decorated, and furnished in meticulous detail. The Dolls' House itself mirrors the Baker Street universe, home to Doyle's puppets, which perhaps inspired him to play a little game with them. In a fairy-sized book, bound in red leather, Doyle handwrote a five-hundred-word story, "How Watson Learned the Trick." It is what Pope Hill would call the master key; tucked away in a secret place is the story to answer and end all the others.[108]

The tiny book returns us to the breakfast table, where Watson is not reading but "watching his companion intently," until Holmes looks up to ask, "What are you thinking about?" That's a strange question coming from a logician who once claimed to be able to fathom a man's inmost thoughts—the first clue that this Holmes story is not what it seems. "About you," Watson replies, which raises its own question. Why can't Holmes read the mind of someone thinking about him? "I was thinking how superficial are those tricks of yours," Watson elaborates, "and how wonderful it is that the public should continue to show interest in them." It begins to look as if Holmes loses his sheer power of mind as soon as someone starts to see through it. To demonstrate that Holmes's methods "are really easily acquired," Watson explains all that he has observed and deduced. Holmes is unshaven, and thus preoccupied; he has failed a client by the name of Barlow, written on a crumpled envelope in his pocket; he is expecting a visitor, having come to breakfast in a coat rather than a dressing gown; and he has overspeculated in the market, which is why he turned first to the financial page. "There are other people in the world," Watson finishes triumphantly, "who can be as clever as you." But Watson is wrong; the trick is beyond him. "I fear your deductions have not been so happy as I should have wished," says Holmes, explaining that his razor is being sharpened, Barlow is a dentist with whom he has an early appointment, and he was checking the cricket results on the opposite page. However, as the title of the story suggests, Watson may now be starting to see through a different trick: his author's. "People have often asked me whether I knew the end of a Holmes story before I started it," Doyle said in 1924, the same year that the Dolls' House was presented to the queen: "Of course I do."[109] When the story is only five hundred words long, its backward composition must be obvious even to its characters, although there is no room for Watson to make his usual protest. Instead, the last word goes to Holmes, who teases his friend and thereby baits all the other people in the world who continue to show interest in the Science of Deduction and Analysis. "But go on, Watson, go on! It's a very superficial trick, and no doubt you will soon acquire it."

NOTES

Introduction

1. Christopher Hitchens, "The Case of Arthur Conan Doyle," *New York Review of Books*, November 4, 1999, 25.
2. Hitchens, *No One*, 88, 93.
3. Hitchens, "Introduction," 8.
4. Hitchens, "Case of Arthur Conan Doyle," 27.
5. Acord, *Life Lessons*, xiii.
6. Smith, *How to Think*, 10–11.
7. Konnikova, *Mastermind*, 6, 12.
8. Bruce, *Strange Case*, x.
9. O'Brien, *Scientific Sherlock*, xiv.
10. Ibid., 154.
11. Konnikova, *Mastermind*, 230–31.
12. Einstein and Infeld, *Evolution*, 4.
13. *Times*, November 25, 1887, 2.
14. Gardner, "Irrelevance," 188.
15. Doyle, *Vital Message*, 66.
16. Messac, *Le "détective novel,"* 507.
17. McDonald, *British Literary Culture*, 167–68.
18. Pearsall, *Conan Doyle*, 56.
19. Doyle, *Complete Sherlock Holmes*, 23. Hereafter cited parenthetically in the text.

Chapter 1

1. *Times*, December 25, 1887, 9, 13.
2. Momerie, "Christmas Day," 201.
3. "An Event," *Times*, November 3, 1887, 9.
4. "The Consecration of Truro Cathedral," *Times*, November 4, 1887, 7.
5. "England and the Vatican," *Times*, December 24, 1887, 5.
6. "Pope Leo XIII," 144; "The Bishop of London and Ritualism," *Times*, December 6, 1887, 7.
7. "The Church Association," *Times*, November 4, 1887, 5.
8. Arthur Conan Doyle, "The Unionist Platform," *Evening News* (Portsmouth, UK), July 6, 1886, 2.

9. Gladstone, *Liberal Programme*, 9.
10. Burleigh, "Attack," 869.
11. "Lord Salisbury at Oxford," *Times*, November 24, 1887, 6.
12. "Sir G. Trevelyan in Denbighshire," *Times*, November 1, 1887, 7.
13. "Lord Salisbury at Oxford," 6.
14. "Lord Selborne on Church Defence," *Times*, December 7, 1887, 6.
15. "Sir G. Trevelyan in Denbighshire," 7.
16. Review of *A Defence of the Church*, 468.
17. Dunkley, *Official Report*, 12, 20.
18. Ibid., 325–26.
19. "The Church Congress," *Times*, October 8, 1887, 9.
20. Dunkley, *Official Report*, 328, 347, 351.
21. Isaac Taylor, "Islam," *Times*, October 26, 1887, 4; Isaac Taylor, "The Progress of Islam II," *Times*, October 31, 1887, 13.
22. "The Letter on Islam," *Times*, October 31, 1887, 9.
23. Malcolm MacColl, "To the Editor," *Times*, November 7, 1887, 13.
24. Isaac Taylor, "The Progress of Islam IV," *Times*, November 17, 1887, 13.
25. MacColl, *Eastern Question*, 380.
26. Review of *On the Track of the Crescent*, by Edmund Cecil Johnson, *Vanity Fair*, July 10, 1886, 28.
27. Taylor, "Progress of Islam IV," 13.
28. Malcolm MacColl, "Bean-Bag Versus Impalement," *Times*, November 23, 1887, 4.
29. Henry Liddon, "Canon Taylor on Islam," *Times*, November 21, 1887, 6.
30. MacColl, "Bean-Bag Versus Impalement," 4.
31. Dunkley, *Official Report*, 411–23.
32. Henry Liddon, "Canon Taylor on Islam," *Times*, November 21, 1887, 6.
33. John Stuart-Glennie, "To the Editor," *Times*, November 23, 1887, 4.
34. A. R. Fairfield, "To the Editor," *Times*, December 5, 1887, 4.

35. Henry Liddon, "To the Editor," *Times*, December 9, 1887, 3; Malcolm MacColl, "To the Editor," *Times*, December 9, 1887, 4; "What the Canons Saw," *Times*, December 9, 1887, 4.

36. *Times*, November 25, 1887, 2.

37. Dunkley, *Official Report*, 19, 412.

38. *Times*, December 21, 1887, 2.

39. Ibid., 3.

40. "The Constitution of the Heavenly Bodies," *Times*, November 18, 1887, 13.

41. "Middlesex Natural History Society," *Times*, November 9, 1887, 10.

42. [Allen], "Fossil," 259; Garnett, "Contemporary Record," 600; "Contemporary Literature," 1164.

43. Proctor, "Gossip," 18.

44. Elmslie, "First Chapter," 815.

45. Dunkley, *Official Report*, 417.

46. "The Miraculous Statue at Saint Lo," *All the Year Round*, October 29, 1887, 371.

47. Dunkley, *Official Report*, 417.

48. *Times*, November 5, 1887, 13.

49. Castelar, "Papacy," 676.

50. Willert, "Service," 58.

51. Ward, "Positivism," 404.

52. "London Sunday Forum," *Pall Mall Gazette*, November 30, 1887, 2.

53. Rossiter, "Artisan Atheism," 120.

54. Gladstone, *Liberal Programme*, 21.

55. "The Party of License and the Party of Law," *Times*, November 1, 1887, 8.

56. Churchill, *Lord Randolph Churchill*, 128.

57. "Sir G. Trevelyan in Denbighshire," 7.

58. "London Sunday Forum," 2–3.

59. "The Defence of Trafalgar-Square," *Times*, November 14, 1887, 6.

60. "To the Editor," *Times*, November 14, 1887, 7.

61. Dunkley, *Official Report*, 413.

62. "To the Editor," *Times*, November 7, 1887, 13.

63. "Echoes of the Pulpit," *Pall Mall Gazette*, December 6, 1886, 11.

64. Ruskin, *Works*, 115.

65. [Allen], "Fossil," 258.

66. Elmslie, "First Chapter," 815–17, 829.

67. Geikie, "Life and Letters," 768.

68. "The Life of Darwin," *Times*, November 19, 1887, 7.

69. "Charles Darwin," 1144–45.

70. "The Life of Darwin," 7.

71. "The Late Mr. Darwin," *Illustrated London News*, December 10, 1887, 686.

72. Argyll, "Power," 760.

73. Argyll, *Unity of Nature*, 438–39, 275.

74. Paley, *Natural Theology*, 16.

75. Bradlaugh, "Is There a God?," 8.

76. Argyll, "Power," 756, 748, 758.

77. Quoted in Darwin, *Life and Letters*, 536.

78. Reginald Wilberforce, "Professor Huxley," *Times*, November 29, 1887, 10; Thomas Huxley, "Bishop Wilberforce and Professor Huxley," *Times*, December 1, 1887, 8.

79. "Echoes of the Pulpit," 11.

80. Huxley, "Scientific and Pseudo-Scientific Realism," 200, 194.

81. Ibid., 197–98, 202–3.

82. Argyll, "Professor Huxley," 328, 331, 334–35.

83. Clay, "Eclipse," 882.

84. Chamier, "Philosophy," 1151, 1159.

85. Review of *The Unity of Nature*, 807.

86. Argyll, "Professor Huxley," 338.

87. Huxley, "Science and Pseudo-Science," 497.

88. Tyndall, *Scientific Use*, 31.

89. Huxley, "Science and Pseudo-Science," 498.

90. Argyll, "Great Lesson," 294, 308.

91. Ward, "Positivism," 404.

92. Huxley, "Science and the Bishops," 639.

93. Argyll, "Power," 760, 764.

94. Huxley, "Science and the Bishops," 625.

95. "Short Reviews," 156.

96. Poole, "Date of the Pentateuch," 350–51.

97. Ibid., 357, 369.

98. "Recent Explorations," 50, 57.

99. Smith, "Archeology," 490, 502, 500.

100. Spurgeon, "Another Word," 397.

101. Wilson, *Essays and Addresses*, 119, 90.

102. Ibid., 113; "Short Reviews," 174.

103. Ebrard, *Apologetics*, 1:xiii, 3:322.

104. Illingworth, "Contemporary Records," 896.

105. Mivart, "Modern Catholics," 47, 35, 41.

106. Mivart, "Catholic Church," 41, 46, 48.

107. Stephen, "Mr. Mivart's Modern Catholicism," 591, 590, 600.

108. Mivart, "Catholicity and Reason," 859, 856.

109. Stephen, "Rejoinder," 115, 119, 125, 123, 121.

110. Mivart, "Catholicity and Reason," 869.

111. Mivart, "Sins of Belief," 560, 561.
112. Mivart, "Happiness in Hell," 899, 918.
113. Mivart, *On the Genesis*, 3.
114. Mivart, review of *The Descent*, 87, 52.
115. Huxley, "Mr. Darwin's Critics," 458.
116. Huxley, "On the Method of Zadig," 931.
117. Doyle, *Memories*, 31.
118. Huxley, "On the Method of Zadig," 932.

Chapter 2

1. Doyle, *Memories*, 32.
2. Doyle, *Our Second American Adventure*, 244.
3. Doyle, *Memories*, 20, 31–32, 83.
4. Ibid., 32–33.
5. Cook, "Does Death," 298.
6. Lellenberg, Stashower, and Foley, *Life in Letters*, 121.
7. Doyle, "Life and Death," 181.
8. Arthur Conan Doyle, "The 'New' Scientific Subject," *British Journal of Photography*, July 20, 1883, 418.
9. William Warner, "A New Scientific Subject," *British Journal of Photography*, July 27, 1883, 440.
10. Arthur Conan Doyle, "The Portsmouth Young Men's Christian Association and Their Rev. Critic," *Evening News* (Portsmouth, UK), March 27, 1884, 2.
11. Doyle, *Narrative*, 46–47.
12. Lellenberg, Stashower, and Foley, *Life in Letters*, 224.
13. Doyle, "My First Book," 637–38.
14. Doyle, *Narrative*, 105–8.
15. Lellenberg, Stashower, and Foley, *Life in Letters*, 224.
16. Burrow, "Gothic Materialism," 313.
17. Doyle, *Narrative*, 65, 91.
18. "Brief Notices," 667.
19. "The Last Glacial Epoch," *Nature*, August 14, 1873, 301.
20. Drayson, *Great Britain*, 53.
21. Alfred Drayson, "The Solution of Scientific Problems by Spirits," *Light*, November 29, 1884, 499.
22. Doyle, *Memories*, 85.
23. Viswanathan, "Ordinary Business," 5–6.
24. [Blavatsky], "What's in a Name?," 6.
25. Sinnett, "Invisible World," 186–87.

26. [Blavatsky], "'Lucifer' to the Archbishop," 243.
27. Doyle, *Memories*, 86.
28. "Report of the Committee," 207.
29. Doyle, *Memories*, 87.
30. Johnston, "Emerson and Occultism," 255–56.
31. Lang, "At the Sign," 234.
32. Sinnett, "Invisible World," 192.
33. Doyle, *Memories*, 86–87.
34. Ellis, "Infant Genius," 296–98.
35. Oppenheim, *Other World*, 7–27.
36. Kerr, *Conan Doyle*, 221.
37. Cottom, *Abyss of Reason*, 27.
38. Luckhurst, *Invention of Telepathy*, 29.
39. Tyndall, "Science and the 'Spirits,'" 504; Huxley quoted in Sword, *Ghostwriting*, 4.
40. Lamont, "Spiritualism," 918.
41. [Blavatsky], "Literary Jottings," 75.
42. Innes, "Where Are the Letters?," 189, 193.
43. "New Books," *Illustrated London News*, November 26, 1887, 629; "Trying the Spirits," 658.
44. Doyle, *Memories*, 83, 86.
45. Arthur Conan Doyle, "A Test Message," *Light*, July 2, 1887, 303.
46. Lycett, *Man Who Created*, 140.
47. Arthur Conan Doyle, "Mr. Hodgson," *Light*, August 27, 1887, 404.
48. Lycett, *Man Who Created*, 141.
49. Arthur Conan Doyle, "A New Revelation," *Light*, November 4, 1916, 357–58.
50. Lamond, *Arthur Conan Doyle*, 38; Pearson, *Conan Doyle*, 172; Carr, *Life*, 255–56; Nordon, *Conan Doyle*, 139, 144; Stashower, *Teller of Tales*, 99; Miller, *Adventures*, 358.
51. Christopher Hitchens, "The Case of Arthur Conan Doyle," *New York Review of Books*, November 4, 1999, 27.
52. [Blavatsky], "Signs of the Times," 83; Doyle, "Test Message," 303.
53. Nordon, *Conan Doyle*, 247; Lightman, "Ideal Reasoner," 29, 32.
54. Frank, *Victorian Detective Fiction*, 143.
55. Sinnett, "Invisible World," 191.
56. Doyle, *Narrative*, 90.
57. Illingworth, "Contemporary Records," 896.
58. Chamier, "Philosophy," 1152.
59. [Collins], "Comments," 9.
60. Doyle, *Narrative*, 61–62.

61. [Blavatsky], "Great Paradox," 120.

62. Quoted in Green, *Sherlock Holmes Letters*, 61.

63. "A New Novelist," *Hampshire Telegraph*, December 3, 1887, 11.

64. Arthur Conan Doyle, *A Study in Scarlet* (London: Ward, Lock, 1888), v.

65. Morley, *Sherlock Holmes*, 2; Barzun, "Detection and the Literary Art," 13; Estleman, "Introduction," xiv; Jaffe, *Arthur Conan Doyle*, 36.

66. McLaughlin, *Writing*, 32.

67. Lecourt, "Mormons," 96–97.

68. Thomas, *Detective Fiction*, 227–28; Fillingham, "Colorless Skein," 685; Agathocleous, "London Mysteries," 144.

69. "In the Name of the Prophet—Smith!," *Household Words*, July 19, 1851, 385.

70. Reynolds, "Our New Religions," 435.

71. Cleere, "Chaste Polygamy," 201.

72. Burton, *City*, 1.

73. Barclay, "New View," 183.

74. [Charlton], *Notes of a Trip*, 49–51.

75. "Portsmouth Literary and Scientific Society," *Hampshire Telegraph*, April 4, 1885, 2.

76. Doyle, *Narrative*, 88.

77. "Spirit Rapping," *National Miscellany*, May 5, 1853, 129.

78. Owen, *Darkened Room*, 35–39.

79. Homer, "Arthur Conan Doyle," 73, 68.

80. Givens, *Viper*, 82.

81. Burton, *City*, 410, 385.

82. Marshall, "Characteristics," 692, 697, 699.

83. McMurrin, *Theological Foundations*, 2.

84. Sword, *Ghostwriting*, 18.

85. Burton, *City*, 398.

86. Robinson, *Sinners and Saints*, 199, 204–5.

87. Burton, *City*, 398.

88. Dilke, *Greater Britain*, 149–50.

89. Dixon, *New America*, 254–55.

90. Burton, *City*, 410, 261.

91. Dixon, *New America*, 188.

92. Burton, *City*, 386, 410.

93. Ibid., 362.

94. Hardy, *Through Cities*, 120.

95. Chandless, *Visit*, 159–60.

96. Ibid., 157; Conybeare, "Mormonism," 374.

97. Brigham Young, "Hearken, O Ye Latter-Day Saints," *Deseret News*, August 23, 1865, 373.

98. Burton, *City*, 441.

99. Dilke, *Greater Britain*, 150, 159.

100. Quoted in Homer, *On the Way*, 79, 158.

101. "In the Name of the Prophet—Smith!," 385.

102. Baudrillard, *Simulacra*, 1–2.

103. Ward, "Positivism," 404.

104. Doyle, "True Story," 346–47.

105. Doyle, *Memories*, 75.

106. Quoted in Green, *Letters*, 60.

107. Quoted in ibid.

108. "Jottings," *Light*, July 14, 1888, 339.

109. Quoted in Green, *Letters*, 63–64.

110. Weber, *Protestant Ethic*, 181.

111. Calhoon, "Detective," 317, 326.

112. Atkinson, *Secret Marriage*, 117.

113. Saler, *As If*, 117.

114. Eliot, "Sherlock," 553, 556.

115. Auden, "Guilty Vicarage," 412, 410.

116. Kissane and Kissane, "Sherlock Holmes," 358, 360.

117. Nordon, *Conan Doyle*, 247.

118. Jann, *Adventures*, 3; Frank, *Victorian Detective Fiction*, 155.

119. Bailey, "Sherlock Holmes," 69.

120. Kern, *Cultural History*, 104.

121. Knight, *Form and Ideology*, 105.

122. Alewyn, "Origin of the Detective Novel," 70.

123. Eagleton, "Flight to the Real," 17–18.

124. Engels, "Natural Science," 308.

125. Ibid., 309.

126. Stephen, "Mr. Mivart's Modern Catholicism," 591.

Chapter 3

1. "Advice to Inquirers," *Light*, January 8, 1887, 24.

2. Huxley, "Scientific and Pseudo-Scientific Realism," 200.

3. Arthur Conan Doyle, "A Test Message," *Light*, July 2, 1887, 303.

4. Doyle, *Micah Clarke*, 221–22.

5. Arthur Conan Doyle, "The Mystery of Cloomber—Chapter XV, Continued," *Pall Mall Gazette*, September 28, 1888, 14.

6. "Local Topics," *Hampshire Telegraph*, September 29, 1888, 5.

7. "The Whitechapel Murders," *Chat* (Portsmouth, UK), November 23, 1888, 7.

8. Quoted in Stavert, *Study in Southsea*, 145–47.

9. "Mr. Shutte's Critic," *Evening News* (Portsmouth, UK), November 20, 1889, 2.

10. Doyle, *Narrative*, 112.

11. "Witches and Witchcraft," *Hampshire Telegraph*, April 5, 1890, 6.

12. Lycett, *Man Who Created*, 160.

13. Ferraris, *Manifesto*, 45–46.

14. Galvan, *Sympathetic Medium*, 146.

15. Most, "Hippocratic Smile," 349.

16. "Conan Doyle on Screen," *New York Times*, May 26, 1929, X4.

17. Ronell, *Stupidity*, 5, 37.

18. Agassi, "Detective Novel," 104, 108.

19. Smith, *Fact and Feeling*, 235–36.

20. Doyle, "Test Message," 303.

21. Steven Byington, "An Introduction to the Book of James," *Liberty* 14, no. 15, November 1903, 5.

22. Arthur Conan Doyle, "The 'New' Scientific Subject," *British Journal of Photography*, July 20, 1883, 418.

23. Tyndall, "Miracles," 649.

24. Blathwayt, "Talk," 50.

25. How, "Day," 186.

26. Quoted in Liebow, *Dr. Joe Bell*, 172.

27. Lellenberg, Stashower, and Foley, *Life in Letters*, 300, 305, 319.

28. Doyle, *Narrative*, 47–48.

29. Lellenberg, Stashower, and Foley, *Life in Letters*, 324.

30. Doyle, *Stark Munro*, 158.

31. Lellenberg, Stashower, and Foley, *Life in Letters*, 326, 358.

32. Doyle, *Stark Munro*, 193.

33. Lellenberg, Stashower, and Foley, *Life in Letters*, 332.

34. Meikle, "Over There," 24.

35. Doyle, *Memories*, 239.

36. Doyle and Stansbury, "In Quest of Truth," 9.

37. Stansbury, *In Quest of Truth*, 150–51, 258.

38. Frank, "Hound," 348.

39. Clausson, "Degeneration," 76; Taylor-Ide, "Ritual," 55.

40. Neill, *Primitive Minds*, 136, 149.

41. Smajić, *Ghost-Seers*, 132–35.

42. Ibid., 134.

43. Kerr, *Conan Doyle*, 225–33.

44. Nichols, "Ungrateful Father," 382, 380.

45. Doyle and Stansbury, "In Quest of Truth," 14, 21.

46. Ibid., 12, 15–18, 22.

47. Sword, *Ghostwriting*, 3.

48. Lodge, *Raymond*, 126, 184, 197.

49. Arthur Conan Doyle to Lily Loder-Symonds, May 15, 1915 (BL).

50. Doyle and Stansbury, "In Quest of Truth," 20.

51. Arthur Conan Doyle, "The New Revelation," *Light*, November 4, 1916, 357.

52. Doyle, "Some Personalia," 533–35.

53. Doyle, *New Revelation*, 50, 33–34.

54. Doyle, "New Revelation," 358.

55. Doyle, *New Revelation*, 71.

56. Doyle, *Vital Message*, 96.

57. Ibid., 62; Doyle, *History of Spiritualism*, 185.

58. Doyle, *Wanderings*, 168–69.

59. Doyle, "Test Message," 303.

60. Doyle, "New Revelation," 357.

61. Cottom, *Abyss of Reason*, 42.

62. Doyle, *Vital Message*, 214.

63. Doyle, *New Revelation*, 43.

64. Doyle, *Wanderings*, 54, 61.

65. Ibid., 16.

66. Doyle, *New Revelation*, 71.

67. Doyle, *Vital Message*, 66.

68. Doyle, *New Revelation*, 101.

69. Sword, *Ghostwriting*, 13.

70. Doyle, *History of Spiritualism*, 307.

71. Doyle, *New Revelation*, 94, 36, 91.

72. Joseph Jastrow, "Conan Doyle, Spiritualist, on Tour," *Independent and Weekly Review*, April 29, 1922, 416.

73. Rational Press Association, *Verbatim Report*, 29, 39.

74. McCabe, "Scientific Men," 446.

75. Doyle, *Spiritualism and Rationalism*, 7, 23.

76. Ibid., 4, 5, 7, 21.

77. Ibid., 3, 19.

78. McCabe, *Spiritualism*, 238.

79. E. T. Raymond, "Sir Arthur Conan Doyle and His Spooks," *Living Age*, January 3, 1920, 33.

80. Laqueur, "Why the Margins," 121.

81. McCabe, *Spiritualism*, 239.

82. Lamond, *Arthur Conan Doyle*, 172.

83. James Douglas, "Is Conan Doyle Mad?," *Sunday Express*, September 25, 1921, 6.

84. Raymond, "Sir Arthur Conan Doyle and His Spooks," 32.

85. Heywood Broun, "It Seems to Heywood Broun," *The Nation*, September 21, 1927, 277.

86. "'Jack the Ripper': How 'Sherlock Holmes' Would Have Tracked Him," *Evening News* (Portsmouth, UK), July 4, 1894, 2; Doyle, "Uncharted Coast," 74.

87. Arthur Conan Doyle, "Sir A. Conan Doyle and Christie Case," *Morning Post* (London), December 20, 1926, 4.

88. Raymond, "Sir Arthur Conan Doyle and His Spooks," 32.

89. Eliot, "Sherlock Holmes," 554.

90. Lamond, *Arthur Conan Doyle*, 38.

91. Crocombe, "World's Happiest Museum," 455.

92. "The Psychic Museum," *Daily News* (London), December 7, 1925, 7; Arthur Conan Doyle, "The Psychic 'Gloves,'" *Daily News* (London), December 9, 1925, 3.

93. Doyle, *Memories*, 395–96.

94. Tyndall, "Miracles," 649.

95. Doyle, *New Revelation*, 79.

96. Doyle, *Our American Adventure*, 19.

97. Lycett, *Man Who Created*, 432.

98. Eagleton, "Flight to the Real," 17.

99. Doyle, *Coming of the Fairies*, 32, 41.

100. Doyle, *New Revelation*, 39.

101. Doyle, *Narrative*, 41, 105.

102. Doyle, *Memories*, 396.

103. Doyle, *New Revelation*, 48.

104. Doyle, *Narrative*, 88–89.

105. Doyle, *Our Second American*, 91, 92, 99, 101, 104.

106. Ibid., 89; "Conan Doyle's London Church," *Reynold's News*, August 26, 1923, 2.

107. Arthur Conan Doyle, "Spiritualism and Christian Evidence," *Sydney Morning Herald*, November 20, 1920, 13.

108. Quoted in Byrne, *Modern Spiritualism*, 55.

109. Arnold Pinchard to Arthur Conan Doyle, July 5, 1920 (BL).

110. Doyle, *Our Reply*, 6.

111. Lellenberg, Stashower, and Foley, *Life in Letters*, 656.

112. "Houdini Hits Conan Doyle," *Los Angeles Times*, October 28, 1924, 17.

113. Doyle, "Houdini the Enigma," 270.

114. Doyle, *Pheneas Speaks*, 26–27.

115. Meikle, "Over There," 28.

116. Doyle, *Pheneas Speaks*, 126.

117. Susan Morrison to Arthur Conan Doyle, October 4, 1927 (BL).

118. Lycett, *Man Who Created*, 439.

119. Nelson, *Spiritualism and Society*, 149.

120. "Spiritualists and the Hidden Hand," *Daily Express*, May 4, 1925, 8.

121. Hazelgrove, *Spiritualism and British Society*, 19.

122. "Father Vaughan and Spiritualism," *Pall Mall Gazette*, June 11, 1917, 5.

123. Quoted in Kollar, "Spiritualism and Religion," 408.

124. Doyle, *Roman Catholic Church*, 5.

125. "Other Armistice Meetings," *Light*, November 23, 1929, 555.

126. Meikle, "Over There," 35.

127. Doyle, *Word of Warning*, 4.

128. Doyle, *Pheneas Speaks*, 78.

129. Meikle, "Over There," 36.

130. "Doyle Predicts a Disaster," *New York Times*, September 17, 1925, 34.

131. Doyle, *Pheneas Speaks*, 183.

132. Meikle, "Over There," 37.

133. "Conan Doyle on Screen," X4.

Chapter 4

1. "Conan Doyle Dead from Heart Attack," *New York Times*, July 8, 1930, 1.

2. "Sir Arthur Conan Doyle's Resignation," 47.

3. William Barrett, "Sir Arthur Conan Doyle and Psychical Research," *Light*, November 11, 1916, 365.

4. "Sir Arthur Conan Doyle's Resignation," 46.

5. Nelson, *Spiritualism and Society*, 159.

6. Doyle, *What Does Spiritualism*, 6.

7. Letters to Arthur Conan Doyle from Flora Waddington, June 17, 1919; Abbie Farr, September 6, 1919; Eli Darrow, February 4, 1922; B. Amos, June 26, 1928; and F. Ballantine, n.d. (HRC).

8. "'Sees' Conan Doyle at London Service," *New York Times*, July 14, 1930, 1, 14.

9. "Conan Doyle Dead from Heart Attack," 9.

10. Nelson, *Spiritualism and Society*, 255.

11. Viswanathan, "Ordinary Business," 9.

12. "'Message' from Doyle," *New York Times*, July 11, 1930, 6.

13. "Spirit Messages Real, Lady Doyle Insists," *New York Times*, July 31, 1930, 8.

14. "Lady Conan Doyle on Spiritualism," *Singapore Free Press*, September 30, 1930, 4.

15. Grace Cooke to Jean Conan Doyle, November 13, 1930 (HRC).

16. "Sir Arthur Conan Doyle and the End of the World," *Times*, July 3, 1931, 4.

17. "Spiritists Wear Gay Attire at Doyle Funeral," *New York Times*, July 12, 1930, 1; Price, "Return," 10.

18. Jean Conan Doyle to *Evening Standard*, July 11, 1930 (HRC).

19. "Conan Doyle Dead from Heart Attack," 9.

20. Horace Leaf to Jean Conan Doyle, August 20, 1930 (HRC).

21. Garland, *Forty Years*, 388.

22. O'Neill, *Spiritualism*, 129.

23. Price, "Return," 94.

24. Séance notes, October 25, 1930 (HRC).

25. "My Husband Comes Back," *Liberty*, June 6, 1931, 18.

26. "Conan Doyle Dead from Heart Attack," 9.

27. "Conan Doyle Comes Through," *Daily Sketch*, October 11, 1932, 5.

28. "Spirit Messages Real, Lady Doyle Insists," 8.

29. Quoted in Lamond, *Arthur Conan Doyle*, 273.

30. Doyle, "Alleged," 723, 725, 721.

31. Doyle, *Edge of the Unknown*, 152.

32. "My Husband Comes Back," 18.

33. "Conan Doyle Comes Through," 5.

34. "Conan Doyle Still of the Family Council," *Daily Sketch*, October 12, 1932, 5, 16.

35. "My Husband Comes Back," 18.

36. "Medium Whose Séances Baffled Scientists Quits Profession," *New York Times*, April 9, 1931, 1; "Resents Medium's Story," *New York Times*, April 10, 1931, 3.

37. Robert Gower to Jean Conan Doyle, April 14, 1931 (PL).

38. Charles Tweedale to Jean Conan Doyle, January 21, January 28, February 12, and April 8, 1931 (PL).

39. T. A. R. Purchas to Jean Conan Doyle, May 5 and August 24, 1931 (PL); Jean Conan Doyle to T. A. R. Purchas, July 22, 1931 (HRC).

40. Quoted in Cooke, *"Thy Kingdom Come,"* 31.

41. Ibid., 77.

42. Ivan Cooke to Jean Conan Doyle, June 3, 1931 (HRC).

43. Cooke, *"Thy Kingdom Come,"* 88–89, 149, 161.

44. Ibid., 121.

45. Cooke, *Return*, ix.

46. "'Spirit Voices' Heard in Plane in Flight," *New York Times*, March 22, 1935, 5.

47. "Lady Doyle's Protest," *Two Worlds*, April 26, 1935, 269.

48. "Alleged Séance Deceptions," *Times*, March 31, 1944, 2.

49. "Lady Conan Doyle, Widow of Author," *New York Times*, June 28, 1940, 19.

50. Denis Conan Doyle to Jean Conan Doyle, April 29, 1938 (PL).

51. Knight, *Form and Ideology*, 105.

52. J. M. Barrie, "My Evening with Sherlock Holmes," *The Speaker*, November 28, 1891, 643–44; "The Real Sherlock Holmes," *National Observer*, October 29, 1892, 606–7.

53. Knox, *Caliban*, 191, 183.

54. Sayers, *Unpopular Opinions*, 7.

55. Knox, "Studies," 148, 159.

56. "Sherlockholmitos," *Times Literary Supplement*, October 27, 1932, 782.

57. Starrett, *Private Life*, 105.

58. Darwin, "Sherlockiana," 87–88.

59. Quoted in Nieminski and Lellenberg, *"Dear Starrett,"* 66.

60. Quoted in Lellenberg, *Irregular Memories*, 166, 175.

61. Smith, *Profile*, 291.

62. Quoted in Lellenberg, *Irregular Memories*, 141, 205.

63. Quoted in ibid., 175; Smith, "Notes," xxiii.

64. Smith, *Profile*, 156.

65. Starrett, "Introduction," 10.

66. Starrett, *221B*, xi.

67. Denis Conan Doyle to Jean Conan Doyle, February 10, 1940 (PL).

68. Pearson, *Conan Doyle*, vii.

69. Doyle, *Wanderings*, 98.

70. Pearson, *Conan Doyle*, 87.

71. "Sherlock Holmes's Identity," *Times*, October 28, 1943, 2.

72. Quoted in Lamond, *Arthur Conan Doyle*, 280.

73. Doyle, *True Conan Doyle*, 14.

74. Carr, *Life*, 194.

75. Lantagne, "Sherlock Holmes," 314.

76. Quoted in Lellenberg, *Irregular Proceedings*, 294, 25.

77. Doyle and Carr, *Exploits*, 4.

78. *Late Night Line-Up*, BBC2, aired April 8, 1969, video, 20:40, Arthur Conan Doyle Encyclopedia, https://www.arthur-conan -doyle.com/index.php/Interview_of_Adrian _Conan_Doyle_at_Lucens_Castle.

79. Poore, "Sherlock Holmes and the Leap of Faith," 159.

80. "Sir Arthur Conan Doyle," Spiritualists' National Union, https://www.snu.org.uk/sir -arthur-conan-doyle.

81. "Publishing Shop," White Eagle Lodge, https://www.whiteagle.org/shop/books /white-eagle-publishing-book-list.

82. "Who Are We?," Conan Doyle Estate, https://arthurconandoyle.co.uk/about.

83. Wojton and Porter, *Sherlock and Digital Fandom*, 29.

84. Hill, *Part One*, 26–27.

85. Hill, *Sherlock Holmes Hoax*, 20.

86. Hill, *Part One*, 27; Adrian Conan Doyle to E. W. MacAlpine, December 13, 1953 (BL).

87. Quoted in Lellenberg, *Irregular Crises*, 48, 347.

88. "Heads or Tails Run Even in 40,000 Flips of a Penny," *New York Times*, October 24, 1933, 26; "Heads or Tails," *New York Times*, June 10, 1934, E4.

89. Hill, *Part One*, 18.

90. Hill, "Final Problem," 149.

91. Wiltse, "So Constant," 119.

92. Sayers, *Unpopular Opinions*, 7–8.

93. Clausen, "Sherlock Holmes," 105.

94. Wiltse, "So Constant," 119.

95. Stein and Busse, "Introduction," 16.

96. Quoted in Lellenberg, *Irregular Crises*, 347.

97. Barthes, "Death of the Author," 146.

98. Foucault, "What Is an Author?," 159.

99. Wimsatt and Beardsley, "Intentional Fallacy," 469, 487.

100. Barthes, "Death of the Author," 146–47.

101. Foucault, "What Is an Author?," 144.

102. Foucault, "Pouvoir et savoir," 404.

103. Knox, "Studies," 145.

104. Buurma and Heffernan, "Interpretation," 619.

105. Knox, "Studies," 146.

106. Ibid., 151, 169.

107. Barthes, "Death of the Author," 148.

108. Brandt, "How Far," 60–61; Graff, *Professing Literature*, 67–68.

109. Tupper, "Textual Criticism," 165, 168–69.

110. Frederick Tupper, "Chaucer and Sherlock," *The Nation*, September 21, 1927, 289–90.

111. Eliot, *Sacred Wood*, 12, 53.

112. Eliot, "Function," 40–41.

113. Eliot, "Sherlock Holmes," 554, 556.

114. Eliot, "Experiment," 229.

115. Schryer, "Fantasies," 665.

116. Kopec, "Digital Humanities," 329.

117. Eliot, "Frontiers," 532–33, 543.

118. Garratt, *Victorian Empiricism*, 198.

119. Macherey, *Theory of Literary Production*, 5.

120. Jameson, "On Raymond Chandler," 645.

121. Lacan, "Seminar," 49.

122. Jameson, "On Raymond Chandler," 645.

123. Belsey, *Critical Practice*, 138–39.

124. Ibid., 111, 116.

125. Jann, "Sherlock Holmes Codes," 705.

126. Thomas, "Fingerprint," 656.

127. Barsham, *Arthur Conan Doyle*, 101.

128. White, "Historical Pluralism," 484.

129. Tucker, "Introduction," ix.

130. Ginzburg, "Clues," 91.

131. Ibid., 109–10.

132. Menand, *Metaphysical Club*, 228–30.

133. Klein and Keller, "Deductive Detective Fiction," 167.

134. Truzzi, "Sherlock Holmes," 70–71.

135. Eco, "Horns, Hooves, Insteps," 217, 220.

136. Mahaffey, *Modernist Literature*, 80.

137. Siddiqi, *Anxieties of Empire*, 15–16.

138. Klein, "Future," 922–23.

139. Moretti, *Distant Reading*, 48.

140. Felski, "After Suspicion," 29; Felski, "Suspicious Minds," 229.

141. Best and Marcus, "Surface Reading," 18.

142. Ibid., 18.

143. Freedgood, *Ideas in Things*, 151–52.

144. Love, "Close Reading," 404.

145. Rooney, "Live Free," 125.

146. Lee, "Evidence, Coincidence," 89.

147. Moretti, *Signs Taken*, 24, 27, 149.

148. Moretti, *Graphs, Maps, Trees*, 57.

149. James English, "Morettian Picaresque," *Los Angeles Review of Books*, June 27, 2013, https://lareviewofbooks.org/article/franco -morettis-distant-reading-a-symposium.

150. Moretti, *Distant Reading*, 75.

151. Allison et al., "Quantitative Formalism," 25.

152. Moretti, *Distant Reading*, 48.

153. Gottschall, *Literature*, 3.

154. Zunshine, *Why We Read Fiction*, 125, 141.

155. Vermeule, *Why Do We Care*, 56, xii.

156. Gottschall, *Storytelling Animal*, 102.

157. Levine, *One Culture*, 5.

158. Latour, *Aramis*, 2, 277.

159. Latour, *Reassembling the Social*, 52.

160. Gross and Levitt, *Higher Superstition*, 45.

161. Takanashi, "Sherlock's 'Brain Attic,'" 261–62.

Chapter 5

1. "Notes of a Sitting with Mrs. Scales," August 31, 1929 (HRC).

2. Cooke, *"Thy Kingdom Come,"* 157.

3. Eagleton, *Event of Literature*, 108.

4. Fred Kroon and Alberto Voltolini, "Fictional Entities," in *Stanford Encyclopedia of Philosophy*, Stanford University, 1997–, article published November 6, 2018, https://plato .stanford.edu/archives/win2018/entries /fictional-entities.

5. Dennett, "Why and How," 8.

6. Argyll, "Great Lesson," 308.

7. Cottom, *Abyss of Reason*, 37.

8. Tyndall, "Science and the 'Spirits,'" 503.

9. "Woman Seeks Death to Be a Spirit Guide," *New York Times*, April 15, 1922, 1.

10. "Topics of the Times," *New York Times*, April 17, 1922, 16.

11. Rouse, "To the Editor," 116.

12. Dunkley, *Official Report*, 12.

13. Doyle, "Some Personalia," 534.

14. Forrest and Gross, *Creationism's Trojan Horse*, 6, 9.

15. "Notes," 315.

16. Behe, *Darwin's Black Box*, 72.

17. Dembski and Witt, *Intelligent Design Uncensored*, 59.

18. Sober, "What Is Wrong," 3.

19. "Departmental Position on Evolution and 'Intelligent Design,'" Biological Sciences,

Lehigh University, https://www.lehigh.edu /~inbios/News/evolution.html.

20. Denton, *Evolution*, 155.

21. Hartwig and Meyer, "Note," 155.

22. Thaxton, "New Design Argument," 21; David Klinghoffer, "The Curious Incident of the Non-Rafting Foxes," *Evolution News*, April 28, 2016, https://evolutionnews.org/2016/04 /the_curious_inc.

23. Doyle and Stansbury, "In Quest of Truth," 21.

24. Dembski, *Design Revolution*, 220, 141.

25. Berlinski, *Devil's Delusion*, 149; Michael Denton, "Aristotle Rediscovered," *Evolution News*, April 21, 2015, https://evolutionnews.org /2015/04/aristotle_redis.

26. Kendrick, *Holy Clues*, 23.

27. Hartwig and Meyer, "Note," 155.

28. Meyer, *Signature in the Cell*, 325.

29. Clancy, *Teaching*, 28.

30. Edward Sisson, "Prominent Atheist Professor of Law and Philosophy Thomas Nagel Calls Intelligent Design Scientific," *Evolution News*, September 2, 2008, https://evolution news.org/2008/09/prominent_atheist_pro fessor_of.

31. Chuck Colson, "Sherlock Holmes Knew What Not to Do," BreakPoint, January 31, 2000, accessed December 1, 2011, http://thepoint .breakpoint.org/bpcommentaries/entry/13 /12438.

32. Dembski, *Design Inference*, 23.

33. O'Leary, *By Design*, 197.

34. Collins, *Science and Faith*, 352.

35. Seiglie, "Intelligent Design," 16–17.

36. Denyse O'Leary, "Why Is Origin of Life Such a Difficult Problem?," *Post-Darwinist* (blog), February 1, 2006, http://post-darwin ist.blogspot.com/2006_02_01_archive.html.

37. Huxley, "On the Method of Zadig," 935.

38. "Evolution, Creationism, Intelligent Design," Gallup, https://news.gallup.com /poll/21814/evolution-creationism-intelligent -design.aspx.

39. Nicholas Matzke, "The Evolution of Antievolution Policies after *Kitzmiller v. Dover*," *Science*, January 1, 2016, 30.

40. "*Kitzmiller* Trial Transcripts: Day 1 PM," National Center for Science Education, https://ncse.ngo/files/pub/legal/kitzmiller /trial_transcripts/2005_0926_day1_pm.pdf.

41. "*Kitzmiller* Trial Transcripts: Day 9 AM," National Center for Science Education, https://ncse.ngo/files/pub/legal/kitzmiller /trial_transcripts/2005_1014_day9_am.pdf.

42. Pigliucci, *Denying Evolution*, 131; Pigliucci, *Nonsense*, 81.

43. Pigliucci, *Nonsense*, 12, 298.

44. Pigliucci, *Denying Evolution*, 203.

45. Dawkins, *Greatest Show*, 18, 279, 281, 404.

46. Ruse, *Darwin and Design*, 44.

47. Ruse, *Darwinism*, 123.

48. Chesterton, "Blue Cross," 31.

49. Dembski, "Foreword," 7.

50. Doyle and Stansbury, "In Quest of Truth," 21.

51. McCabe, "Scientific Men," 448.

52. Harrington, "Terror, Nostalgia," 81.

53. Thomas, *Detective Fiction*, 224.

54. Eliot, "Sherlock Holmes," 553.

55. Holroyd, *Seventeen Steps*, 13.

56. Quoted in Vanessa Thorpe, "Sherlock Holmes and Dr. Watson in the 21st Century," *The Observer*, March 20, 2010, 18.

57. Harrington, "Terror, Nostalgia," 71.

58. Ibid., 71, 73.

59. Leitch, *Film Adaptation*, 221.

60. Polasek, "Sherlockian Simulacra," 196.

61. "A Scandal in Belgravia," *Sherlock*, BBC, aired January 1, 2012.

62. Basu, "(Re)Invention," 198, 205–6.

63. "A Scandal in Belgravia."

64. "A Study in Pink," *Sherlock*, BBC, aired July 25, 2010.

65. "The Reichenbach Fall," *Sherlock*, BBC, aired January 15, 2012.

66. "The Great Game," *Sherlock*, BBC, aired August 8, 2010.

67. "Great Game," "Scandal in Belgravia," and "The Empty Hearse," *Sherlock*, BBC, aired August 8, 2010, January 1, 2012, and January 1, 2014.

68. "Pilot," *Elementary*, CBS, aired September 27, 2012.

69. "Flight Risk," *Elementary*, CBS, aired November 8, 2012.

70. "Heroine," *Elementary*, CBS, aired May 16, 2013.

71. Keller and Klein, "Detective Fiction," 51.

72. Rational Press Association, *Verbatim Report*, 29.

73. Hannen Swaffer, "The Plot to Destroy Us," *Psychic News*, June 18, 1932, 1.

74. "The Woman," *Elementary*, CBS, aired May 16, 2013.

75. Rea, *Mounting Evidence*, xi, 460–61.

76. Wheen, *How Mumbo-Jumbo*, 144.

77. Ruppert, *Crossing*, 251; Zwicker, *Towers*, 220.

78. "The 9/11 Conspiracy Movement," BBC News, February 14, 2007, http://news.bbc .co.uk/2/hi/programmes/conspiracy_files /6354679.stm; Jonathan Cole, "9/11 Experiments: Eliminate the Impossible," June 21, 2012, YouTube video, 14:16, https://www.youtube .com/watch?v=qGCWBDFZ5Zs.

79. Bevin Chu, "9/11: Controlled Demolitions," *China Desk* (blog), September 10, 2011, http://thechinadesk.blogspot.com/2011/09 /911-controlled-demolitions.html; Len Hart, "Fatal Holes Destroy Bush's Lies About 911," *Existentialist Cowboy* (blog), March 25, 2012, https://existentialistcowboy.blogspot.com /2012_03_25_archive.html.

80. "Some Thoughts of a Newcomer to the 9/11 Truth Movement," *Vineyard of the Saker* (blog), February 3, 2010, https://thesaker.is /some-thoughts-of-a-newcomer-to-the-911 -truth-movement.

81. Michael Rivero, "The Secret Service at Booker Elementary: The Dog That Did Not Bark," *What Really Happened*, http://www .whatreallyhappened.com/WRHARTICLES /9-11secretservice.html; David Ray Griffin, "Was America Attacked by Muslims on 9/11?," OpEdNews, September 9, 2008, https://www .opednews.com/articles/8/Was-America -Attacked-by-Mu-by-David-Ray-Griffin -080909-536.html; Rea, *Mounting Evidence*, 513.

82. J. Bonington Jagworth, "9/11 Was an Inside Job," *Mustn't Grumble* (blog), September 26, 2006, http://jagworth.blogspot.com /2006/09.

83. Phil Howe, post in "Uncovered: The Rat's Nest of 9/11" forum, Break for News, February 9, 2006, http://www.breakfornews .com/forum/viewtopic.php?p=373.

84. Douglas Herman, "Sherlock Holmes and 911," Rense, April 16, 2006, https://rense.com /general70/sherlock.htm.

85. Ellis Roberts, "Sherlock Holmes and Certain Critics," *Light*, November 16, 1918, 362.

86. Neil Slade, *Captain Sherlock Solves 9/11*, video, 1:16:00, accessed June 14, 2013, https://www.neilslade.com/911.html.

87. Cort, *American Hiroshima*, n.p.

88. Albert Pastore, *Stranger Than Fiction: An Independent Investigation of 9/11 and the War on Terrorism*, n.d., 2, https://archive.org/details/StrangerThanFiction-9-11AndZionism-ByDr.AlbertD.PastorePhd.

89. Stead, *Wanted*, v.

90. Ken Bensinger and Andrea Chang, "Boston Bombings: Social Media Spirals Out of Control," *Los Angeles Times*, April 20, 2013, https://www.latimes.com/nation/la-xpm-2013-apr-20-la-fi-boston-bombings-media-20130420-story.html.

91. Michela Del Vicario et al., "The Spreading of Misinformation Online," *Proceedings of the National Academy of Sciences*, January 19, 2016, 554.

92. Andrew Griffin, "False-Flag Hints on Episode of 'Sherlock'?," *Red Dirt Report*, May 8, 2012, accessed June 14, 2013, http://www.reddirtreport.com/Story.aspx/22220.

93. Mark Anderson, "'Game of Shadows' Makes Conspiracy Believable," *American Free Press*, January 6, 2012, https://americanfreepress.net/web-exclusive-game-of-shadows-makes-conspiracy-believable.

94. "Google Meets Sherlock Holmes," United States Department of Homeland Security, October 2007, https://www.dhs.gov/science-and-technology/google-meets-sherlock-holmes.

95. Interview with Peter McCormack, Defiance, September 27, 2019, https://www.defiance.news/def004-mike-cernovich.

96. Andrew Marantz, "Trolls for Trump," *New Yorker*, October 31, 2016, 46.

97. Latour, "Why Has Critique," 229.

98. @cernovich, Twitter, January 24, 2020.

99. David Halperin, "Trump Team Disgracefulness Power Rankings—Week 4," *Huffington Post*, June 29, 2017, https://www.huffpost.com/entry/trump-team-disgracefulness-power-rankings-week-4_b_59554881e4b0326c0a8doebb.

100. *Late Night with Seth Meyers*, CBS, aired September 10, 2018.

101. McCabe, "Scientific Men," 448.

102. Tom Harris and Timothy Ball, "Avalanches of Global Warming Alarmism," Heartland Institute, November 15, 2017, https://www.heartland.org/news-opinion/news/avalanches-of-global-warming-alarmism.

103. Joseph Bast, "Why Democrats Lose on Global Warming," Heartland Institute, December 1, 2017, https://www.heartland.org/news-opinion/news/why-democrats-lose-on-global-warming.

104. Ross McKitrick, "Despite Hurricanes Harvey and Irma, Science Has No Idea If Climate Change Is Causing More (or Fewer) Powerful Hurricanes," Cato Institute, September 6, 2017, https://www.cato.org/publications/commentary/despite-hurricanes-harvey-irma-science-has-no-idea-climate-change-causing.

105. Tom Segalstad, "The Construction of Dogmas in Climate Science," Committee for a Constructive Tomorrow, August 1, 2006, https://www.cfact.org/2006/08/01/the-construction-of-dogmas-in-climate-science.

106. Bud Ward, "Whodunnit?: The Case of Global Warming," Yale Climate Connections, January 7, 2016, https://www.yaleclimateconnections.org/2016/01/whodunnit-the-case-of-global-warming.

107. Christopher Hitchens, "The Case of Arthur Conan Doyle," *New York Review of Books*, November 4, 1999, 25.

108. Reprinted in "Queen's Dolls Have Priceless Library," *New York Times*, August 24, 1924, XX3.

109. Doyle, *Memories*, 106.

BIBLIOGRAPHY

References to Arthur Conan Doyle's *The Complete Sherlock Holmes* (Garden City, NY: Doubleday, 1930) are cited parenthetically in the text. References to websites, television episodes, daily newspapers, weekly/semimonthly periodicals, and archival materials are cited in the notes. The archives referenced are the British Library (BL), the Harry Ransom Center (HRC), and the Portsmouth Central Library (PL). Unless otherwise noted, all websites were accessed on July 1, 2020.

Acord, David. *Success Secrets of Sherlock Holmes: Life Lessons from the Master Detective.* New York: Perigee, 2011.

Agassi, Joseph. "The Detective Novel and the Scientific Method." *Poetics Today* 3 (1982): 99–108.

Agathocleous, Tanya. "London Mysteries and International Conspiracies: James, Doyle, and the Aesthetics of Cosmopolitanism." *Nineteenth-Century Contexts* 26 (2004): 125–48.

Alewyn, Richard. "The Origin of the Detective Novel." In *The Poetics of Murder: Detective Fiction and Literary Theory*, edited by Glenn Most and William Stowe, 62–78. New York: Harcourt Brace Jovanovich, 1983.

[Allen, Grant]. "A Fossil Continent." *Cornhill Magazine* 9 (September 1887): 258–70.

Allison, Sarah, Ryan Heuser, Matthew Jockers, Franco Moretti, and Michael Witmore. "Quantitative Formalism: An Experiment." *Pamphlets of the Stanford Literary Lab* 1 (January 15, 2011): 1–26.

Argyll, Duke of (George Douglas Campbell). "A Great Lesson." *The Nineteenth Century* 22 (September 1887): 293–309.

——. "The Power of Loose Analogies." *The Nineteenth Century* 22 (December 1887): 745–65.

——. "Professor Huxley on Canon Liddon." *The Nineteenth Century* 21 (March 1887): 321–39.

——. *The Unity of Nature.* London: Alexander Strahan, 1884.

Atkinson, Michael. *The Secret Marriage of Sherlock Holmes.* Ann Arbor: University of Michigan Press, 1996.

Auden, W. H. "The Guilty Vicarage." *Harper's* 196 (May 1948): 406–12.

Bailey, Steve. "Sherlock Holmes Meets Art Bell: Masters of Knowledge at the Fin-de-Siècle." *Popular Culture Review* 13 (2002): 67–76.

Barclay, James. "A New View of Mormonism." *The Nineteenth Century* 15 (January 1884): 167–84.

Barsham, Diana. *Arthur Conan Doyle and the Meaning of Masculinity.* Aldershot, UK: Ashgate, 2000.

Barthes, Roland. "The Death of the Author." In *Image, Music, Text*, translated by Stephen Heath, 142–48. New York: Hill and Wang, 1977.

Barzun, Jacques. "Detection and the Literary Art." In *The Delights of Detection*, 9–23. New York: Criterion, 1961.

Basu, Balaka. "*Sherlock* and the (Re)Invention of Modernity." In *"Sherlock" and Transmedia Fandom: Essays on the BBC Series*, edited by Louisa Ellen Stein and Kristina Busse, 196–209. Jefferson, NC: McFarland, 2012.

Baudrillard, Jean. *Simulacra and Simulation.* Translated by Sheila Faria Glaser. Ann Arbor: University of Michigan Press, 1994.

Behe, Michael. *Darwin's Black Box: The Bio-chemical Challenge to Evolution*. New York: Simon and Schuster, 1996.

Belsey, Catherine. *Critical Practice*. London: Routledge, 1980.

Berlinski, David. *The Devil's Delusion: Atheism and Its Scientific Pretensions*. New York: Crown Forum, 2008.

Best, Stephen, and Sharon Marcus. "Surface Reading: An Introduction." *Representations* 108 (2009): 1–21.

Blathwayt, Raymond. "A Talk with Dr. Conan Doyle." *Bookman* 2 (May 1892): 50–51.

[Blavatsky, Helena]. "The Great Paradox." *Lucifer* 1 (October 1887): 120–22.

———. "Literary Jottings." *Lucifer* 1 (September 1887): 71–75.

———. "'Lucifer' to the Archbishop of Canterbury." *Lucifer* 1 (December 1887): 241–51.

———. "The Signs of the Times." *Lucifer* 1 (October 1887): 83–89.

———. "What's in a Name?" *Lucifer* 1 (September 1887): 1–7.

Bradlaugh, Charles. "Is There a God?" In *Theological Essays*, 1–8. London: Bradlaugh Bonner, 1895.

Brandt, H. C. G. "How Far Should Our Teaching and Text-Books Have a Scientific Basis?" *PMLA* 1 (1884–85): 57–63.

"Brief Notices," *Eclectic Review* 1 (June 1859): 666–72.

Bruce, Colin. *The Strange Case of Mrs. Hudson's Cat: And Other Science Mysteries Solved by Sherlock Holmes*. Reading, MA: Helix, 1997.

Burleigh, Lord Balfour of (Alexander Hugh Bruce). "The Attack on the Scottish Church." *Contemporary Review* 52 (December 1887): 867–79.

Burrow, Merrick. "Conan Doyle's Gothic Materialism." *Nineteenth-Century Contexts* 35 (2013): 309–23.

Burton, Richard. *The City of the Saints*. New York: Harper, 1862.

Buurma, Rachel Sagner, and Laura Heffernan. "Interpretation, 1980 and 1880." *Victorian Studies* 55 (2013): 615–28.

Byrne, Georgina. *Modern Spiritualism and the Church of England, 1850–1939*. Woodbridge, UK: Boydell, 2010.

Calhoon, Kenneth. "The Detective and the Witch: Local Knowledge and the Aesthetic Pre-History of Detection." *Comparative Literature* 47 (1995): 307–29.

Carr, John Dickson. *The Life of Sir Arthur Conan Doyle*. New York: Harper, 1949.

Castelar, Emilio. "The Papacy and the Temporal Power." *Fortnightly Review* 42 (November 1887): 676–95.

Chamier, Edward. "Philosophy and Common-Sense." *Westminster Review* 128 (December 1887): 1147–160.

Chandless, William. *A Visit to Salt Lake: Being a Journey Across the Plains and a Residence in the Mormon Settlements at Utah*. London: Smith, 1857.

"Charles Darwin." *Westminster Review* 128 (December 1887): 1136–46.

[Charlton, James?]. *Notes of a Trip from Chicago to Victoria, Vancouver's Island, and Return*. Chicago: Rand, McNally, 1885.

Chesterton, G. K. "The Blue Cross." In *The Innocence of Father Brown*, 1–32. London: Cassell, 1911.

Churchill, Winston. *Lord Randolph Churchill*. New York: Macmillan, 1906.

Clancy, Patrick. *Teaching the Controversy: A How-To Guide for Public (Government) School Biology*. Longwood, FL: Xulon Press, 2008.

Clausen, Christopher. "Sherlock Holmes, Order, and the Late-Victorian Mind." *Georgia Review* 38 (1984): 104–23.

Clausson, Nils. "Degeneration, Fin-de-Siècle Gothic, and the Science of Detection." *Journal of Narrative Theory* 35 (2005): 60–87.

Clay, Edmund. "Eclipse of the Soul II." *Westminster Review* 128 (October 1887): 882–97.

Cleere, Eileen. "Chaste Polygamy: Mormon Marriage and the Fantasy of Sexual Privacy in *East Lynne* and *Verner's Pride*." *Victorian Studies* 57 (2015): 199–224.

Collins, C. John. *Science and Faith: Friends or Foes*? Wheaton, IL: Crossway, 2003.

[Collins, Mabel]. "Comments on 'Light on the Path,'" *Lucifer* 1 (September 1887): 8–14.

"Contemporary Literature: Science." *Westminster Review* 128 (December 1887): 1161–67.

Conybeare, William John. "Mormonism." *Edinburgh Review* 102 (April 1854): 319–82.

Cook, Joseph. "Does Death End All?" In *The Boston Monday Lectures*, 275–322. London: Dickinson, 1881.

Cooke, Ivan. *The Return of Arthur Conan Doyle*. Hampshire, UK: White Eagle, 1956.

———. *"Thy Kingdom Come": A Presentation of the Whence, Why, and Whither of Man.* London: Wright & Brown, 1933.

Cort, Hugh. *The American Hiroshima: Osama's Plan for a Nuclear Attack, and One Man's Attempt to Warn America.* Bloomington, IN: iUniverse, 2009.

Cottom, Daniel. *The Abyss of Reason: Cultural Movements, Revelations, and Betrayals.* New York: Oxford University Press, 1991.

Crocombe, Leonard. "The World's Happiest Museum." *Strand Magazine* 73 (May 1927): 451–58.

Darwin, Bernard. "Sherlockiana: The Faith of a Fundamentalist." In *Every Idle Dream*, 87–96. London: Collins, 1948.

Darwin, Francis, ed. *The Life and Letters of Charles Darwin*. New York: Appleton, 1887.

Dawkins, Richard. *The Greatest Show on Earth: The Evidence for Evolution.* New York: Free Press, 2009.

Dembski, William. *The Design Inference: Eliminating Chance Through Small Probabilities.* Cambridge, UK: Cambridge University Press, 1998.

———. *The Design Revolution: Answering the Toughest Questions About Intelligent Design.* Downers Grove, IL: InterVarsity Press, 2004.

———. "Foreword." In *Darwin Strikes Back: Defending the Science of Intelligent Design*, by Thomas Woodward, 7–8. Grand Rapids, MI: Baker, 2006.

Dembski, William, and Jonathan Witt. *Intelligent Design Uncensored: An Easy-to-Understand Guide to the*

Controversy. Downers Grove, IL: InterVarsity Press, 2010.

Dennett, Daniel. "Why and How Does Consciousness Seem the Way It Seems?" In *Open MIND*, edited by Thomas Metzinger and Jennifer Windt, 1–11. Frankfurt am Main: MIND Group, 2015.

Denton, Michael. *Evolution: A Theory in Crisis.* Chevy Chase, MD: Adler and Adler, 1986.

Dilke, Charles Wentworth. *Greater Britain: A Record of Travel in English-Speaking Countries During 1866 and 1867.* London: Macmillan, 1868.

Dixon, William Hepworth. *New America.* London: Hurst and Blackett, 1867.

Doyle, Adrian Conan. *The True Conan Doyle.* London: John Murray, 1945.

Doyle, Adrian Conan, and John Dickson Carr. *The Exploits of Sherlock Holmes.* New York: Ace Books, 1954.

Doyle, Arthur Conan. "The Alleged Posthumous Writings of Great Authors," *Fortnightly Review* 122 (December 1927): 721–35.

———. *The Coming of the Fairies.* London: Hodder and Stoughton, 1922.

———. *The Complete Sherlock Holmes.* Garden City, NY: Doubleday, 1930.

———. *The Edge of the Unknown.* New York: John Murray, 1930.

———. *The History of Spiritualism.* Vol. 1. New York: George Doran, 1926.

———. "Houdini the Enigma." *Strand Magazine* 74 (August and September 1927): 134–43, 265–70.

———. "Life and Death in the Blood." *Good Words* 24 (March 1883): 178–81.

———. *Memories and Adventures.* London: Hodder and Stoughton, 1924.

———. *Micah Clarke.* London: Longmans, Green, 1889.

———. "My First Book." *Idler* 2 (January 1893): 633–40.

———. *The Narrative of John Smith.* Edited by Jon Lellenberg, Daniel Stashower, and Rachel Foss. London: British Library, 2011.

———. *The New Revelation.* New York: George Doran, 1918.

———. *Our American Adventure*. New York: George Doran, 1923.

———. *Our Reply to the Cleric*. Halifax, UK: Spiritualists' National Union, 1920.

———. *Our Second American Adventure*. Boston: Little, Brown, 1924.

———. *Pheneas Speaks*. New York: George Doran, 1927.

———. *The Roman Catholic Church: A Rejoinder*. London: Psychic Press, 1929.

———. "Some Personalia About Mr. Sherlock Holmes." *Strand Magazine* 54 (December 1917): 531–35.

———. *Spiritualism and Rationalism*. London: Hodder and Stoughton, 1920.

———. *The Stark Munro Letters*. Bloomington, IN: Gaslight, 1982.

———. "The True Story of Sherlock Holmes." In *The Uncollected Sherlock Holmes*, edited by Richard Lancelyn Green, 345–51. Harmondsworth, UK: Penguin, 1983.

———. "The Uncharted Coast, No. II: A New Light on Old Crimes." *Strand Magazine* 59 (January 1920): 65–74.

———. *The Vital Message*. London: Hodder and Stoughton, 1919.

———. *The Wanderings of a Spiritualist*. London: Hodder and Stoughton, 1921.

———. *What Does Spiritualism Actually Teach and Stand For?* London: Psychic Bookshop, 1928.

———. *A Word of Warning*. London: Psychic Press, 1928.

Doyle, Arthur Conan, and Hubert Stansbury. "In Quest of Truth: Being a Correspondence Between Sir Arthur Conan Doyle and Captain Stansbury." *Rationalist Press Association Annual* (1914): 9–22.

Drayson, Alfred. *Great Britain Has Been and Will Once Again Be in the Tropics*. London: Dalziel, 1859.

Dunkley, Charles, ed. *The Official Report of the Church Congress, Held at Wolverhampton, October 1887*. London: Bemrose, 1887.

Eagleton, Terry. *The Event of Literature*. New Haven, CT: Yale University Press, 2012.

———. "The Flight to the Real." In *Cultural Politics at the Fin de Siècle*, edited by

Sally Ledger and Scott McCracken, 11–21. Cambridge, UK: Cambridge University Press, 1995.

Ebrard, Johannes. *Apologetics; or, The Scientific Vindication of Christianity*. Translated by William Stuart and John Macpherson. 3 vols. Edinburgh: Clark, 1886–87.

Eco, Umberto. "Horns, Hooves, Insteps: Some Hypotheses on Three Types of Abduction." In *The Sign of Three: Dupin, Holmes, Peirce*, edited by Umberto Eco and Thomas Sebeok, 198–220. Bloomington: Indiana University Press, 1983.

Einstein, Albert, and Leopold Infeld. *The Evolution of Physics*. London: Cambridge University Press, 1938.

Eliot, T. S. "Experiment in Criticism." *Bookman* 70 (November 1929): 225–33.

———. "The Frontiers of Criticism." *Sewanee Review* 64 (1956): 525–43.

———. "The Function of Criticism." *Criterion* 2 (1923): 31–42.

———. *The Sacred Wood: Essays on Poetry and Criticism*. New York: Knopf, 1921.

———. "Sherlock Holmes and His Times." *Criterion* 32 (April 1929): 552–56.

Ellis, William Ashton. "An Infant Genius." *Lucifer* 1 (December 1887): 296–98.

Elmslie, William Gray. "The First Chapter of Genesis." *Contemporary Review* 52 (December 1887): 815–30.

Engels, Frederick. "Natural Science and the Spirit World." In *Dialectics of Nature*, edited and translated by Clemens Dutt, 297–310. New York: International, 1940.

Estleman, Loren. "Introduction." In *Sherlock Holmes: The Complete Novels and Stories*, by Arthur Conan Doyle, 1:vii–xviii. 2 vols. New York: Bantam, 1986.

Felski, Rita. "After Suspicion." *Profession* 8 (2009): 28–35.

———. "Suspicious Minds." *Poetics Today* 32 (2011): 215–34.

Ferraris, Maurizio. *Manifesto of New Realism*. Translated by Sarah De Sanctis. Albany: State University of New York Press, 2014.

Fillingham, Lydia Alix. "'The Colorless Skein of Life': Threats to the Private Sphere

in Conan Doyle's *A Study in Scarlet."
ELH* 56 (1989): 667–88.

Forrest, Barbara, and Paul Gross. *Creationism's Trojan Horse: The Wedge of Intelligent Design.* Oxford, UK: Oxford University Press, 2004.

Foucault, Michel. "Pouvoir et savoir." In *Dits et écrits: 1954–1988,* edited by Daniel Defert and François Ewald, 2:399–414. Paris: Gallimard, 2001.

———. "What Is an Author?" In *Textual Strategies: Perspectives in Post-Structuralist Criticism,* edited by Josué Harari, 141–60. Ithaca, NY: Cornell University Press, 1979.

Frank, Lawrence. "*The Hound of the Baskervilles,* the Man on the Tor, and a Metaphor for the Mind." *Nineteenth-Century Literature* 54 (1999): 336–72.

———. *Victorian Detective Fiction and the Nature of Evidence.* Basingstoke, UK: Palgrave Macmillan, 2003.

Freedgood, Elaine. *The Ideas in Things: Fugitive Meaning in the Victorian Novel.* Chicago: University of Chicago Press, 2006.

Galvan, Jill. *The Sympathetic Medium: Feminine Channeling, the Occult, and Communication Technologies, 1859–1919.* Ithaca, NY: Cornell University Press, 2010.

Gardner, Martin. "The Irrelevance of Conan Doyle." In *The Night Is Large: Collected Essays 1938–1995,* 183–92. New York: St. Martin's Griffin, 1996.

Garland, Hamlin. *Forty Years of Psychic Research: A Plain Narrative of Fact.* New York: Macmillan, 1936.

Garnett, William. "Contemporary Record: Physical Science." *Contemporary Review* 52 (October 1887): 599–604.

Garratt, Peter. *Victorian Empiricism: Self, Knowledge, and Reality in Ruskin, Bain, Lewes, Spencer, and George Eliot.* Madison, NJ: Fairleigh Dickinson University Press, 2010.

Geikie, Archibald. "The Life and Letters of Charles Darwin." *Contemporary Review* 52 (December 1887): 757–69.

Ginzburg, Carlo. "Clues: Morelli, Freud, and Sherlock Holmes." In *The Sign of Three: Dupin, Holmes, Peirce,* edited by Umberto Eco and Thomas Sebeok, 81–118. Bloomington: Indiana University Press, 1983.

Givens, Terryl. *The Viper on the Hearth: Mormons, Myths, and the Construction of Heresy.* New York: Oxford University Press, 1997.

Gladstone, William. *The Liberal Programme for Great Britain and Ireland.* London: Liberal Publication Department, 1887.

Gottschall, Jonathan. *Literature, Science, and a New Humanities.* New York: Palgrave Macmillan, 2008.

———. *The Storytelling Animal: How Stories Make Us Human.* Boston: Houghton Mifflin Harcourt, 2012.

Graff, Gerald. *Professing Literature: An Institutional History.* Chicago: University of Chicago Press, 1987.

Green, Richard Lancelyn, ed. *The Sherlock Holmes Letters.* Iowa City: University of Iowa Press, 1986.

Gross, Paul, and Norman Levitt. *Higher Superstition: The Academic Left and Its Quarrels with Science.* Baltimore: Johns Hopkins University Press, 1998.

Hardy, Lady Duffus [Mary Anne]. *Through Cities and Prairie Lands: Sketches of an American Tour.* London: Chapman and Hall, 1881.

Harrington, Ellen Burton. "Terror, Nostalgia, and the Pursuit of Sherlock Holmes in *Sherlock.*" In *"Sherlock" and Transmedia Fandom: Essays on the BBC Series,* edited by Louisa Ellen Stein and Kristina Busse, 70–84. Jefferson, NC: McFarland, 2012.

Hartwig, Mark, and Stephen Meyer. "A Note to Teachers." In *Of Pandas and People: The Central Question of Biological Origins,* by Percival Davis and Dean Kenyon, 153–63. 2nd ed. Dallas: Haughton, 1993.

Hazelgrove, Jenny. *Spiritualism and British Society Between the Wars.* Manchester, UK: Manchester University Press, 2000.

Hill, Pope. "The Final Problem: An Exemplification of the Substructure Theory." *Baker Street Journal* 5 (1955): 149–53.

———. *Part One*. Athens, GA: Self-published, 1947.

———. *The Sherlock Holmes Hoax*. Athens, GA: Self-published, 1952.

Hitchens, Christopher. "Introduction: Certitude and Its Discontents." In *Certitude: A Profusely Illustrated Guide to Blockheads and Bullies*, edited by Adam Begley, 7–10. New York: Harmony, 2009.

———. *No One Left to Lie To: The Triangulations of William Jefferson Clinton*. London: Verso, 1999.

Holroyd, James, ed. *Seventeen Steps to 221B: A Collection of Sherlockian Pieces by English Writers*. London: George Allen, 1967.

Homer, Michael. "Arthur Conan Doyle and His Views on Mormonism." *Journal of the Arthur Conan Doyle Society* 2 (1991): 66–81.

———, ed. *On the Way to Somewhere Else: European Sojourners in the Mormon West, 1834–1930*. Spokane, WA: Arthur H. Clark, 2006.

How, Harry. "A Day with Dr. Conan Doyle." *Strand Magazine* 4 (August 1892): 182–88.

Huxley, Thomas Henry. "Mr. Darwin's Critics." *Contemporary Review* 18 (November 1871): 443–76.

———. "On the Method of Zadig: Retrospective Prophecy as a Function of Science." *The Nineteenth Century* 7 (June 1880): 929–40.

———. "Science and Pseudo-Science." *The Nineteenth Century* 21 (April 1887): 481–98.

———. "Science and the Bishops." *The Nineteenth Century* 22 (November 1887): 625–41.

———. "Scientific and Pseudo-Scientific Realism." *The Nineteenth Century* 21 (February 1887): 191–205.

Illingworth, John Richardson. "Contemporary Records: Apologetic Theology." *Contemporary Review* 52 (December 1887): 895–99.

Innes, Alexander Taylor. "Where Are the Letters? A Cross-Examination of Certain

Phantasms." *The Nineteenth Century* 22 (August 1887): 174–94.

Jaffe, Jacqueline. *Arthur Conan Doyle*. Boston: Twayne, 1987.

Jameson, Fredric. "On Raymond Chandler." *Southern Review* 6 (1970): 624–50.

Jann, Rosemary. *The Adventures of Sherlock Holmes: Detecting Social Order*. New York: Twayne, 1995.

———. "Sherlock Holmes Codes the Social Body." *ELH* 57 (1990): 685–708.

Johnston, Charles. "Emerson and Occultism." *Lucifer* 1 (December 1887): 252–57.

Keller, Joseph, and Kathleen Gregory Klein. "Detective Fiction and the Function of Tacit Knowledge." *Mosaic* 23 (1990): 45–60.

Kendrick, Stephen. *Holy Clues: The Gospel According to Sherlock Holmes*. New York: Vintage, 2000.

Kern, Stephen. *A Cultural History of Causality: Science, Murder Novels, and Systems of Thought*. Princeton, NJ: Princeton University Press, 2004.

Kerr, Douglas. *Conan Doyle: Writing, Profession, and Practice*. Oxford, UK: Oxford University Press, 2013.

Kissane, James, and John Kissane. "Sherlock Holmes and the Ritual of Reason." *Nineteenth-Century Fiction* 17 (1963): 353–62.

Klein, Kathleen Gregory, and Joseph Keller. "Deductive Detective Fiction: The Self-Destructive Genre." *Genre* 19 (1986): 155–72.

Klein, Richard. "The Future of Literary Criticism." *PMLA* 125 (2010): 920–23.

Knight, Stephen. *Form and Ideology in Crime Fiction*. Bloomington: Indiana University Press, 1980.

Knox, Ronald. *Caliban in Grub Street*. London: Sheed and Ward, 1930.

———. "Studies in the Literature of Sherlock Holmes." In *Essays in Satire*, 145–75. London: Sheed and Ward, 1928.

Kollar, René. "Spiritualism and Religion: Sir Arthur Conan Doyle's Critique of Christianity and a Roman Catholic Response." *Recusant History* 24 (1999): 397–413.

Konnikova, Maria. *Mastermind: How to Think Like Sherlock Holmes*. New York: Viking, 2013.

Kopec, Andrew. "The Digital Humanities, Inc.: Literary Criticism and the Fate of a Profession." *PMLA* 131 (2016): 324–39.

Lacan, Jacques. "Seminar on 'The Purloined Letter.'" Translated by Jeffrey Mehlman. *Yale French Studies* 48 (1972): 39–72.

Lamond, John. *Arthur Conan Doyle: A Memoir*. London: John Murray, 1931.

Lamont, Peter. "Spiritualism and a Mid-Victorian Crisis of Evidence." *Historical Journal* 47 (2004): 897–920.

Lang, Andrew. "At the Sign of the Ship." *Longman's* 11 (December 1887): 234–40.

Lantagne, Stacey. "Sherlock Holmes and the Case of the Lucrative Fandom." *Michigan Telecommunications and Technology Law Review* 21 (2015): 263–315.

Laqueur, Thomas. "Why the Margins Matter: Occultism and the Making of Modernity." *Modern Intellectual History* 3 (2006): 111–35.

Latour, Bruno. *Aramis, or the Love of Technology*. Translated by Catherine Porter. Cambridge, MA: Harvard University Press, 1996.

———. *Reassembling the Social*. Oxford, UK: Oxford University Press, 2005.

———. "Why Has Critique Run Out of Steam?" *Critical Inquiry* 30 (2004): 225–48.

Lecourt, Sebastian. "The Mormons, the Victorians, and the Idea of Greater Britain." *Victorian Studies* 56 (2013): 85–111.

Lee, Maurice. "Evidence, Coincidence, and Superabundant Information." *Victorian Studies* 54 (2011): 87–94.

Leitch, Thomas. *Film Adaptation and Its Discontents*. Baltimore: Johns Hopkins University Press, 2007.

Lellenberg, Jon, ed. *Irregular Crises of the Late 'Forties: An Archival History of the Baker Street Irregulars, Summer 1947–December 1950*. New York: Baker Street Irregulars, 1999.

———. *Irregular Memories of the 'Thirties: An Archival History of the Baker Street Irregulars' First Decade, 1930–1940*. New York: Fordham University Press, 1990.

———. *Irregular Proceedings of the Mid 'Forties: An Archival History of the Baker Street Irregulars, Autumn 1943–June 1947*. New York: Baker Street Irregulars, 1995.

Lellenberg, Jon, Daniel Stashower, and Charles Foley, eds. *Arthur Conan Doyle: A Life in Letters*. New York: Penguin, 2007.

Levine, George, ed. *One Culture: Essays in Science and Literature*. Madison: University of Wisconsin Press, 1987.

Liebow, Ely. *Dr. Joe Bell: Model for Sherlock Holmes*. Bowling Green, OH: Bowling Green University Popular Press, 1982.

Lightman, Bernard. "Conan Doyle's Ideal Reasoner: The Case of the Reluctant Scientific Naturalist." *Journal of Literature and Science* 7 (2014): 19–36.

Lodge, Oliver. *Raymond, or Life and Death*. London: Methuen, 1916.

Love, Heather. "Close Reading and Thin Description." *Public Culture* 25 (2013): 401–34.

Luckhurst, Roger. *The Invention of Telepathy, 1870–1901*. Oxford, UK: Oxford University Press, 2002.

Lycett, Andrew. *The Man Who Created Sherlock Holmes: The Life and Times of Sir Arthur Conan Doyle*. New York: Free Press, 2007.

MacColl, Malcolm. *The Eastern Question: Its Facts and Fallacies*. London: Longmans, Green, 1877.

Macherey, Pierre. *A Theory of Literary Production*. Translated by Geoffrey Wall. London: Routledge and Kegan Paul, 1978.

Mahaffey, Vicki. *Modernist Literature: Challenging Fictions*. Malden, MA: Blackwell, 2007.

Marshall, Charles. "Characteristics of Mormonism." *Fraser's Magazine* 3 (June 1871): 692–702.

McCabe, Joseph. "Scientific Men and Spiritualism." *English Review* 30 (May 1920): 439–48.

———. *Spiritualism: A Popular History from 1847*. London: Fisher Unwin, 1920.

McDonald, Peter. *British Literary Culture and Publishing Practice, 1880–1914*. Cambridge, UK: Cambridge University Press, 1997.

McLaughlin, Joseph. *Writing the Urban Jungle: Reading Empire in London from Doyle to Eliot*. Charlottesville: University Press of Virginia, 2000.

McMurrin, Sterling. *The Theological Foundations of the Mormon Religion*. Salt Lake City: University of Utah Press, 1965.

Meikle, Jeffrey. "'Over There': Arthur Conan Doyle and Spiritualism." *Library Chronicle of the University of Texas at Austin* 8 (1974): 23–37.

Menand, Louis. *The Metaphysical Club*. New York: Farrar, Straus and Giroux, 2001.

Messac, Régis. *Le "detective novel" et l'influence de la pensée scientifique*. Paris: Encrage, 2011.

Meyer, Stephen. *Signature in the Cell: DNA and the Evidence for Intelligent Design*. New York: HarperOne, 2009.

Miller, Russell. *The Adventures of Arthur Conan Doyle: A Biography*. New York: St. Martin's, 2008.

Mivart, St. George. "The Catholic Church and Biblical Criticism." *The Nineteenth Century* 22 (July 1887): 31–51.

———. "Catholicity and Reason." *The Nineteenth Century* 22 (December 1887): 850–70.

———. "Happiness in Hell." *The Nineteenth Century* 32 (December 1892): 899–919.

———. "Modern Catholics and Scientific Freedom." *The Nineteenth Century* 18 (July 1885): 30–47.

———. *On the Genesis of Species*. London: Macmillan, 1871.

———. Review of *The Descent of Man*, by Charles Darwin. *Quarterly Review* 131 (July 1871): 47–90.

———. "Sins of Belief and Sins of Unbelief." *The Nineteenth Century* 24 (October 1888): 548–68.

Momerie, Alfred Williams. "Christmas Day." In *Inspiration, and Other Sermons Delivered in the Chapel of the Foundling Hospital*, 196–209. London: Blackwood, 1889.

Moretti, Franco. *Distant Reading*. London: Verso, 2013.

———. *Graphs, Maps, Trees: Abstract Models for Literary History*. London: Verso, 2007.

———. *Signs Taken for Wonders: Essays in the Sociology of Literary Form*. London: Verso, 1988.

Morley, Christopher, ed. *Sherlock Holmes and Dr. Watson: A Textbook of Friendship*. New York: Harcourt, Brace, 1944.

Most, Glenn. "The Hippocratic Smile: John le Carré and the Traditions of the Detective Novel." In *The Poetics of Murder: Detective Fiction and Literary Theory*, edited by Glenn Most and William Stowe, 341–65. New York: Harcourt Brace Jovanovich, 1983.

Neill, Anna. *Primitive Minds: Evolution and Spiritual Experience in the Victorian Novel*. Columbus: Ohio State University Press, 2013.

Nelson, Geoffrey. *Spiritualism and Society*. New York: Schocken, 1969.

Nichols, Beverley. "Sir Arthur Conan Doyle, or, An Ungrateful Father." In *The Uncollected Sherlock Holmes*, edited by Richard Lancelyn Green, 379–82. Harmondsworth, UK: Penguin, 1983.

Nieminski, John, and Jon Lellenberg, eds. *"Dear Starrett—" / "Dear Briggs—": A Compendium of Correspondence Between Vincent Starrett and Gray Chandler Briggs (1930–1934)*. New York: Fordham University Press, 1989.

Nordon, Pierre. *Conan Doyle: A Biography*. New York: Holt, Rinehart and Winston, 1967.

"Notes." *Journal of the British Astronomical Association* 4 (1893–94): 311–17.

O'Brien, James. *The Scientific Sherlock Holmes: Cracking the Case with Science and Forensics*. Oxford, UK: Oxford University Press, 2013.

O'Leary, Denyse. *By Design or by Chance? The Growing Controversy on the Origins of Life in the Universe*. Minneapolis: Augsburg, 2004.

O'Neill, Herbert. *Spiritualism as Spiritualists Have Written of It*. London: Burns, Oates, and Washbourne, 1944.

Oppenheim, Janet. *The Other World: Spiritual-
ism and Psychical Research in England,
1850–1914.* Cambridge, UK: Cam-
bridge University Press, 1985.
Owen, Alex. *The Darkened Room: Women,
Power and Spiritualism in Late Victorian
England.* London: Virago, 1989.
Paley, William. *Natural Theology.* Oxford, UK:
Oxford University Press, 2006.
Pearsall, Ronald. *Conan Doyle: A Biographical
Solution.* New York: St. Martin's, 1977.
Pearson, Hesketh. *Conan Doyle: His Life and
Art.* London: Methuen, 1943.
Pigliucci, Massimo. *Denying Evolution:
Creationism, Scientism, and the Nature
of Science.* Sutherland, MA: Sinauer,
2002.
———. *Nonsense on Stilts: How to Tell Science
from Bunk.* Chicago: University of
Chicago Press, 2010.
Polasek, Ashley. "Sherlockian Simulacra:
Adaptation and the Postmodern Con-
struction of Reality." *Literature/Film
Quarterly* 40 (2012): 191–96.
Poole, Reginald Stuart. "The Date of the
Pentateuch: Theory and Facts." *Con-
temporary Review* 52 (September 1887):
350–69.
Poore, Benjamin. "Sherlock Holmes and the
Leap of Faith: The Forces of Fandom
and Convergence in Adaptations
of the Holmes and Watson Stories."
Adaptation 6 (2013): 158–71.
"Pope Leo XIII." *London Quarterly Review* 9
(October 1887): 144–55.
Price, Harry. "The Return of Conan Doyle."
Nash's Pall Mall Magazine 86 (January
1931): 10–13, 91–94.
Proctor, Richard. "Gossip." *Knowledge* 10
(November 1886): 18–19.
Rational Press Association. *Verbatim Report of
a Public Debate on "The Truth of Spiri-
tualism."* London: Watts, 1920.
Rea, Paul. *Mounting Evidence: Why We Need a
New Investigation into 9/11.* Blooming-
ton, IN: iUniverse, 2011.
"Recent Explorations in Palestine." *London
Quarterly Review* 9 (October 1887):
44–57.
"Report of the Committee Appointed to
Investigate Phenomena Connected

with the Theosophical Society."
*Proceedings of the Society for Psychical
Research* 3 (1885): 201–400.
Review of *A Defence of the Church of England
Against Disestablishment,* by Roundell
Palmer, Earl of Selborne. *Quarterly
Review* 165 (October 1887): 468–99.
Review of *The Unity of Nature,* by the Duke of
Argyll. *American Naturalist* 18 (August
1884): 807–8.
[Reynolds, Henry Robert]. "Our New
Religions." *British Quarterly Review* 21
(1855): 408–41.
Robinson, Phil. *Sinners and Saints: A Tour
Across the States, and Round Them; with
Three Months Among the Mormons.*
Boston: Roberts Brothers, 1883.
Ronell, Avital. *Stupidity.* Urbana: University of
Illinois Press, 2002.
Rooney, Ellen. "Live Free or Describe: The
Reading Effect and the Persistence of
Form." *differences* 21 (2010): 112–39.
Rossiter, William. "Artisan Atheism." *The Nine-
teenth Century* 22 (July 1887): 111–26.
Rouse, Charles. "To the Editor." *Occult Review*
44 (August 1926): 116–17.
Ruppert, Michael. *Crossing the Rubicon: The
Decline of the American Empire at the
End of the Age of Oil.* Gabriola Island,
BC: New Society, 2004.
Ruse, Michael. *Darwin and Design: Does Evolu-
tion Have a Purpose?* Cambridge, MA:
Harvard University Press, 2003.
———. *Darwinism and Its Discontents.* Cam-
bridge, UK: Cambridge University
Press, 2006.
Ruskin, John. *The Works of John Ruskin.* Vol.
36. Edited by E. T. Cook and Alexan-
der Wedderburn. London: George
Allen, 1909.
Saler, Michael. *As If: Modern Enchantment
and the Literary Prehistory of Virtual
Reality.* New York: Oxford University
Press, 2012.
Sayers, Dorothy. *Unpopular Opinions.*
London: Gollancz, 1946.
Schryer, Stephen. "Fantasies of the New Class:
The New Criticism, Harvard Sociol-
ogy, and the Idea of the University."
PMLA 122 (2007): 663–78.

Seiglie, Mario. "Intelligent Design's Sherlock Holmes." *Vertical Thought* 17 (2007): 16–17.

"Short Reviews and Brief Notices: Theology." *London Quarterly Review* 9 (October 1887): 156–75.

Siddiqi, Yumna. *Anxieties of Empire and the Fiction of Intrigue.* New York: Columbia University Press, 2008.

Sinnett, Alfred. "The Invisible World." *Lucifer* 1 (November 1887): 186–92.

"Sir Arthur Conan Doyle's Resignation," *Journal of the Society for Psychical Research* 26 (March 1930): 45–52.

Smajić, Srdjan. *Ghost-Seers, Detectives, and Spiritualists: Theories of Vision in Victorian Literature and Science.* Cambridge, UK: Cambridge University Press, 2010.

Smith, Daniel. *How to Think Like Sherlock.* London: Michael O'Mara, 2012.

Smith, Edgar. "Notes on the Collation." In *The Adventures of Sherlock Holmes*, by Arthur Conan Doyle, xix–xxiii. New York: Heritage Press, 1950.

———, ed. *Profile by Gaslight: An Irregular Reader About the Private Life of Sherlock Holmes.* New York: Simon and Schuster, 1944.

Smith, Jonathan. *Fact and Feeling: Baconian Science and the Nineteenth-Century Literary Imagination.* Madison: University of Wisconsin Press, 1994.

Smith, William Robertson. "Archeology and the Date of the Pentateuch." *Contemporary Review* 52 (October 1887): 490–503.

Sober, Elliott. "What Is Wrong with Intelligent Design?" *Quarterly Review of Biology* 82 (2007): 3–8.

Spurgeon, Charles. "Another Word Concerning the Down-Grade," *Sword and the Trowel* 23 (August 1887): 397–400.

Stansbury, Hubert. *In Quest of Truth: A Study of Religion and Morality.* London: Watts, 1913.

Starrett, Vincent, ed. *221B: Studies in Sherlock Holmes.* New York: Macmillan, 1940.

———. "Introduction." In *Appointment in Baker Street*, edited by Edgar Smith, 9–11. New York: Pamphlet House, 1938.

———. *The Private Life of Sherlock Holmes.* New York: Macmillan, 1933.

Stashower, Daniel. *Teller of Tales: The Life of Arthur Conan Doyle.* New York: Holt, 1999.

Stavert, Geoffrey. *A Study in Southsea: The Unrevealed Life of Doctor Arthur Conan Doyle.* Portsmouth, UK: Milestone, 1987.

Stead, William. *Wanted: A Sherlock Holmes! A Chance for Amateur Detectives.* London: Review of Reviews Office, 1895.

Stein, Louisa Ellen, and Kristina Busse. "Introduction: The Literary, Televisual and Digital Adventures of the Beloved Detective." In *"Sherlock" and Transmedia Fandom: Essays on the BBC Series*, edited by Louisa Ellen Stein and Kristina Busse, 9–26. Jefferson, NC: McFarland, 2012.

Stephen, James Fitzjames. "Mr. Mivart's Modern Catholicism." *The Nineteenth Century* 22 (October 1887): 581–600.

———. "A Rejoinder to Mr. Mivart." *The Nineteenth Century* 23 (January 1888): 115–26.

Sword, Helen. *Ghostwriting Modernism.* Ithaca, NY: Cornell University Press, 2002.

Takanashi, Kyoko. "Sherlock's 'Brain Attic': Information Culture and the Liberal Professional Dilemma." *PMLA* 132 (2017): 250–65.

Taylor-Ide, Jesse Oak. "Ritual and the Liminality of Sherlock Holmes in *The Sign of Four* and *The Hound of the Baskervilles.*" *English Literature in Transition* 48 (2005): 55–70.

Thaxton, Charles. "A New Design Argument." *Cosmic Pursuit* 2 (1998): 13–21.

Thomas, Ronald. *Detective Fiction and the Rise of Forensic Science.* Cambridge, UK: Cambridge University Press, 1999.

———. "The Fingerprint of the Foreigner: Colonizing the Criminal Body in 1890s Detective Fiction and Criminal Anthropology." *ELH* 61 (1994): 655–83.

Truzzi, Marcello. "Sherlock Holmes: Applied Social Psychologist." In *The Sign of Three: Dupin, Holmes, Peirce*, edited by Umberto Eco and Thomas Sebeok,

55–80. Bloomington: Indiana University Press, 1983.

"Trying the Spirits." *Cornhill Magazine* 9 (December 1887): 646–58.

Tucker, Herbert. "Introduction." *New Literary History* 42 (2011): vii–xii.

Tupper, Frederick. "Textual Criticism as a Pseudo-Science." *PMLA* 25 (1910): 164–81.

Tyndall, John. "Miracles and Special Providences." *Fortnightly Review* 7 (1867): 645–60.

——. "Science and the 'Spirits.'" In *Fragments of Science*, 1:496–504. 6th ed. 2 vols. London: Longmans, Green, 1879.

——. *The Scientific Use of the Imagination*. London: Longmans, Green, 1870.

Vermeule, Blakey. *Why Do We Care About Literary Characters?* Baltimore: Johns Hopkins University Press, 2010.

Viswanathan, Gauri. "The Ordinary Business of Occultism." *Critical Inquiry* 27 (2000): 1–20.

Ward, Wilfrid. "Positivism in Christianity." *The Nineteenth Century* 22 (September 1887): 403–14.

Weber, Max. *The Protestant Ethic and the Spirit of Capitalism*. Translated by Talcott Parsons. New York: Scribner's, 1958.

Wheen, Francis. *How Mumbo-Jumbo Conquered the World: A Short History of Modern Delusions*. New York: Perseus, 2004.

White, Hayden. "Historical Pluralism." *Critical Inquiry* 12 (1986): 480–93.

Willert, Paul Ferdinand. "The Service of Man." *National Review* 10 (September 1887): 46–58.

Williams, William Mattieu. "Science Notes." *Gentlemen's Magazine* 263 (November 1887): 512–17.

Wilson, James. *Essays and Addresses: An Attempt to Treat Some Religious Questions in a Scientific Spirit*. London: Macmillan, 1887.

Wiltse, Ed. "'So Constant an Expectation': Sherlock Holmes and Seriality." *Narrative* 6 (1998): 105–22.

Wimsatt, W. K., and M. C. Beardsley. "The Intentional Fallacy." *Sewanee Review* 54 (1946): 468–88.

Wojton, Jennifer, and Lynnette Porter. *Sherlock and Digital Fandom: The Meeting of Creativity, Community and Advocacy*. Jefferson, NC: McFarland, 2018.

Yellen, Sherman. "Sir Arthur Conan Doyle: Sherlock Holmes in Spiritland." *International Journal of Parapsychology* 7 (1965): 33–63.

Zunshine, Lisa. *Why We Read Fiction: Theory of Mind and the Novel*. Columbus: Ohio State University Press, 2006.

Zwicker, Barrie. *Towers of Deception: The Media Cover-Up of 9/11*. Gabriola Island, BC: New Society, 2006.

INDEX

Works by Arthur Conan Doyle are indexed by title, omitting "The Adventure of" from Sherlock Holmes stories.

Cleere, Eileen, 53
Clinton, Bill, 1, 7
Clinton, Hillary, 165
confirmation bias, 15–17, 28–31, 62, 80, 87, 94,
    121
  and the internet, 134, 142, 164
  and literary criticism, 124, 126, 134–37
conspiracy theory, 7, 21, 130
  9/11 Truth movement, 142, 161–65
  and *Elementary*, 159–61
  and McKinley assassination, 77–78, 161
  right-wing, 165–66
  and *Sherlock*, 155–56, 164
  and spiritualism, 93, 101–2, 114, 159
Conybeare, William, 59
Cook, Joseph, 38, 40
Cooke, Grace, 106, 111–12, 119, 138
Cooke, Ivan, 111–12, 119, 138–39
Copernicus, 23, 33, 68, 92, 149
"Copper Beeches, The," 91
Cottom, Daniel, 44, 91, 140
Cuvier, Georges, 35, 81
  See also paleontology

Darwin, Bernard, 115
Darwin, Charles, 67, 71–73
  Descent of Man, The, 24, 35
  and intelligent design (ID), 142–44, 148,
    151–52
  and literary criticism, 135–36
  On the Origin of Species, 23, 25, 30, 35, 38
  theory of evolution, 23–30, 39, 43, 87
Dawkins, Richard, 150
deductive logic, 6–7, 61, 64, 75, 126, 134–35
Dembski, William, 143–47, 151
Dennett, Daniel, 139
Denton, Michael, 144, 147
Der Mann, der Sherlock Holmes War (film), 113
Derrida, Jacques, 128, 130, 132
"Devil's Foot, The," 87, 114
Dickens, Charles, 109
Dilke, Charles, 57, 59
Dixon, William, 57
Doyle, Adrian Conan, 105–9, 116–19, 121, 123
Doyle, Arthur Conan
  biographies of, 1–2, 46–48, 116–17
  and Catholicism, 4, 35, 38, 45, 71, 101–2
  conversion to spiritualism, 45–48, 70–73,
    78, 83–84
  debate with McCabe, 93–95, 159
  debate with Stansbury, 84–89
  and fairy photographs, 2–3, 98

literary estate of, 5, 106, 117–20
medical practice of, 38–39, 81
memorial service for, 104–5
missionary work of, 2, 37, 97–103
  and Mormonism, 54–55, 65, 99–100
  public conversion, 89, 95–97
  scientific education of, 35, 38, 41, 47, 49, 76
  spirit messages from, 105–12
  and theosophy, 41–45, 92
Doyle, Denis Conan, 106, 113–14, 116–17, 121
Doyle, Jean Conan (née Leckie), 88, 101,
    105–12, 116–17, 138
Doyle, Kingsley Conan, 88–89, 101, 105
Doyle, Lena Jean Conan, 112
Doyle, Louisa Conan (née Hawkins), 83, 88, 138
Doyle, Mary (née Foley), 38, 40–41, 81, 83, 101
Doyle, Mary Louise Conan, 88
Drayson, Alfred, 41–43, 62, 64, 91, 142
"Dying Detective, The," 89, 98

Eagleton, Terry, 69, 139
Ebrard, Johannes, 32
Eco, Umberto, 131
Edalji, George, 90
Edge of the Unknown, The, 109
Einstein, Albert, 3
Elementary (television series), 158–62
Eliot, T. S., 67, 96, 127–29, 132–33, 136, 153
Ellis, William, 43
Elmslie, William, 19, 23, 25
empiricism, 6, 15, 22, 31, 40, 49–50, 68–69, 72,
    85–87
  and intelligent design (ID), 144–45
  and literary criticism, 124–36
  and theosophy, 43–44
  See also spiritualism, evidence for
"Empty House, The," 87
Engels, Friedrich, 69
English, James, 135
Estleman, Loren, 52, 122
Euclid, 7, 43, 49, 72

"Fate of the Evangeline, The," 78
Felski, Rita, 132–33
Fenian bombings, 21, 53, 153
Ferraris, Maurizio, 74
Fillingham, Lydia Alix, 53
"Final Problem, The," 82–83, 85, 154, 159
First World War, 3, 84, 88–89, 95
"Five Orange Pips, The," 79, 81
Forrest, Barbara, 142
Foucault, Michel, 123–24, 128

Ruse, Michael, 150–51
Ruskin, John, 23

Saler, Michael, 66, 68, 70, 115, 119–20
Sayers, Dorothy, 114, 122–23
"Scandal in Bohemia, A," 79–80
Schryer, Stephen, 127
scientific method, 2–3, 35–36, 48–51, 68–69,
    76–77, 85
    See also empiricism; naturalism, method-
    ological; pseudoscience
Sebeok, Thomas, 131
Second World War, 67, 154–56
September 11 terrorist attacks, 2, 153–59, 165
Sherlock (television series), 119, 153–60, 163–64
Sherlockiana, 113–15, 118, 120, 122–23
Siddiqi, Yumna, 132
Sign of Four, The, 74–76, 90–91
"Silver Blaze," 1, 69, 80, 128, 143, 151, 162
Sinnett, Alfred, 42–43, 48–49
Slater, Oscar, 90
Smajić, Srdjan, 86
Smith, Daniel, 2
Smith, Edgar, 115–16, 118, 121
Smith, Jonathan, 77
Smith, Joseph, 53–57, 99–100
Smith, William Robertson, 31
Sober, Elliott, 143
Society for Psychical Research, 45–46, 73,
    83–84, 104–5
"Some Personalia About Mr. Sherlock
    Holmes," 90
"Speckled Band, The," 68, 80–81
spiritualism, 3–7, 65, 88, 105–7, 119, 123, 140–41,
    166
    evidence for, 44–45, 68–69, 90–92, 97
    logic of, 92–93, 97–99, 109, 152
    and Mormonism, 53–60, 99–100
    and theosophy, 44, 105, 111–12, 140
Spiritualists' National Union, 101, 119
Spurgeon, Charles, 32–33
Stansbury, Hubert, 84–85, 87–89, 142, 145, 152
Stark Munro Letters, The, 83–85
Starrett, Vincent, 115–16
Stashower, Daniel, 47
Stavert, Geoffrey, 73
Stead, William, 101, 163–64
Stein, Louisa Ellen, 122
Stephen, James, 33–34, 64, 70, 93, 95
Strand Magazine, 78–83, 85, 87, 89

Study in Scarlet, A
    "Book of Life, The" in, 7–8, 15, 35, 48–51,
        60, 82–83, 92, 103, 165
    composition of, 63–64
    "Country of the Saints, The" in, 51–65, 89,
        100, 137
    publication of, 3, 17, 29, 46, 70
    reviews of, 52, 64–66
    and spiritualism, 4, 46–48, 71–76
"Sussex Vampire, The," 86, 98
Sword, Helen, 56, 88, 92

Takanashi, Kyoko, 137
Taylor, Isaac, 13–15
Taylor-Ide, Jesse Oak, 86
Thaxton, Charles, 144
theosophy, 41–45, 48–50, 60, 92, 105, 111–12,
    140
Thomas, Ronald, 53, 130, 153
Trump, Donald, 166
Truzzi, Marcello, 131
Tucker, Herbert, 130
Tupper, Frederick, 126, 132
Tweedale, Charles, 106, 110
Tyndall, John, 29, 44–45, 48, 80, 84–85, 97, 140

Universal Pictures, 113, 154–56

Valley of Fear, The, 89, 154
Vermeule, Blakey, 136
Viswanathan, Gauri, 42, 105
Vital Message, The, 91

Wanderings of a Spiritualist, The, 91
Ward, Wilfrid, 20, 29, 61
Warner, William, 39–40, 64, 78
Weber, Max, 66, 68
Wheen, Francis, 161–62
White, Hayden, 130
Williams, William Mattieu, 18
Wilson, James, 32
Wiltse, Ed, 122
Wimsatt, W. K., 123–24
Witchcraft Act, 101, 112, 140
Witt, Jonathan, 143
Wojton, Jennifer, 120

Young, Brigham, 52–54, 56–59, 62–64

Zunshine, Lisa, 135–36